Positive as Sound

Positive as Sound

Emily Dickinson's Rhyme

J U D Y   J O   S M A L L

The University of Georgia Press

Athens and London

© 1990 by the University of
Georgia Press
Athens, Georgia 30602
All rights reserved
Designed by Mary Mendell
Set in 10/13 Palatino
The paper in this book meets the guide-
lines for permanence and durability of
the Committee on Production Guidelines
for Book Longevity of the Council on
Library Resources.

Printed in the United States of America
94 93 92 91 90   5 4 3 2 1

Library of Congress Cataloging in Publication Data
Small, Judy Jo.
Positive as sound : Emily Dickinson's
rhyme / Judy Jo Small.
p.   cm. Includes bibliographical references.
ISBN 0-8203-1227-4 (alk. paper)
1. Dickinson, Emily, 1830–1886—Versification.   I. Title.
PS1541.Z5S63   1990   811'.4—dc20
89-29073 CIP
British Library Cataloging in Publication
Data available

for Tom

This World is not Conclusion
A Species stands beyond –
Invisible, as Music –
But positive, as Sound –

   —Emily Dickinson

Contents

Acknowledgments

A number of generous people assisted me in this study. Above all, I am grateful to Everett Emerson, who first urged me to undertake the project, guided me through Dickinson studies, and offered unflagging encouragement and sound advice every step of the way. He has been a steadfast friend. William Harmon, in many patient hours of conversation, helped to refine my ideas about rhyme and poetry. Connie Eble's linguistic expertise and good judgment were a reliable support. Thoughtful suggestions given by George Lensing, Robert Bain, and Robert Kirkpatrick were of considerable benefit. I deeply appreciate the precise criticism each of them has offered.

I am indebted to the labors of previous Dickinson scholars, particularly to Thomas H. Johnson and R. W. Franklin for their meticulous work with the Dickinson texts. I am especially grateful to Jane Eberwein and Cristanne Miller, whose careful readings of the manuscript and astute comments about matters of substance and detail have been invaluable. Their advice prompted important revisions. Mary De Jong freely shared ideas and information and gave me some important leads. Karen Dandurand and Agnieska Salska offered helpful comments. Of the many other critics to whom I am indebted, a word is due here to David Porter: though I argue with several of his positions, I appreciate the considerable merit of his books and his personal kindness to me.

I wish to thank the department of English at the University of North Carolina at Chapel Hill for a fellowship, awarded in honor of the late C. Hugh Holman, which enabled me to travel to Massachusetts for research at libraries in Cambridge and in Amherst. The staff of the Houghton Library, Harvard, kindly supplied me with materials from their collection and assisted me in a variety of other ways. The Robert Frost Library of Amherst College made available to me on microfilm their Dickinson manuscripts, and the staff of the archives there provided me with significant information. Elaine Trehub, College History Librarian at Mount Holyoke College, provided documents pertaining to Dickinson's experiences at Mount Holyoke; I am grateful for permission to quote from one of those documents. Daniel Lombardo, Curator of Special Collections of the Jones Library, Amherst, furnished several useful bits of information. The library staff of the University of North Carolina gave valuable assistance in procuring research materials.

My colleagues at North Carolina State University have been encouraging and helpful. In particular, Jim Clark, Peggy King, and Sharon Setzer have kindly given useful suggestions. Wayne Haskin and Lou Rosser have each read portions of the manuscript, shared their enthusiasm for Dickinson with me, and contributed specific, beneficial advice. Students too have helped me to see clearly.

During the long course of this project, personal friends and the members of my family have patiently listened and understood and believed. My husband has reached out into a field not his own to help me in making countless decisions, many of them stylistic. I owe special thanks to my mother, Helen Worley, and to my daughter, Jane, for their insights into individual poems. My son, Ben, helped prepare the index. To my uncle, James Worley, poet and long-time lover of Emily Dickinson, I wish to express thanks for his persistent interest, his perceptions, and the refining power of his sharp-edged objections.

I have been exceedingly fortunate in my friends.

Selections from Emily Dickinson's poetry are reprinted by permission of the publishers and the Trustees of Amherst College from *The Poems of Emily Dickinson,* Thomas H. Johnson, ed., Cambridge, Mass.: The Belknap Press of Harvard University Press, Copyright 1951, © 1955, 1979, 1983 by the President and Fellows of Harvard College; and from *The Complete Poems of Emily Dickinson*, edited by Thomas H. Johnson. Copyright 1914, 1929, 1935, 1942 by Martha Dickinson Bianchi; Copyright © renewed 1957, 1963 by Mary L. Hampson. Reprinted by permission of Little, Brown and Company.

Selections from Emily Dickinson's letters are reprinted by permission of the publishers from *The Letters of Emily Dickinson*, edited by Thomas H. Johnson, Cambridge, Mass.: The Belknap Press of Harvard University Press, Copyright © 1958, 1986 by the President and Fellows of Harvard College.

Poems #309 and #316 are reprinted with permission from *Face to Face*, edited by Martha D. Bianchi. Copyright 1932 by Martha Dickinson Bianchi. Copyright © renewed 1960 by Alfred Leete Hampson. Reprinted by permission of Houghton Mifflin Company.

Letters #1072 and #1453 are reprinted with permission from *Life and Letters of Emily Dickinson* by Emily Dickinson, edited by Martha D. Bianchi. Copyright 1924 by Martha Dickinson Bianchi. Copyright renewed © 1952 by Alfred Leete Hampson.

Positive as Sound

Introduction

A century after her death, Emily Dickinson remains enigmatic. Her poems, though compelling, are strangely elusive. Biographers try to provide some key to the mystery of who Dickinson was, what drove her to write those hundreds of short, disturbing lyrics, and why she did not publish more than a handful of them. Critics strive to place her in this or that tradition or to piece together from her poems a comprehensive philosophy. These concerns, though, are tangential to the central issue: what is the nature of her artistic achievement? Evaluation of the poems is still strongly influenced by the now legendary image of the woman in white, a recluse wracked by volcanic inner forces that spilled over into verse. That persistent conception of Dickinson carries the suggestion that she lacked proper artistic control and that her poems on the whole are not well wrought. Even much of the acclaim for her poetry is laden with provisos and disparaging nods at her characteristic technical lapses, the most striking of which is her unconventional rhyme. That her poems have gained and sustained a wide, growing, and devoted readership in spite of pervasive formal flaws, though, is a notion that strains credibility. Poetry survives not only because of its sentiments or even because of the depth of its philosophical and psychological insights. It survives because it says what it says *well*.

Because Dickinson was a woman, and largely removed from

an artistic or poetic community, it has taken readers some time to realize that her departures from conventional form resulted not from technical ineptitude but from deliberate art. Because her art is radically original, and frequently strange and obscure, it has taken some time to appreciate her subtle mastery and the craftsmanship she demonstrates in her selection and placement of words. Readers *felt* the power of her tightly compressed style long before they began to acknowledge that it resulted from something more than a spontaneous overflow of turbulent emotion. The image of Dickinson as an eccentric genius bursting with psychic energies she could not control has been a persistent fascination, and critics have been fond of quoting this statement from her fifth letter to Thomas Wentworth Higginson (August 1862): "I had no Monarch in my life, and cannot rule myself, and when I try to organize – my little Force explodes – and leaves me bare and charred – ." That letter was published in the *Atlantic Monthly* in October 1891, less than a year after the first volume of poems appeared, and again in 1894, in the first collection of letters. Although her lament about the difficulty of organizing expresses sentiments that might belong to any beginning writer, especially one seeking advice from an established professional, ever since then her statement has clung to her, distorting assessments of her poetic merit. Seldom has it been noticed that the disclaimer itself is beautifully organized. It is dramatic, figurative, rhythmical, poetic—and it blends a modesty calculated to appeal to a preceptor with the sly brag of a young genius claiming volcanic powers of inspiration. Dickinson cultivated the image of herself as an ingenuous, eccentric genius, but she was never so ingenuous as she appeared; her brother Austin said of her that she "definitely posed" in the letters to Higginson (quoted from Mabel Loomis Todd's journal, Sewall 538). At this distance and with access to her manuscripts, it is possible to see that her fiery genius was compounded with laborious, dedicated revising of words and lines and with careful, conscious art.

Increasingly, the critical community has taken Dickinson

seriously as an artist, and in recent decades the applause of leading literary figures and a series of important scholarly studies have done much to dispel the image of a half-cracked poetess who was occasionally, and almost accidentally, great. Growing attention to her use of language has helped to clarify the technical side of her achievement. All students of Dickinson are indebted to Charles R. Anderson for his *Emily Dickinson's Poetry: Stairway of Surprise*. Methodical and intelligent analysis by Brita Lindberg-Seyersted has made an important contribution to criticism, as have the works of Albert Gelpi and the articles of Roland Hagenbüchle. Most recently, several feminist studies have shed light on Dickinson's role as an outsider to the (masculine) tradition, working partly within but also against that tradition. It now seems clear that her position on the margins of literary culture may have allowed her "a space, a crucial discontinuity that provide[d] her the freedom to experiment," as Joanne Feit Diehl puts it in *Dickinson and the Romantic Imagination* (7), which explores the poet's divergences from her male Romantic precursors. Feminist criticism has directed attention to Dickinson's antagonism to masculine power and has helpfully explained her departures from social and literary convention as means of circumventing the rigid roles allotted to women and to women poets. That Dickinson suffered from the cultural subordination of women, that she had a healthy resentment of masculine prerogative and power, that she maintained a long struggle against an arbitrary patriarchal God—all that has been elucidated. Partly through the influence of feminist criticism, Dickinson's style has been viewed increasingly as innovative rather than as flawed.

In their zeal to locate in Dickinson's work a consciousness that undermines the structures of patriarchal power, however, feminist critics have occasionally fallen into facile generalizations that identify formal features of her poetry as gender-based linguistic maneuvers intended to subvert masculine authority. To suppose, as Wendy Martin does in the new *Columbia Literary History of the United States*, that Dickinson's use of oxymoron and synesthesia constitutes a political act subversive of "masculine linguistic hierarchy" and "male epistemology" (619) is to ignore the obvious: while such poetic devices do indeed break down binary oppositions traditional to logical thinking, they are devices that appear not only in the works of writers defiant of hierarchical social structures, gender-based or otherwise, but also in works of writers whose political attitudes are quite reactionary. Margaret Homans's far more persuasive arguments that Dickinson's "different kind of language" represents "a reaction against phallogocentrism" and its structures of literal meaning (*Women Writers* 36) and especially against the subject-object hierarchy fundamental to phallogocentric language ("Vision" 124–32) still leaves troublesome questions about whether and to what extent such stylistic traits as she describes (double meanings, repetitions, metonymy) are in fact linguistic expressions of a particular poet's consciousness of gender politics, or—as seems more likely—they are manipulations that characterize poetic language generally, and baroque and modern poetic language especially. Cristanne Miller, in *Emily Dickinson: A Poet's Grammar*, intelligently addresses those questions; she recognizes the correspondence between Dickinson's creative deviations from conventional language patterns and the imaginative constructs of "woman's writing" (*écriture féminine*) in current feminist theory (177), but she also acknowledges that "[m]ultiplicity of meaning, irrational or metaphorical progressions, disruptive or marginal discourse characterize much of the poetry of every age" (182). Adroitly, Miller balances the argument that gender is important in setting Dickinson's "antagonistic stance," her "opposition to an existing order" (184), with an understanding that Dickinson's language is influenced by multiple determinants. The excitement of Dickinson's poetry derives in large part from her daringly innovative handling of traditional poetic forms, but plainly what we hear in her poetry is not just "woman" but a voice uniquely her own.

None of the more recent considerations of Dickinson's style, curiously, gives more than a passing glance to the innovation that most obviously characterizes that voice—her strangely deviant rhymes. Rhyme is pervasive in her poetry; very nearly all of her poems are rhymed in one way or another, and in most of them rhymes occur at the end of the lines where one expects them, in accordance with traditional stanzaic forms. The rhymes, though, differ markedly from established poetic norms. They are unexpected, disruptive, unsettling. They do not sound like the rhymes of other poets. Yet, however different or faint they sometimes may be, they provide a structural backbone for the poetry, marking a fundamental stanzaic regularity underlying the frequently jagged, disjunctive syntax. And they provide a strangely distinctive sound, recognizably Dickinson's. Rhyme was important to her. When Higginson evidently suggested that she amend or discard her rhymes, she answered with a polite refusal: "I could not drop the Bells whose jingling cooled my Tramp" (L 265),[1] and she persisted in rhyming in her own way. The importance of those rhymes and of her experiments with aural effects in her poetry we have scarcely yet begun to understand.

From the start, readers of her poetry have found it difficult to come to terms with her rhymes. When Mabel Loomis Todd and Thomas Wentworth Higginson brought out the first volume of Dickinson's poems after her death, they felt it necessary to "correct" many of her rhymes to accord with public taste—and one suspects, with their own tastes as well. Higginson's notice of the soon-to-be-published volume makes apologies for deficiencies: "one can no more criticise a faulty rhyme here and there than a defect of drawing in one of Blake's pictures. When a thought takes one's breath away, who cares to count the syllables?" ("Open Portfolio" 393). The volume they published was a modest popular success, but in spite of the numerous editorial "improvements" the prevailing critical response was to censure Dickinson's departures from formal convention, particularly the rhymes.[2]

Uncertainty about the value of those rhymes has lingered ever since, and no consensus has been reached on the question of whether her rhymes constitute a serious defect, an eccentric quirk, or a major accomplishment. Poetic experiments in this century have broadened public taste and accustomed readers to rhymes that are not "right" by traditional standards. Still, a general expectation remains that the sound of a poem will somehow correlate with the ideas and feelings in the poem. Rightly so. Alexander Pope's dictum that "The sound must seem an echo to the sense" is as valid now as it ever was. Modern criticism has emphasized that the meaning of a poem derives quite as much from *how* it says something as from what it says. Deviations from convention, in particular, require explanation in terms of their aesthetic and semantic purposes. But critics who have considered Dickinson's practice have not agreed that her odd rhymes do in fact serve those purposes.

Susan Miles argued in 1925 that Dickinson's technical irregularities are artistically valuable in mirroring "a cleft and unmatching world"; partial rhymes, she believed, are a means of implying "defeat, incongruity, suspense, failure, struggle, frustration, disillusion, thwarting, disruption, or escape" (158, 147). Gay Wilson Allen wrote in 1935, however, that Dickinson was "simply careless in composing the verse and too indifferent to revise it carefully afterward" (317). George Frisbie Whicher, similarly, in 1939 found "no subtlety of intention," merely an unwillingness to let "the bonds of rhyme . . . cause her to bend her thoughts" (248). Carelessness of poetic form is a fairly serious charge to bring against a poet, and it is not surprising that admirers of Dickinson have persisted in defending her approach, all more or less along the lines originally set forth by Miles. Frederic Carpenter has claimed that the unorthodox rhymes suggest the "imperfect correspondence" between dreams and harsh reality (114). Henry Wells, while admitting that there is "no simple formula," still holds that "[i]n the richly modulated music of her lyrics, full rhyme may be compared to the musician's major mode, half rhyme to the minor mode. The latter connotes indecision, pensiveness, quiet grief, or spiritual numbness" (267). Charles Anderson argues that "Exact correspondences of sound could not convey the dissonances that reached her ears from a fractured universe, though she could use them in moments of renewed faith or as ironic musical symbols of a world whose orderliness was illusory" (27).

James Reeves is more cautious: "on the whole though not invariably, full rhyme accompanies her moods of confidence and assonance [partial rhyme, apparently] her moods of uncertainty. But the exceptions are significant" (xlviii). (He does not say what they signify.) There are in fact so many exceptions that Brita Lindberg-Seyersted, a linguist of considerable analytic skill, hesitates to draw any general conclusions other than that partial rhymes help to relieve the monotony of the hymn stanza and contribute to a poetic voice that is "private," "colloquial," and "slant"; otherwise, she doubts the possibility of drawing conclusions about rhyme beyond the level of individual poems (156, 166).[3]

Perhaps the critical uncertainty on the issue is best illustrated by David Porter, who in his first book wrote that "the intrusion of discordant sounds makes audible the noises of this less-than-perfect world as against the formal perfection of exact rhyme correspondence" (*Early* 120–21). He had changed his mind by the time he wrote his second study of Dickinson's poetry, where he gives the subject a terse dismissal: "Rhyming was not Dickinson's forte, and the hymn never taxed that faculty" (*Idiom* 100).

The critical confusion surrounding the evaluation of Dickinson's rhymes results in part from lack of understanding of the principles by which rhyme operates. The recurrent idea that full rhymes indicate happiness or confidence while partial rhymes indicate sorrow or doubt has a strong appeal to common sense; the idea is elegant in its simplicity. It seems fitting that an "off-rhyme," like a deliberately "sour" note in music, should constitute some kind of ironic gesture referring either to the nature of the world or to the nature of one's feelings. But as critics have seen, this appealing theory does not work very well unless we are willing to choose poems that accord with the theory and ignore many others. The widely admired poem "There's a certain Slant of light" (P 258),[4] for example, has full rhymes in an *abcb* arrangement throughout even though it deals with the conviction of despair. And the whimsical, even merry, poem "Between the form of Life and Life" (P 1101) contains only partial rhymes.

Comparison of two poems that seem nearly identical in theme illustrates the difficulty. The famous poem "I felt a Funeral, in my Brain" has a pattern of rhyme that coordinates well with the meaning, but another poem, "I felt a Cleaving in my Mind," has rhymes that apparently conflict with the meaning. An analysis of these poems demonstrates the sort of problems one confronts when seeking out correlations between meaning and sound in Dickinson's poetry.

> I felt a Funeral, in my Brain,
> And Mourners to and fro
> Kept treading – treading – till it seemed
> That Sense was breaking through –
>
> And when they all were seated,
> A Service, like a Drum –
> Kept beating – beating – till I thought
> My Mind was going numb –
>
> And then I heard them lift a Box
> And creak across my Soul
> With those same Boots of Lead, again,
> Then Space – began to toll,
>
> As all the Heavens were a Bell,
> And Being, but an Ear,
> And I, and Silence, some strange Race
> Wrecked, solitary, here –

And then a Plank in Reason, broke,
And I dropped down, and down –
And hit a World, at every plunge,
And Finished knowing – then –

(P 280)

The theme of the poem is supported by strangely evocative images of funeral rites conducted noisily in some obscure mental space—"here," it says jarringly (in line sixteen), leaving the reader groping to comprehend that too-immediate word. The metrical disruptions are not extreme, but the slight disturbance of iambic rhythm in line one, the insistent trochaic feeling given by the caesurae in lines three and seven, the catalexis in line five, and the caesurae before the final syllable in lines seventeen and twenty—all these lend a metric instability that contributes to the trembling unease of this powerful poem. The rhyme-pairs form full rhymes in the three middle stanzas; this pattern correlates with the "Sense" that seems to break through in these stanzas in a drama almost coherent until finally the "Plank in Reason" breaks, dropping the speaker into an unfamiliar, grave-like abyss. The rhymes, then, reinforce the structure suggested by the discursive content of the poem: a speaker struggles to communicate an overwhelming mental experience by presenting it in terms of the most painful ceremony of the exterior world. The conventional "correctness" of the rhymes in the middle of the poem contrasts with the oddness of the rhymes in the framing stanzas, which parallel the speaker's initial disorientation and the ultimate failure of his or her desperate attempt at formal control. The concluding consonantal rhyme "incoheres," as it were, in a superbly coherent way, according well with the critical theory that such rhymes support tones of doubt and despair.

It can be seen, furthermore, that the lexical ambiguity of "breaking through" augments the undercurrent of doubt that pervades even the middle section of the poem. Because "breaking through" may mean either "emerging" or "shattering," the reader is stranded between two interpretive possibilities: is intelligibility emerging into lucidity or crumbling into nonsense? The "Plank" of rational sense does not break until the final stanza, yet even so the sensory details in the center of the poem import an incipient terror. Further, the poetic voice, by speaking—however metaphorically—of its own death as a past event, arouses a disquiet, which becomes intense when that living voice declares, eerily, that it has "Finished knowing." Consequently, one cannot be sure whether the last line indicates a final dissolution of consciousness or a release from the confining "Box" of rationality and physical sense into some higher mode of knowing that the "I" in "Silence" attends. (The variant for "Finished" is "Got through," a phrase that even more strongly suggests the possibility of passage from the realm of "Sense" into the realm of "Soul.") The dashes before and after the final word "then" seem to be markers of inconclusiveness, of hesitation before the unspoken or unspeakable, and they, along with the partial rhyme, unsettle the ending.

A theme similar to that in "I felt a Funeral, in my Brain," however, appears in "I felt a Cleaving in my Mind," a poem that contains only full rhymes, rhymes that perhaps cohere too well to suit the explicitly stated idea of the poem. As a result, the poem has aroused some controversy:

> I felt a Cleaving in my Mind –
> As if my Brain had split –
> I tried to match it – Seam by Seam –
> But could not make them fit.
>
> The thought behind, I strove to join
> Unto the thought before –
> But Sequence ravelled out of Sound
> Like Balls – upon a Floor.
>
> (P 937)

The poem describes an experience of mental disintegration, and it has generally been interpreted in that way, as a serious portrayal of psychological strain bordering on madness, perhaps experienced by Dickinson and here confessed and described. Formally, however, it is as regular a poem as she ever wrote, more regular than most. It flows in flawless iambic rhythm, is exactly rhymed, and joins its thoughts to one another in perfect sequence, although the speaker says that is precisely what he or she cannot do. All the "seams" of the poem are perfectly matched. Though Dickinson's verse is often called cryptic or elliptical or gnomic, here there is nothing of the sort; the final simile of balls of yarn unravelling as they roll across the floor is easy enough, even homely, and there is no disruption of form to reflect the theme of mental disturbance. The sound does not seem to echo the sense, but in fact is directly opposed to it.

I rather suspect that if "I felt a Cleaving" were dated 1858 instead of 1864, it would make, in contrast with "I felt a Funeral" (dated 1861 by Johnson, 1862 by Franklin), an ideal illustration for a pedagogue's purposes of the awkward fitting of form to subject by a poet who had not yet mastered her craft. But it is not an early poem, and critics are left with an awkward problem. Lindberg-Seyersted has considered the problem and still reads the poem as a "powerful expression of a disturbance of the mind," successful, she says, not in spite of but "because of the very contrast embodied in the high degree of accord among the rhyme words as against the theme of the poem" (169). She does not comment further, leaving us to ponder this befuddling statement. How are we to stretch our sensibilities to encompass such an antithesis and to come to an understanding of the *tone* of the poem? If we listen to it, it jingles, especially in the first verse, where *split* is rhymed with *fit*. The rhymes of the second verse are mellower in sound, but the only thing disturbing a serene, even a cheery tone, is the intellectual content of the words apart from their sound.[5]

If form and content should be compatible, then either the poem is seriously flawed or the apparently conflicting sound and sense do in fact work together in some complex way. Perhaps the poem is a wry commentary on the way one can hold externals under maniacal control while one's inner self is crumbling? Sharon Cameron offers a reading akin to this, pointing to the order that is imposed on feelings of chaos so that "the very sequence the speaker claims she is at a loss to reconstruct is that structure which elements the poem" (205). Or perhaps we are meant to feel the artistic mastery (if that is what it is) as a liberating anodyne to the psychic distress so that the two are poised in delicate balance? I think that must be what Lindberg-Seyersted had in mind. Or, maybe the poem is a Dickinsonian joke, a parody ridiculing conventional verse technique for its absurd unfittedness to this kind of theme and laughing, "So *this* is how they want me to write!" More likely, the poem is a feat of linguistic acrobatics based on the two antithetical senses of the word "cleave"—"to split" and "to adhere to"—and complicated by the fact that "ravel" is synonymous with "unravel" and that both of those words mean not only "separate" but also "entangle"; then the "Cleaving" of *lexis* and *melos* is at once a perfect split and a perfect fit. This interpretation is plausible in view of Dickinson's love of her lexicon and her love of paradox, and it allows for an unimpassioned tone such as the regular versification suggests.[6]

But the theory about rhyme active behind these deliberations, that full rhyme is somehow indicative of security while partial rhyme is indicative of insecurity, has been questioned by—among others—Lindberg-Seyersted, the most thoroughgoing analyst of Dickinson's technique. She points out that "such overall distinctions" do not apply: "It is only possible to point to individual poems where either kind of rhyme is appropriate to the meaning" (165–66). But then on what theoretical basis is one to determine the appropriateness of a kind of rhyme to an individual poem other than by appeal to the same dichotomy? (Consider in this regard the curious hedging in Lindberg-Seyersted's comment on the "contrast" between the full rhymes and the unhappy theme of "I felt a Cleaving.") Until we grasp some sort of general principles governing the relation of partial and full rhyme to aesthetic possibilities, how can we begin to understand whether Dickinson, or any other poet using partial rhymes, demonstrates technical brilliance or technical ineptitude?

Rhyme, like sound in poetry generally, is hard to deal with analytically. In an effort to understand Dickinson's rhyming procedures, several scholars have classified her rhymes as to type and a few have done some tentative counting to determine the frequency of each kind. T. Walter Herbert, the earliest to attempt a classification, divided the partial rhymes (which he defends for their "rare, refreshing tang") into twelve categories that indicate the wide variety of kinds of sound-resemblance she employs as end rhyme (446–52). Whicher grouped the rhymes into five categories—exact, identical, vowel, imperfect, and suspended; his study has the merit of systematizing a point that Herbert laid the groundwork for, namely that Dickinson's practice shows that she recognized and sometimes used in rhyme the equivalence of nasals (m, n, and ng), sibilants (s, z, sh, and ch), dentals (d, t/nd, nt; t/ct; d/vd), or such groups as t and p, z and soft g, k and nk (244–45). (He sees, as noted earlier, no aesthetic or semantic value in these departures from convention.) Thomas H. Johnson, who brought forth in 1955 what is regarded as the authoritative edition and who was therefore the first to work with an accurate text of the poems, divides the rhymes into the same five types as Whicher but differs from him in arguing that "Examination of the intent of a poem usually reveals a motive for the variations" (87). (He adds a warning that rhymes on worksheet drafts should not be considered equally with those on finished copies.) Porter's analysis of the early poems indicates the relative frequency of the types of rhyme (exact—over half; suspended—over a quarter; imperfect—very few; vowel —one-twelfth) but, because he treats only the poems dated 1861 and earlier plus the sixteen poems sent to Higginson, he leaves out of consideration most of the poems (110–14).

Lindberg-Seyersted revises the terminology of her predecessors in line with more recent usage, preferring the term "consonant rhyme" for the previous "suspended rhyme" and "assonant rhyme" for the previous "imperfect rhyme." More important, she adds to her classification a sixth category, which she calls "unaccented rhymes" because one or more syllables not receiving full stress are involved; these rhymes, remarkably abundant in Dickinson's verse, had been largely ignored by previous analysts, whose attention had been directed to phonological similarity alone. Since classification according to stress overlaps with classification according to phonological similarity, Lindberg-Seyersted's focus on unaccented rhyme brings into question earlier counts. Strictly speaking, no rhyme can be "exact" if one or both syllables involved are unstressed; similarly, a consonantal rhyme is rather different in effect if it involves an unstressed syllable. Actually, the category "unaccented rhyme" is scarcely adequate, for it does not distinguish between rhymes wherein one (or both) rhyming syllables receive a secondary stress in normal speech and a metrical promotion stress in the poem (*be/Authority*) and those wherein one of the rhyming syllables receives neither speech nor metrical stress (*Honey/variety*); the inequality of stress in rhymes of the latter type is significantly greater. In the Holman-Harmon *Handbook,* the name "promotion rhyme" is given to rhymes of the former type and the name "ironic" to the latter (431).[7] Lindberg-Seyersted's own approximate counts, while they suggest interesting possibilities, are far from complete.

More nearly complete is a recent count made by Timothy Morris, who has compiled the following information (30):

Of 4,840 rhymes in Dickinson's poems, 2,006 (41.4%) are exact (of the type see/me, 1732); 167 (3.5%) pair a vowel with a reduced version of itself (me/immortality, 712); 80 (1.6%) are assonantal (breath/quench, 422); 731 (15.1%) are vowel (blew/sky, 354); 1,535 (31.7%) are consonantal (mean/sun, 411); 164 (3.4%) pair a consonant with a cluster containing that consonant (night/erect, 419); 23 pair a cluster with another cluster that shares one consonant with it (disclosed/blind, 761); 2 rhyme a cluster with the same cluster reversed (used/birds, 430); 84 (1.7%) rhyme one nasal consonant with another (thing/begun, 565); 20 rhyme one fricative with another (breeze/divorce, 896); 2 rhyme one voiced stop with another (sob/wood, 45); 5 rhyme one unvoiced stop with another (frock/night, 584); 21 rhyme-positions show less close approximations to exact rhyme, and cannot be considered rhyme at all (for instance, blaze/forge in 365).

These statistics, and the chronological charts Morris provides that show in the development of Dickinson's style a growing reliance on inexact rhymes, are significant, though it is not clear why Morris's accounting omits identical rhymes. Still, the main shortcoming of all these analyses is their vagueness about the aesthetic importance of any of the specific types of partial rhyme.

At an early stage of my research into the subject of Dickin-

Table 1. Basic Types of Rhyme in Dickinson's Verse

Full Rhyme	hands/sands
Partial Rhyme	
Assonantal	green/dream
Consonantal	wheel/mill
Semi-consonance	rides/is
Zero-consonance (or Vowel rhyme)	way/sea
Rich consonance	deed/dead
Unaccented	
stressed syllable + promoted syllable	be/eternity
promoted syllable + promoted syllable	malignity/obliquity
unstressed syllable + promoted syllable	honey/variety
Identical Rhyme (or Rime Riche)	sea/see

son's rhyme, it was suggested to me that the best way to proceed was to classify and count all of Dickinson's rhymes so that I could base conclusions about her stylistic purposes and development on mathematically accurate tables listing rhymes according to incidence and type. Computers enable such study, I was assured. Though I set forth gamely with this approach, it was not long before I began to realize that the obstacles are virtually insurmountable.

The first problem is textual. As is well known, Johnson's dating of the poems is suspect since it is based on the hand-writing styles of extant copies that may be transcriptions of poems actually composed earlier; hence, firm conclusions about stylistic development are impossible.[8] Even Franklin's meticulous and valuable rearrangement of Dickinson's manu-scripts does not resolve all such questions, since it too includes copies of poems written earlier. Then there is the problem of weighing rough or intermediate drafts, scraps, fragments, and ditties meant for gift enclosures along with finished, serious poetry: the Dickinson corpus may in some sense be equivalent to what we would have if we treated not the pub-lished poems of some other poet but the entire contents of his or her desk drawers. Consequently, a statistical analysis based on a lumping together of all extant verses would be of questionable value.[9]

A more complex problem that faces any analyst of rhyme, but especially an analyst of verse replete with partial rhymes, concerns the issue of partial rhymes that have become con-ventional through common use and the closely related issue of the historical evolution of the language. Unaccented rhyme (promotion rhyme) is a type of partial rhyme that has ample precedent in English poetry, though not so prominently as in Dickinson's verse; Shakespeare rhymed *die* with *dignity*, for example, Milton rhymed *thee* with *Liberty*, Pope rhymed *sky* and *company*, and numerous similar examples are easy to find in the work of almost any poet. Some partial rhymes became conventional because of a shortage of rhyming words avail-

able in the language to match a common, necessary word—
heaven and *given*, for example (*seven* and *eleven* and *leaven* will
not serve conveniently all the time).

Other partial rhymes have found acceptance in tradition
because of an actual full rhyme that did exist at some historical time and place—the pair *love* and *prove* is the most
familiar of these. Among phonological features of language,
vowel sounds are particularly unstable, showing considerable fluctuation across time and region; consonant pronunciation remains more nearly uniform. There would appear
to be a connection between this fact and the fact that assonantal rhymes are very rare in English poetry (as they are
in Dickinson's) whereas consonantal rhymes are relatively
common. Frequently, words that now appear as consonantal rhymes reflect full rhymes according to the pronunciation
of the poet's time and place. On the other hand, some consonantal rhymes were used by poets *as* consonantal rhymes
carried over from previous tradition. The precise correlation
between eye-rhymes and changing pronunciation is a matter
of scholarly debate.[10] But it is clear that as pronunciation has
shifted, the relics of earlier pronunciations are preserved as
conventionalized partial rhymes for subsequent generations
of readers, whose ears become accustomed to certain departures from full rhyme, especially in the form of eye rhymes.
As Michael Shapiro has observed, "in the poetic traditions
of the Western languages, it is quite common to observe the
continued, fossilized implementation of rhyme rules which
reflect the defunct pronunciation of earlier stages of the language's evolution; or that of dialects which retain the phonological rules but have lost their prestige status for literary
purposes" (196). Rhymes such as *wind/mind,* or *prove/love,* or
alone/none, hallowed by centuries of use, or any of the common
unaccented rhymes lack the force of surprise that we associate with some of Dickinson's other rhymes such as *pause/
decays* or *ascend/Diamond*. Although the historical background
of conventional practice is important in governing stylistic ex-

pectations, a catalog of rhymes cannot very well differentiate between partial rhymes that have been honored by abundant historical precedent, those that have been used occasionally before, and those that are making their first appearance in English poetry.

The degree of phonological distance between words paired as partial rhymes is another important determinant of the effect of a rhyme, particularly an unusual one. It is possible to lump into one category conventional eye-rhymes (*come/home*), unconventional rhymes near in sound (*star/swear*), and unconventional rhymes distant in sound (*Blind/unmoved*); all these are consonantal rhymes. But the net result of such a count will be a lot of numbers that blur significant distinctions. Numerous sub-categories might alleviate that difficulty, but even then the study is likely to ignore the issue that matters most: how do the partial rhymes relate to the meanings of the poems?

A more immediate stumbling block is the unsteadiness of rhyme pattern in many of Dickinson's poems. Here is the first stanza of poem 348, for example:

> I dreaded that first Robin, so,
> But He is mastered, now,
> I'm some accustomed to Him grown,
> He hurts a little, though –

The common meter stanza employed here is one traditionally associated with a rhyme scheme *abab* or *abcb*. Instead, the reader hears *so* at the end of line one echoed by a partial vowel rhyme, *now* at the end of line two, then by an assonantal rhyme, *grown*, at the end of line three, and finally by the full rhyme *though* at the end of line four; the full rhyme that finally occurs does not conform either to the paradigm associated with the metrical pattern or with the rhyme scheme of the other six stanzas of the poem, which turns out to be *abcb*. Should one count here merely the consonantal rhyme (a zero-consonance) of *now* and *though* (dictated by the dominant rhyme scheme) while ignoring the full rhyme of *so* and *though*, or do the opposite and count the full rhyme only, or count them both, or count them both and also the assonantal rhyme of lines one and three? None of these solutions is satisfactory. The predominant feature of the rhymes as a reader experiences them is the effect of uncertainty lent by the ambiguous pattern. Since disorientation is the subject of the poem as well as the impression the rhyme pattern produces, that effect is more important than anything a statistical table can register. [11]

Finally, irregularities in line arrangement present a major obstacle to a quantitative approach to rhyme. In stanza two of this poem, for example, the analyst is confronted with a choice:

> Their Hight in Heaven comforts not –
> Their Glory – nought to me –
> 'Twas best imperfect – as it was –
> I'm finite – I cant see –
>
> The House of Supposition –
> The Glimmering Frontier that
> skirts the Acres of Perhaps –
> To Me – shows insecure –
>
> The Wealth I had – contented me –
> If 'twas a meaner size –
> Then I had counted it until
> It pleased my narrow Eyes –
>
> Better than larger values –
> That show however true –
> This timid life of Evidence
> Keeps pleading – "I dont know."
>
> (P 696)

Should *that* and *insecure* be registered as a non-rhyme? Or should the lines be rearranged in accord with the metrical pattern of the other stanzas, moving *that* into position as the first word of the next line, so that *Frontier* and *insecure* can be registered (as they are heard anyway) as a consonantal rhyme? The latter arrangement was used by Dickinson's editors when the poem was first published in 1891, and it is defensible, to be sure. But the "corrective" rearrangement obscures the significant tension between what the ear hears and what the eye sees in these lines, which are about the insecurity of one caught within finite limits, trying but unable to see across those limits to a "Glimmering" realm dimly intuited but disturbingly beyond the grasp of knowledge; the irregularity of the line arrangement provides the reader with a similar experience of insecurity as he gropes for a rhyme that, echoing almost invisibly, partly seems to be there and partly seems not to be. What good is a mere count—no matter what choice a counter makes—at capturing what matters here? What matters is precisely the ambiguity of the liminal, which evades "Evidence."

Lindberg-Seyersted correctly observes of the irregularities of Dickinson's line arrangements: "It is not possible to tell how conscious and intentional (if at all) this unorthodoxy was with the poet. The size of the paper she wrote on, especially when she made the penciled drafts, may sometimes have occasioned the irregularity." Although "a slight reordering" frequently establishes a regular meter, she believes that irregularities of line arrangement "probably served [Dickinson's] need to put emphasis on certain words or phrases" (138–39). The example of poems such as "Their Hight in Heaven" definitely indicates deliberate manipulation, but the increasing size of the poet's handwriting (as her eyesight dimmed, probably) meant that she often could not fit a whole line of poetry onto a page; as a result, it is sometimes hard to determine whether she intends a line to be broken or not, and thus whether there is or is not a real deviation from "normal" arrangement. A further and formidable difficulty is that the line divisions in Johnson's edition do not always coincide with those of the manuscripts. He assumes, and rightly, that her line breaks are often necessitated by arriving at the edge of the paper before a line is complete, but in many individual instances his reorderings are questionable.[12] Complicating the problem, Dickinson herself rearranged lines in different copies of the same poem.

Though I abandoned the statistical approach to rhyme, in the process of studying rhymes mathematically, I did achieve one substantial gain. By a careful examination and count of Dickinson's variant rhyme words (reproduced from her manuscripts in Johnson's variorum edition), I ascertained that her rhymes cannot be the result of casual neglect, that the variants demonstrate she was very firm in her sense of how her poems should be rhymed. Higginson says in his preface to the 1890 *Poems* that Dickinson "often altered a word many times to suit an ear which had its own tenacious fastidiousness" (xx). We may smile in wondering how often he had struggled against her tenacious ear; at times he must have thought it merely stubborn. Nevertheless, it is surprising that such a small proportion of the suggested variant words in her manuscripts are rhyme words. She tinkered with her poetry extensively, revising, polishing, debating between choices; we see the proof of her toil in the textual variants. Essential oils, she knew, come because they are wrung (P 675). While one might suppose that any poet working in rhymed stanzas would exert a large part of the labor of revision on the rhyming words, Dickinson's variants offer proof that she did not. Of the thousands of variant words the variorum edition shows she considered in the process of composition, there are, according to my count, fewer than two hundred instances where she either alters or considers altering one of the words that make up an end rhyme. About her rhyme words she was particularly tenacious.

Even when she does offer variants for rhyme words, about three-quarters of those would not appreciably alter the sound character of the words they would replace. That is, full rhymes usually would stay full, and partial rhymes usually would stay partial. Moreover, in partial rhymes that have partial rhymes as variants, Dickinson tended to preserve about the same degree of difference of sound between the rhyme word and its partner. For example, in "The Lilac is an ancient shrub" (P 1241), the draft gives *Blind/detained* as the final rhyme and lists *Blind/profaned* as a possible alternative; she clearly is weighing the conceptual and connotative values of the two words, not striving to produce a more (or less) nearly exact rhyme. Similarly, in "I asked no other thing" (P 621), *denied/sneered* has as its variant *denied/smiled;* the substitute word is slightly closer in sound to its partner by virtue of a shared stressed vowel, but the difference in sound is negligible compared with the difference in meaning. That she did not use partial rhymes merely because she could not or did not bother to think of full ones is indicated by a number of instances where she actually changes a full rhyme to a partial rhyme in a later version of a poem. The revisions demonstrate, however, that usually she adhered to an original rhyme pattern with remarkable persistence. If we add to this firmness about rhyme the corresponding firmness about rhythm pointed out by Lindberg-Seyersted,[13] we may conclude that Dickinson had a strong, relatively unwavering sense of how she wanted her poems to sound and that she pursued that end deliberately.

An interesting sample of her process of composition is offered in the worksheet for a redaction of "Two Butterflies went out at Noon" (P 533; Fig. 1), which Johnson dates 1878, about sixteen years after the original version of the poem.[14] The stanzaic pattern, common meter rhyming *abcb*, is constant; that pattern and the rhyme words almost constitute a frame *within* which her mind, pouring forth multiform alternatives, works at finding the right word. There are partial rhymes in all three verses, and the creative process leaves them nearly untouched. *Farm/him* and *sun/noon* are not considered for alteration; and, though in the last stanza *Fatuity* and *Biography* are contemplated as possible rhymes for *entomology,* either would form a partial rhyme echoing a similarity of sound on the basis of ending in two unaccented syllables

Figure 1. Worksheet for redaction of Poem 533

[stanza 1]   Two Butterflies went out at Noon
And waltzed upon a Farm
And then espied Circumference
Then overtook –
And caught a ride with him –
   and took a Bout with him –

[stanza 2]   Then lost themselves and found themselves
      staked   lost
      chased   caught
In eddies of the sun –
  Fathoms in
  Rapids of
  Gambols with
      of
For Frenzy zies of
  antics in
    with
Till Rapture *missed them*
    missed her footing –
      Peninsula

  Gravitation chased
    humbled –
    ejected
    foundered
    grumbled
Until a Zephyr pushed them
    chased –
    flung –
    spurned
    scourged
And Both were wrecked in Noon –
    drowned –
    quenched –
    whelmed –
And they were hurled from noon –

[stanza 3]   To all surviving Butterflies
Be this Fatuity
  Biography –
Example – and monition
To entomology –

(the latter syllable receiving a promotion stress from the iambic rhythm) and ending on the same final vowel—that is, they are nearly equidistant from *entomology* in sound. (*Biography* does have the same stressed vowel as *entomology*, but it seems unlikely that such a slight phonic difference would have been of as much import as the more weighty denotative and connotative differences of the two variant words.) The testimony of this worksheet is consistent with the evidence provided by variants in her other worksheets (see poems 1207, 1386, and 1416) and in her poetry as a whole.

If we grant that the textual variants demonstrate that Dickinson's rhymes are not the result of casual neglect, however, still the larger question remains: to what purpose was her tenacity? Since a mathematical analysis of rhyme in the poems is of little aid in answering that question, the only approach that *can* be used is interpretive analysis of structures of rhyme in relation to their context.

The single universally admired critical venture into the relation of rhyme and poetic meaning is William Wimsatt's "One Relation of Rhyme to Reason," a pioneer work exploring the role in Pope's and Byron's poetry of rhyme-words from disparate grammatical and semantic regions, words which by their surprising "chime" contribute to effective paradox and wit. Among the examples Wimsatt quotes are these lines from Pope's "The Rape of the Lock":

> One speaks the glory of the British Queen,
> And one describes a charming Indian screen.
>
> (162)

This rhyme is intriguing not only because of its conventional phonic fit but also because of the unexpected semantic distance between the substantial grandeur of the British monarchy and the trivial splendor of an imported luxury item, a distance that ironically comments on the chatter of a shallow society that has lost a proper hierarchy of values. From

Byron, Wimsatt quotes such passages as this, from *Beppo: A Venetian Story:*

> He was a Turk, the colour of mahogany;
> And Laura saw him, and at first was glad,
> Because the Turks so much admire philogyny.
>
> (164)

In this triple rhyme, too, the sharp disjuncture of meaning between words similar in sound contributes to the intellectual surprise and the comic effect as "an ingenious affinity in meaning is established" (165). Thus, Wimsatt insists, rhyme words may "impose upon the logical pattern of expressed argument a kind of fixative counterpattern of alogical implication"; or, as he goes on to say, "they are the icon in which the idea is caught" (153, 165).

Important though Wimsatt's insights are, in detail at least they turn out to be of somewhat limited usefulness in the analysis of Dickinson's poetry. The diligent efforts of Lindberg-Seyersted to apply them are not very productive (170–80). Her conclusion is merely that grammatic and semantic affinities between words that rhyme only partially may strengthen a "weak" rhyme; by arguing that Dickinson uses an approach opposite to Pope's to compensate for a phonic disparity acknowledged to be a weakness, the critic overlooks the brilliance of Dickinson's own, divergent, procedure. Wimsatt is examining the effects of full rhymes in the end-stopped couplets of Pope and in the ottava rima of Byron, and the principles he discovers there are not easily transferable to a poetry that is heavily enjambed and that uses a large proportion of partial rhymes. In fact, there may be a clue to a different and important principle in Byron's *mahogany/philogyny*. Though Wimsatt never mentions it, these words do not quite rhyme. Surely it is not only the "ingenious affinity in meaning" to which the effect of this rhyme is attributable but also the ingenious incongruity in their sounds.

Dickinson seldom wrote lines that can be construed as end-stopped couplets. There are a few instances:

> Our's be the tossing – wild though the sea –
> Rather than a Mooring – unshared by thee.
>
> (P 368)

> Title divine – is mine!
> The Wife – without the Sign!
>
> (P 1072)

> The Riddle we can guess
> We speedily despise –
> Not anything is stale so long
> As Yesterday's surprise –
>
> (P 1222)

The last of these examples, a quatrain that could be rearranged as a poulter's measure couplet, has an epigrammatic force that might be called Popeian. But by and large the quick click of wit that we associate with Pope, or with Byron, is not her aim. The feature of her rhyme that demands to be understood is her use of rhyme-words unexpectedly different in sound. As Pope and Byron increased the grammatical and semantic distance between rhyming words, she increased the phonic distance. Part of her poetic artistry inheres in the subtle ways she uses that distance in relation to meaning.

Rhymes have whatever meaning they do have only in the context of a rhyme pattern, which exists in the context of the whole pattern of words, ideas, rhythms, and other sounds of a poem, and that pattern in turn exists against the historical background of previous poetry. A reader's response to a given rhyme is affected by all of these, most immediately by the pattern of the individual poem. This is doubtless what Lindberg-Seyersted meant when she wrote that it is only in individual poems that one can see whether a partial or a full rhyme is appropriate to the meaning. Her discussion does not make sufficiently clear, however, that this principle holds true for all poets, for all poems; it is not an eccentricity peculiar to Dickinson.

What is offered here is a reappraisal of the aural aspect of Emily Dickinson's poetry generally, with particular emphasis on her rhyme. The first chapter examines her ideas about language and about sound and music to suggest a theoretical basis for her approach to rhyme. She did not share our hesitancies about the "musical" aspect of poetry but in fact often thought of poetry as song and of herself as a singer. Moreover, there is considerable evidence that she thought about the emotional impact of sound and the subtle meaning it conveys. The second chapter considers distinct patterns of rhyme within the poems in relation to lyrical movement and structure. The third chapter discusses freer and more experimental uses of rhyme. The fourth is an excursus on the subject of Dickinson's use of *rime riche*, an area that has hitherto received scant critical attention.[15] The last chapter deals with rhyme in relation to the problem of Dickinson's reputedly weak endings.

One question underlies the several aspects of this study. If it is true, as has been asserted, that the discursive content of a poem influences a reader's interpretation of its sounds, we must ask to what extent the converse is true: how do the sounds of a poem affect a reader's intuitions about the significance of its discursive content? Specifically, and most important for the study of Dickinson, how do the sounds of her rhymes relate to meaning? Since sound (phonology) is, as Wimsatt says, alogical, like Wimsatt we will be seeking relations between rhyme and reason, between the alogical and the logical in poetry, but the relations will doubtless be *other* relations than he discovered in Pope and Byron.

Rhyme terminology is often confusing and not widely agreed upon. Generally, I have tried to be precise without departing too far from the terminology existing in previous Dickinson criticism, particularly that of Lindberg-Seyersted. Least satisfactory perhaps of the terms I employ are the terms "full" and "partial." Other terminological pairs, however, such as "exact" and "inexact," "perfect" and "imperfect," or "perfect" and "deficient," while they denote the same categories, were rejected because they attach negative value to anything short of full/exact/perfect rhymes. Other terms including "half-rhyme," "pararhyme," "off rhyme," and "slant rhyme" have been used so diversely that they have become confusing. I have settled on the broad terms "full" and "partial" as words that are understandable and not laden with overtones pejorative or otherwise. Beyond that, striving for clarity, I have chosen a few basic types of rhyme that deviate from full rhyme and have avoided proliferating sub-subcategories.

The distinctive difference of Dickinson's poetry depends in large part on her intentionally quirky rhymes. Experimenting with rhyme, she devised a poetry with a radically new *sound*. Her subtle manipulations of rhyme often contribute importantly to the effect and meaning of individual poems. Her work as an innovator in the field of rhyme, furthermore, has permanently altered the ears of poets and readers. Robert Frost might have been thinking of her when he wrote

> Never again would birds' song be the same.
> And to do that to birds was why she came.
>
> (452)

ONE

A Musical Aesthetic

As a teenager, Dickinson wrote to a friend, "you know how I hate to be common" (L 5). The statement is a telling one, for it marks a trait in her temperament that proved to be permanent: cultivation of an elite self defiant of conventional authority. Her deliberate separation from the common would extend to stylistic revision of traditional practices of the literary establishment. Her peculiar rhymes in particular are part of a "fuller tune" that she set out to give to the sounds of poetry.

> I shall keep singing!
> Birds will pass me
> On their way to Yellower Climes –
> Each – with a Robin's expectation –
> I – with my Redbreast –
> And my Rhymes –
>
> Late – when I take my place in summer –
> But – I shall bring a fuller tune –
> Vespers – are sweeter than Matins – Signor –
> Morning – only the seed of Noon –
>
> (P 250)

This poem is something of a poetic manifesto, and its phrasing emphasizes the poet's awareness of herself as belated, part of a poetic process active long before her arrival. Whatever anxiety she may have felt with regard to her precursor poets, however, the tone here betrays no sense of impotence; on the contrary, with a mock-deferential bow to "Signor," she expresses confident assurance that she will bring a superior fullness to the tradition. Significantly, as she does again and again, she speaks of poetry as music, as song, and she expresses her revisionary intent in musical terms.

Much has been written about Emily Dickinson's visual and visionary power; the power of her auditory imagination, however, has been relatively neglected. The prominence in her poetry of sound and music, both as content and as acoustic texture, merits far more attention. Her poems often rely on auditory images and aural figures referring to metaphysical concepts. She writes repeatedly about the effects of sound on the hearer. And her poems and letters indicate not only that she had a keen auditory sensitivity but also that she had given thought to the ways sound conveys meaning. Her ideas about sound and about music hold implications relevant to her handling of sound devices in poetry and specifically to her uncommon handling of rhyme.

"*My* business is to *sing*," she wrote to her friends the Hollands (L 269). In the context of her letter, the statement, attributed to a bird that has been singing in her garden, stands as part of a parable with meaning immediately applicable to her writing a second letter when her previous one had received no answer. Her statement also must have had, at least for Dickinson, meaning applicable to her dedication to a poetic career, particularly since she wrote the letter some time in or around 1862, at about the same time she wrote to Higginson the more famous and cryptic statement "My Business is Circumference" (L 268). Much earlier, in 1850, struggling with a temptation that seemed irreligious, she had written to Jane Humphrey: "The path of duty looks very ugly indeed – and the place where *I* want to go more amiable – a great deal – it is so much easier to do wrong than right – so much pleasanter to be evil than good, I dont wonder that good angels weep – and bad ones sing songs" (L 30). Even then, she seems to have been thinking of her real vocation as a kind of singing.

Writing to Higginson for artistic guidance, she wonders, "Could you tell me how to grow – or is it unconveyed – like Melody – or Witchcraft?" (L 261). In the same letter, she confesses, "I had a terror – since September – I could tell to none – and so I sing, as the Boy does by the Burying Ground – because I am afraid – ." To her Norcross cousins she writes some time after the death of Elizabeth Barrett Browning, "I noticed that Robert Browning had made another poem, and was astonished – till I remembered that I, myself, in my smaller way, sang off charnel steps" (L 298). She asks in one poem,

> Why – do they shut Me out of Heaven?
> Did I sing – too loud?
>
> (P 248)

She thought of herself as a singer, and it is no coincidence that her poetry is full of singing birds, which often carry metaphorical value relevant to artistic expression. She frequently describes herself as like a bird—a wren (L 268), a phoebe (P 1009), a bobolink (L 223), or, as in "I shall keep singing," quoted above, a robin.

In depicting herself as a songbird, Dickinson is aligning herself with the contemporary female poets, who were commonly referred to as little birds sweetly chirping spontaneous lays.[1] Not only female poets were regarded as singers—the metaphor is an ancient one, of course, and derives from the time when poetry and song were in fact one art. Dickinson's linking of herself and Robert Browning as singers makes it clear that she by no means considered herself as part of an exclusively female tradition. Nevertheless, when she adopts the stance of a simple songbird singing either sweetly or "too loud," she evokes the standard image of the nineteenth-century poetess, a distorted image with which Dickinson has often been mistakenly identified. Though indeed her writing should be viewed in the context of a flourishing subculture of women writing and publishing popular lyrics, it is important not to lose sight of the fact that Dickinson's uses of gender stereotypes are frequently subversive.

Caroline May's *The American Female Poets* (1869) is a representative treasury of the clichés current about women who wrote poetry and thus of what might be called "the songbird tradition." In the preface, May says appreciatively, "poetry, which is the language of the affections, has been freely employed among us to express the emotions of woman's heart." The profusion of women's verse in periodical literature, she says, unwittingly deprecating the product she praises, "has led many to underrate the genuine value, which upon closer examination will be found appertaining to these *snatches* of American song" (v) [emphasis added]. Of Caroline Gilman she writes: "Her poems are unaffected and sprightly; inspired by warm domestic affection, and pure religious feeling" (115). Of Sarah Louisa P. Smith: "The qualities of her heart were superior to those of her head; and bright as the shining intellect was, the lustre of her love and truth and purity far outshone it . . . ; and when we are assured that to beauty, genius, and amiability, there was added the most ardent and unaffected piety, we may well believe that she was fitted while on earth for singing among the seraphs in heaven" (298). Of Lydia Jane Peirson: "Her privations and inconveniences were many, and her sorrows, too; but she poured out her soul in song, and found—to use her own words—that her 'converse with poetry, wild-flowers, and singing birds, was nearly all that made life endurable' " (303). Of Catherine H. Esling: "Her poems are smoothly and gracefully written; always pleasing, from the deep and pure affection they display. . . . [She never] left her home for a greater distance than forty miles, or for a longer period than forty-eight hours. Well may such a nestling bird sing sweetly of home's quiet joys!" (328). And of Amelia B. Welby: "her rhythm is always correct, and always full of melody, worthy of expressing the ardent impulses of a true and guileless heart. Pure friendship, undivided admiration for the beautiful, and ever-gushing love for the gifts of loving Nature, seem to be the chief incentives to her song" (471). The composite picture of these poets is indistinguishable from that offered by Henry Coppee in his introduction to *A Gallery of Distinguished English and American Female Poets* (1860): ". . . from secluded homes, from the midst of household duties,—woman's truest *profession*,—the daughters of song send forth, bird-like, sweet heart-melodies, which can no more be restrained than the voice of the morning lark, or the plaintive sounds of the nightingale" (xv). Obviously, the image of Dickinson in legend and in popular perception bears more than a passing resemblance to the nineteenth-century idea of the "female poet."

The disparity between this debased image of the woman poet and the real lives of women who wrote and struggled to have their works regarded seriously has become increasingly evident through feminist scholarship in recent years.[2] Dickinson was influenced by the writings of female poets, but she appropriated the stereotyped image of the female poet for her own ends. In her study of American women's poetry, *Nightingale's Burden,* Cheryl Walker has identified a number of poetic subjects that Dickinson derived from that women's tradition —"the concern with intense feeling, the ambivalence toward power, the fascination with death, the forbidden lover and secret sorrow" (116). She might have added, as her title implies, the sweet bird pouring out her heart's joys and pains in melody. For Walker shrewdly observes that Dickinson "toyed in her poems with that stock character the poetess, craftily using the conventions of the role to serve her own purposes and then rewriting the part to suit herself" (87). That is precisely what happens when Dickinson takes up the role of the songbird.

In that role, as so often happens in her self-presentations, "what looks like demurral, reticence, and self-abnegation can also be interpreted as a stubborn assertion of self-importance" (Juhasz 35). While the songbird metaphor types the woman writer as guileless, instinctive, scarcely conscious of matters of art (except, perhaps, correctness of rhythm), Dickinson is only *apparently* the guileless warbler, pouring forth her soul artlessly. She is, at least in part, posing. When she writes of the motives for song, she is drawing upon the tradition: sometimes a song is a way to use the idle time of life's waiting and "To Keep the Dark away" (P 850), sometimes it is a remedy for pain (P 755), and sometimes it is just "For Extasy – of it" (P 653) or "for joy to Nobody" but one's own "seraphic self" (P 1465). Elsewhere, when she ponders *why* a bird sings—"to earn the Crumb" (P 880) or not to earn the crumb (P 864), she makes more original use of the conventional subjects but remains within the tradition; the actual question, surely, is whether public recognition and remuneration should or should not be part of a poet's aim, an issue of considerable concern to women writers, who were not supposed to care about such things. But when she sings too loud and with mock remorse offers to sing "a little 'Minor' / Timid as a Bird" (P 248), she is standing the tradition on its head, parodically offering to mimic the timid little songs of timid little poetesses who do their best not to trouble the gentlemen who control the gateways to power. And when she decides (P 324) to "keep the Sabbath" not at church but in her own backyard "With a Bobolink for a Chorister" and another little bird for a "Sexton," she uses the conventional role of the female poet as home-loving and sensitive to nature while at the same time flouting the sentimental piety conventionally associated with the role. When she, artfully artless, daringly constructs irregular rhythms and eccentric rhymes that seem to have gushed willy-nilly from a simple heart, she reshapes the whole idea of verse melodies, bringing in fact "a fuller tune."

Lydia Huntley Sigourney was known as the "Sweet Singer of Hartford." Lydia Jane Pierson was called "the forest minstrel." Dickinson too set out to be a singer, but—hating to be common—a singer of a superior sort. In "I cannot dance upon my Toes," she exults in her ability as poet-musician.

I cannot dance upon my Toes –
No Man instructed me –
But oftentimes, among my mind,
A Glee possesseth me,

That had I Ballet knowledge –
Would put itself abroad
In Pirouette to blanch a Troupe –
Or lay a Prima, mad,

And though I had no Gown of Gauze –
No Ringlet, to my Hair,
Nor hopped for Audiences – like Birds,
One Claw upon the Air,

Nor tossed my shape in Eider Balls,
Nor rolled on wheels of snow
Till I was out of sight, in sound,
The House encore me so –

Nor any know I know the Art
I mention – easy – Here –
Nor any Placard boast me –
It's full as Opera –

(p 326)

As Anderson points out, the phrase "A Glee possesseth me" refers to minstrelsy and hence to bardic inspiration (23). More immediate to Dickinson's experience, though, were popular songs called "glees" and the glee clubs, popular in towns throughout America, such as existed at Amherst College. In this poem, all the balletic details are a surface decoration deflecting attention, like an epic simile, from the poem's main concern, for she says this "Glee," that is, this song in her mind that is also her joy, *would* express itself in ballet but *does* not because she has no gown, no ballet steps, no ballet knowledge— we may remark the string of negatives. The "Art" she knows and practices "out of sight, in sound" (and why else would she use this phrase?) is the "Glee," the art of poetic song, and at this art she is a virtuoso and knows it, proclaiming "gleefully," "It's full as Opera."

As a singer of glees, as bobolink, as robin, as wren, Dickinson exploits the songbird convention of contemporary female poetry, then, but her references to song and music should be seen in relation to a broader historical context as well, the general interest of the nineteenth century in the music of poetry. Of Dickinson's immediate forebears, Edgar Allan Poe had focused attention on the musical aspect of poetry; in the preface to his *Poems* of 1831, he argued that the object of poetry is "an *indefinite* instead of a *definite* pleasure . . . to which end music is an *essential*, since the comprehension of sweet sound is our most indefinite conception. Music, when combined with a pleasurable idea, is poetry . . ." ("Letter" 17). Poe's theories were to influence the French symbolist poets, whose aesthetic stressed the suggestive nuance, the melody of language: "De la musique avant toute chose," Verlaine's "Art poétique" declared (326)—"Music before everything." Emerson's essay "The Poet" claimed that "whenever we are so finely organized that we can penetrate into that region where the air is music, we hear those primal warblings and attempt to write them down . . ." (5–6). Earlier, Thomas Carlyle (whose portrait Dickinson kept on her wall) had written in his discussion of the hero as poet, "A *musical* thought is one spoken by a mind that has penetrated into the inmost heart of the thing; detected the inmost mystery of it, namely the *melody* that lies hidden in it; the inward harmony of coherence which is its soul . . . (108–9). See deep enough, and you see musically, the heart of Nature *being* everywhere music, if you can only reach it. . . ." Sidney Lanier wrote a treatise probing the links between verse and music, *The Science of English Verse*. Walt Whitman found poetic inspiration in the opera. The association of music with sublimity permeated the age. Music, as Joseph Kerman says, "became the paradigmatic art for the

Romantics because it was the freest, the least tied down to earthly manifestations such as representation in painting and denotation in literature" (65). Walter Pater's pronouncement in *The Renaissance* that "[a]ll art constantly aspires towards the condition of music" (106) must not be thought extravagant: it merely articulates an aesthetic belief then very widely held. [3]

Twentieth-century theorists have tended to recoil from the Romantic fascination with the music of poetry. When Irving Babbitt discussed the turning away of Romantic poets from the classical doctrine of *ut pictura poesis* towards musical suggestiveness, his essay became a diatribe against confusion of the arts, warning that "The constant menace that hangs over the whole ultra-impressionistic school is an incomprehensible symbolism" (185, 169). Such criticism has been profoundly influential, to the extent that many students of literature have become contemptuous of discussions of the "music of poetry" and uncomfortable even with discussions of the sound of poetry, which can seem all too subjective. The relationship of sound and meaning is admittedly a murky area. It is not yet clear to what extent the mere sound of a word, beyond the level of onomatopoeia, can be said to convey meaning at all. Since sounds do not have correspondent meanings in any universal system of signification, either musical or linguistic, talk about "the music of poetry," based on a dubious analogy, is unscientific and can indeed seem impressionistic. René Wellek and Austin Warren have held that "[t]he term 'musicality' (or 'melody') of verse should be dropped as misleading. The phenomena we are identifying are not parallel to musical 'melody' at all . . ." (159).

Still, I would like to urge, Dickinson shared the Romantic concern with the ineffable power of music; further, it is precisely because music and sound generally are so indefinite in their suggestiveness, so resistant to analysis, that she found them appealing. Music, she wrote, "suggests to our Faith" rather than to "our Sight," which must be "put away" (P 797). [4] Like other Romantic writers, she criticized the cast of mind that, demanding certainty, is stupidly insensitive to sublimity. Logical analysis quickly becomes a murderous dissection, for example, in this satirical poem:

> Split the Lark – and you'll find the Music –
> Bulb after Bulb, in Silver rolled –
> Scantily dealt to the Summer Morning
> Saved for your Ear when Lutes be old.
>
> Loose the Flood – you shall find it patent –
> Gush after Gush, reserved for you –
> Scarlet Experiment! Sceptic Thomas!
> Now, do you doubt that your Bird was true?
>
> (P 861)

As it so often does in her poetry, "Music" here represents the elusive sublime. The "Sceptic," whose doubt in the presence of the miraculous links him in shame with the disciple who demanded to touch the wounds of the resurrected Christ, is determined to probe and pry until he locates the song of the lark. The song, though, is impalpable, not contained in the physical mechanism of the bird's body, and it cannot be separated from the secret of its life. Remembering Dickinson's frequent presentations of herself as a poetic songbird, the analyst of her poetry may find in this poem a warning against improper skepticism. Her first letter to Higginson besought him to tell her if her poetry was "alive," if it "breathed." Together, the abundance of her musical references and the persistence of her uncommon phonetic practices argue that she knew that "Music" was part of the vital life of her poetry.

The epistemological question latent in "Split the Lark" is answered in poem 1279, which opens with these lines:

> The Way to know the Bobolink
> From every other Bird
> Precisely as the Joy of him –
> Obliged to be inferred.

Only through inference from the sound of the song, that is, however elusive that sound may seem, can one hope to gain true knowledge of the bird. That this poem is at one level self-referential becomes clear in the second and third stanzas:

> Of impudent Habiliment
> Attired to defy,
> Impertinence subordinate
> At times to Majesty.

> Of sentiments seditious
> Amenable to Law –
> As Heresies of Transport
> Or Puck's Apostacy.

She, too, could be "Amenable to Law" but was more frequently "impudent," "seditious," puckish, or defiant as she manipulated her language to give it an uncommon, individual voice. Indeed, we know her by her distinctive music. As she wrote of the robin, we "know Her – by Her Voice" (P 634).

Other poets of the era experimented with verse-music quite deliberately. Poe, Lanier, Tennyson, and Swinburne lavished their poetry with musical effects. Though they tended to the mellifluous, others broke away from lushness of sound in a variety of ways. Hopkins's experiments with word-sounds, rhythms, and rhymes are distantly akin to Dickinson's, though the two poets worked in ignorance of each other. Emerson may have been a direct influence; his dicta encouraged disregarding the rules of prosody when they cramped lofty thought. His ideas are put forth most clearly in "Merlin":

> No jingling serenader's art,
> Nor tinkle of piano strings,
> Can make the wild blood start
> In its mystic springs.
> The kingly bard
> Must smite the chords rudely and hard,

> As with hammer or with mace;
> That they may render back
> Artful thunder, . . .
>
> .   .   .   .
>
> He shall not his brain encumber
> With the coil of rhythm and number;
> But, leaving rule and pale forethought,
> He shall aye climb
> For his rhyme.
>
> (120–21)

Emerson's verse is correspondingly jagged, not infrequently reckless of rhythm and rhyme, because he was convinced of the primacy of poetic *thought*. "For it is not meters, but meter-making argument that makes a poem," he said in his essay "The Poet" (6). Influenced by Emerson, of course, Whitman developed free verse; but, whereas Emerson, cultivating impulsiveness, was inclined simply to ignore conventional notions of verse-music when they got in the way of expression, Whitman more consciously developed the musical aspect of his poetic language as he tried to shape it into a grander, freer music. Robert Browning experimented with roughened diction and rhythm in poems where it seemed thematically appropriate. And Elizabeth Barrett Browning, whom Dickinson ardently admired, deliberately introduced into some of her poems rhymes she knew critics would complain of as incorrect, evidently aiming for expressive effect in contexts where some disharmony is the poem's subject —"The Cry of the Children," for example, and "The Death of Pan."[5] But the departures that Dickinson makes from full rhyme, except in the fact that they *are* departures, are not like Barrett Browning's. Barrett Browning uses a greater variety of verse forms, abundant double—or "feminine"— rhymes (while Dickinson uses almost none), and few consonantal rhymes (which make up most of Dickinson's unconventional rhymes). Emerson's nonstandard rhymes (including *foot/fruit, once/bones, horse/purse, solitudes/woods, wreath/breath*) are more like Dickinson's in kind than Browning's (including *faces/presses, children/bewildering, shower/know her, mouth/youth, silence/islands, Aethiopia/mandragora, driven/heaving, from/storm, benches/influences*), but Browning and Dickinson both seem to use deviant rhymes toward more specific aesthetic and semantic purposes than Emerson usually did. [6]

Isaac Watts is the predecessor who is ordinarily assumed to be the greatest influence on Dickinson's prosody. Though Watts indeed wrote hymns with deviant rhymes, the narrow linking of her forms with his is erroneous. The notion of her reliance on the verse structures of English hymnody and particularly on those of Watts is so pervasive in commentary on her work that the issue needs to be addressed at some length. Gay Wilson Allen had already pointed out in 1935 in his *American Prosody* (312–14) the fundamental similarity of most of her rhythms to those of traditional ballad quatrains, when Whicher noted the similarity of her meters to those in the hymnals available in her family library (240). Ever since Johnson worked out this insight in detail in his interpretive biography (84–86), commentators have tended to accept it as the central, incontrovertible fact of her poetics. Some have viewed her use of hymn meters in a derogatory light, considering it an index of her provincialism and aesthetic naïveté, if not downright laxness (Walsh 136; Porter, *Idiom* 99, 106, 137). Others have praised her handling of the meters, seeing them as ironically poised against the subject matter of her poems, which is frequently skeptical, sometimes even blasphemous, and generally subversive of the simple religious piety associated with hymns and supposedly "echoing" in the meters (England 120; Porter, *Early* 68, 74; Wolosky 14–16, 118). She can hardly have used the hymn meters for *both* reasons—because that form was at hand in Amherst for a poet who lacked the sophistication to handle more complex forms *and* because she was expertly manipulating and deviating from those forms to criticize religious pieties. All in all, the influence of the hymn form on her prosody has been greatly exaggerated.

Her partial rhymes do bear some resemblance to those of Watts, Wesley, and other hymnodists. Her familiarity with hymns may have encouraged her in the use of such rhymes, as James Davidson, Martha England, and others have indicated. It is unwarranted, though, to suppose that her departures from conventional rhyme offer an oblique, ironic commentary on the hymn by providing "a counterpoint of worldliness to the tonal connotations of the ideal associated with the hymn form" (Porter, *Early* 120) or, on the other hand, that her rhymes are naïvely copied from hymns (Porter, *Idiom* 100). Again, the connection of her rhymes to hymns cannot operate in both ways. The fact is that it scarcely operates either way.

Notably, the actual number of poems that have been shown to refer directly to any particular hymn is extremely small. In an early and frivolous Valentine poem (P 3, not included in any of the fascicles) Dickinson does quote (not quite exactly) a line from Watts's "How doth the little busy bee" and (exactly) part of a line from his "There is a land of pure delight," as England has pointed out (122–23). Less convincing, though, is her contention that the numerous bees throughout Dickinson's poetry provide "a defiant counter-emblem" to Watts's industrious bee (122); these bees frequently are, as England says, idle and irresponsible, "seducers, traitors, buccaneers, given over to apostacy [*sic*] and heresies," but in most of the bee poems Watts seems much too far in the background for any but the faintest of overtones. Similarly, though the poet's allusion to Moses' vision of the promised land in Watts's "There is a land of pure delight" in poem 3 and again in poem 112 is indisputable, it does not seem likely that the references to Moses in poems 168 and 597 represent any attempt "to turn Watts' leading character against Watts" (England 123). Metrically the poems do not parallel the Watts hymn, and generally they seem aimed in other directions.[7] St. Armand (159) suggests three additional hymns that he thinks are "mocked" by Dickinson's "Safe in their Alabaster Chambers" (P 216), "I heard a Fly buzz – when I died – " (P 465), and "I cannot live with You" (P 640), but, though the subjects are similar, there are no parallel phrases and the meters are different in two of the instances. It seems more likely that the mockery of the poems is directed towards broad conceptions than towards any specific hymns.[8]

Moreover, the use of the word "hymn" in the poems shows no trace of ironic intent. It appears eight times, in poems 157, 196, 260, 616 (twice), 746, 944, and 1177. Sometimes it refers to a song that offers spiritual strength, but she also speaks of a "Biscayan Hymn" (P 746) and a "Bailiff's Hymn" (P 1177), both clearly secular. A "Bailiff's Hymn," presumably, is simply the cry "Oyez, Oyez" with which an official silences the court; she compares it to a bluejay in boldness. "Biscayan Hymn" refers to a rousing song about a shipwreck, a popular favorite in Dickinson's day, "The Bay of Biscay."[9] In her letters she uses the word "hymn" in the broadest possible way, including reference to secular poems and even to birdsong. The early letter, L 110, where she teases Austin for having written a pious poem and offers to send him "Village Hymns" is an exception. Elsewhere, she refers to Higginson's poem "Decoration" as a "beautiful Hymn" (L 418). And when she solicits Higginson's advice about poems she is planning to give to a charitable organization to "aid unfortunate Children," she calls these poems "Hymns" (L 676, L 674). The four poems she encloses for his approval (having promised three to the charity and evidently intending with his help to select three from these four) seem surprisingly unhymnlike by today's definition in subject, in diction, in cadence, and in tone: the group consists not only of the Christmas poem she entitles "Christ's Birthday" (P 1487), but also of a homily on anger she calls "Cupid's Sermon" (P 1509), the patriotic poem "My

Country's Wardrobe" (P 1511), and the famous "A Humming-bird" (P 1463), now generally known by its first line as "A Route of Evanescence" (L 675).

The assertion that a "hymn vocabulary" impregnated hers (England 119) amounts to little more than a recognition of her use of a generalized religious vocabulary not specific to hymns. Then, too, so many poems depart so widely from hymn meters and hymn vocabulary that any relation is too tenuous even to be ironic.[10] In fact, the two meters most frequent in Dickinson's verse after common meter—sevens and sixes (7-6-7-6) and common particular meter (8-8-6-8-8-6)—are not used by Watts, whose rhythms supposedly permeated her thoughts (Lindberg-Seyersted 130); they do appear in the work of other hymn writers but may be found in a great many secular poems as well.

Attention to Dickinson's debt to hymn forms has tended to obscure the fact that these stanzaic patterns are by no means exclusive to hymnody. Long meter is a pattern fundamental throughout Indo-European literature. Common meter is the same as ballad meter and apparently derives from seven-stress couplets ("fourteeners") rearranged in quatrain form. Short meter is the poulter's measure (alexandrine plus four-teener) arranged as four lines instead of two. Common particular meter is the same as the romance-six. These stanzas and numerous variants of them have long been abundant in English lyric poetry, especially in the fifteenth to seventeenth centuries. They have always been the mainstay of popular poetic forms including songs and hymns. They regained their importance to the poetry of high culture in the late eighteenth century, after the ballad revival. It is noteworthy that the common meter stanza and variations on it occur more frequently than any other in Wordsworth's poetry, followed only by the common particular meter (O'Donnell 16). Coleridge wrote *The Rime of the Ancient Mariner* in common meter, freely extended. Blake's *Poetical Sketches* and *Songs of Innocence and of Experience* show his fondness for long meter and common meter.[11]

Whittier's most frequently used measures are long meter and common meter (Allen 131, 139). And a great deal of the poetry in the magazines and newspapers of Dickinson's day was composed in these meters.

The *Odeon*, a collection of secular songs available at Mount Holyoke when Dickinson was a student there, contains a dozen lyrics in common meter, including "Hark! the Lark" from Shakespeare's *Cymbeline*, "The Harp, that once through Tara's Halls" by Thomas Moore, and a lyric called "County Guy" by Sir Walter Scott to the tune most of us associate with (and in the meter of) Ben Jonson's "Drink to Me Only with thine Eyes"; there are more than a dozen in long meter, including Robert Burns's popular Scottish lyric "Bonnie Doon," to which Dickinson refers in the same early Valentine poem (P 3) that quotes Isaac Watts. It also includes "My Country, 'tis of Thee," which except for an additional line is in the same stanza pattern as Dickinson's poem beginning "An antiquated Grace" (P 1345). Other collections of secular lyrics available in her day reveal similar metric patterns. Hence, we should be leery of the kind of criticism that makes much of the fact that a certain poem can be sung to the tune of "Oh God Our Help in Ages Past"; we should remember that it can also be sung to the tune of "Auld Lang Syne," which Dickinson also knew and played on the piano.

It is probably appropriate to hear a hymn resonance in such poems as the famous "I never saw a Moor" (P 1052), which Davidson likens to these lines by Watts:

> My gracious God, how plain
> Are thy directions giv'n!
> O may I never read in vain
> But find the path to heaven
> (144)

But many other poems, especially those with a narrative element, are more closely kin to ballads—"I started Early – Took my Dog – / And visited the Sea" (P 520), for example, or

"My Life had stood – a Loaded Gun – " (P 754). Some have an element that aligns them partly with children's verse or nursery rhyme, as several critics have noted. "The Mushroom is the Elf of Plants" (P 1298) is one such example, as is this fanciful poem:

> Did the Harebell loose her girdle
> To the lover Bee
> Would the Bee the Harebell *hallow*
> Much as formerly?
>
> Did the "Paradise" – persuaded –
> Yield her moat of pearl –
> Would the Eden *be* an Eden,
> Or the Earl – an *Earl?*
>
> (P 213)

Though Dickinson may not have known the jingle "How much wood would a woodchuck chuck," the harebell poem has a similar tongue-twister quality and a similar delight in preposterousness; its jingling trochaic rhythm and its chimey rhyme are resonant of Mother Goose rather than of Isaac Watts, in spite of the reference to "Eden." Sober analyses that meditate on the revelation in this poem of the poet's psychosexual anxieties overlook both its whimsical treatment of a poetic subject at least as old as the Wife of Bath and its generic alliance with such poems as Thomas Moore's "What the Bee is to the Floweret," a dialogue including these verses:

> HE: What the bee is to the floweret,
>   When he looks for honey-dew,
>   Through the leaves that close embower it,
>   That, my love, I'll be to you.
>
> SHE: What the bank, with verdure glowing,
>   Is to waves that wander near,
>   Whispering kisses, while they're going,
>   That I'll be to you, my dear.

But they say, the bee's a rover,
　Who will fly when sweets are gone;
And, when once the kiss is over,
　Faithless brooks will wander on.
　　　　　　　　　(57–58)

Though both may be traceable to the same origins, these owe practically nothing to the hymn genre. Likewise, a number of the poems belong to the genre of the epitaph, and some to that of the gift-card. But most are varieties of lyric too diverse to categorize—love poems, nature poems, meditations, riddles, and so forth. [12]

Certainly, Dickinson uses traditional stanza patterns as the basis of her poetic structure and she did not compose sonnets or odes or villanelles, but Anthony Hecht is surely right when he asserts his conviction that "one of the commonplaces that is due for serious revision is her supposedly narrow indebtedness to the hymnals, and to Dr. Watts in particular" (5). For Wordsworth and Coleridge, who sought an alternative to Augustan form, "Ballads afforded a model of prosodic innocence" (Wesling, *New Poetries* 30). Similarly, I believe, Dickinson chose her stanza forms because of their apparent simplicity and because of their connection with the roots of lyric poetry. It was a choice: her knowledge of poetry was broad, and she undoubtedly *could* have written sonnets had she wanted to. It was, moreover, a significant gesture; she wrote not in the pentameters of a predominantly patriarchal tradition but in the simplest and commonest of song forms, from which she made melodies uncommonly fine.

As for rhyme, it is quite true that Dickinson's rhymes bear some similarity to Watts's, but her practice is considerably more radical.[13] Moreover, many of the simple consonantal rhymes found in Watts's hymns (*abode/God* and *obey/sea* for example) are by no means exclusive to Watts or to hymns but have come down through centuries of work by other poets (to some of whom, once, such pairs had been full rhymes and to the later of whom such pairs had become traditional). As pronunciations change, once-full rhymes alter in character. By Dickinson's time, readers accepted as a matter of course a few consonantal and unaccented rhymes in all kinds of poetry. In hymns and ballads they accepted a great many more consonantal rhymes. It may be that Dickinson heard in the non-matching rhymes of poetry she knew a potential she might exploit to a fuller poetic effect. But the example of none of her precursors can encompass, or account for, the radical nature of her prosodic rebellion. They may have offered an impetus, but she had no models.

It is worth remembering that Dickinson had a fairly extensive musical experience—not just in church, where she heard and sang hymns, but beyond that as well. Her aunt Lavinia fondly describes Emily at age two and a half playing the piano and talking about the "moosic" (L 11, editor's note). More important is the fact that she studied voice at Mr. Woodman's singing school in Amherst (L 5, L 6)[14] and that she studied piano, beginning in 1845 when her father purchased one, as a student of her Aunt Selby (L 7). She wrote to her friend Abiah Root about her piano-playing with great enthusiasm, and she evidently practiced two hours a day up until the time she entered Mount Holyoke (L 8, L 9, L 12, L 14). It is not clear that there was any teacher of piano at Mount Holyoke, but she writes that she was practicing an hour every afternoon there (L 18). A classmate recounts a peculiar episode from this year. She begins her story in a visionary vein, then subsides into ordinary remembrance:

> Again we see them, a flock of new-comers, as they crowd into the hall for the opening exercises, some comely and graceful, and some destined to win admiration by their shining virtues and talents. We mark one modest, pale-faced maiden crowned with a wealth of auburn hair. Who could have divined that Emily Dickinson's brain teemed with rare notes that would ring through the land? . . .

E. was my friend and schoolmate in early youth, and together we entered the junior class [the first-year class] at Mount Holyoke Seminary. After our novitiate, and before our studies had become of engrossing interest, we began to feel our limitations and fear lest "in many things we offend all". The dignity of our senior room-mates was a restraint upon us. We had been singers in our respective churches at home, and now were pining for our choir-mates and rehearsals.

One day E. came to my room, singing-book in hand. "I can stand it no longer," she said. "Come with me." We took the road to the ferry as the most sequestered, and having walked our required distance, we ventured to delay in the spaceway—the broad spaceway bounded by the horizon. Then, perched upon the topmost rail of a fence, we opened the book and our mouths, drew the diapason stops of our vocal organs, and sang tune after tune,—long metres, short metres, hallelujah metres, *et id omne genus,*—chants, rounds, fugues, anthems, etc., etc., carrying two parts, and by snatches three or four, as the score demanded. We sang and sang till the valley rang "with our hymns of lofty cheer". Our only visible auditors were two or three cows that had been quietly feeding in a pasture near. They were too well-bred to obtrude with double-base bellowing or with horn accompaniment, but they ceased their cropping and stood in silent amazement at the unusual sight and sound. We needed no plaudits, for we were a joy to ourselves. We had found a remedy for depression, repression, suppression and oppression, and no two maidens returned that day from open-air exercises more exhilarated than we. The seminary choirs were ere long arranged for regular practise, which was the tonic and safety-valve we needed. [15]

Mount Holyoke did have an instructor of vocal music, Harriet Hawes, and Dickinson sang for a half hour each day in Seminary Hall, probably with all or most of the student body (L 18). [16]

Though there is no evidence of any formal musical instruction afterward, music certainly played a large role in the parlor entertainments and in the Amherst College ceremonies attended by the poet in her youth. [17] A volume of Dickinson's collected sheet music (preserved at the Houghton Library, along with her piano) shows her familiarity with a large range of popular songs, waltzes, marches, and quicksteps, extending from adaptations of Beethoven to "Ethiopian Melodies," with lyrics in dialect, from contemporary minstrel shows. The difficulty of the selections indicates that she must have been a moderately accomplished pianist.

As provincial as she was—and she admits "I see . . . Provincially" (P 285), she managed to come in contact with some of the leading musical developments of her time, in addition to participating in the singing-school movement and the genteel growth of piano-playing. She probably heard at Mount Holyoke a performance by the most popular of the touring family singing groups, the Hutchinson Family, "whose programs included sentimental songs along with folk hymns and often temperance and abolition songs" (Sablosky, *American* 59), and two of whose songs are in her collected sheet music. She went to two concerts in Boston in 1846, which she mentions in a letter of September 8; Leyda indicates that these were a program "of secular music and songs" presented by the "Teachers' Class of the Boston Academy" and a performance of Haydn's oratorio "The Creation" (Leyda 1: 112). She attended concerts by the celebrated Jenny Lind, whom Dwight's Journal called "the dear and sovereign Queen of Song" (Sablosky, *What* 25), and by the Germania Musical Society, a touring band of about twenty players, based in Boston, with a repertoire including symphonic works by Mozart, Beethoven, Haydn, Mendelssohn, Weber, Schumann, and Rossini (Sablosky, *What* 17–21). [18]

As is well known, one of the delights of her later years of

seclusion was to have visitors play and sing for her. A curious reminiscence of one of these occasions is that of Clara Bellinger Green, who recounts a visit made in 1877 after Dickinson asked to hear Clara's sister Nora sing a solo version of the Twenty-third Psalm as she had sung it earlier in the village church; the poet listened from upstairs, then came down to meet the two sisters and their brother in the library and to express her pleasure:

> "Except for the birds," she said, "yours is the first song I have heard for many years. I have long been familiar with the voice and the laugh of each one of you, and I know, too, your brother's whistle as he trudges by the house." . . . She told us of her early love for the piano and confided that, after hearing Rubinstein [?]—I believe it was Rubinstein—play in Boston, she had become convinced that she could never master the art and had forthwith abandoned it once and for all, giving herself up then wholly to literature. [19]

This recollection suggests two rather remarkable things: first, that Dickinson may once have had serious musical ambitions that she relinquished for poetry, and second, that she had an auditory relationship to a town and its people that she had closed out of her sight.[20] What part her persistent eye problems may have played in magnifying the importance of her hearing one can only guess.

Other friends recall her piano playing. Kate Scott Anthon, for example, remembers Emily Dickinson "playing weird and beautiful melodies, all from her own inspiration . . ." (Leyda, 1: 367). Writing to her friend John Graves in 1856, Dickinson reminds him of old times together and remarks, "I play the old, odd tunes yet, which used to flit about your head after honest hours – and wake dear Sue, and madden me, with their grief and fun . . ." (L 184). Richard Sewall, her biographer, writes, "Her particular talent, it seems, was for improvising"; implicit in his statement is a surmise that she may have experimented with extending the conventional range of music as she extended the conventions of poetry (407). The suggestion is intriguing, particularly if we think of her main extension of the phonic conventions of poetry—her "weird" rhymes.

At the simplest level, sound enters Dickinson's poetry as content in descriptions of the wind, birdsong, thunder, the buzzing of bees, or the low wail of crickets. These sounds make up a natural music something like the voice of nature. "The earth," she writes, "has many keys. / Where melody is not / Is the unknown peninsula" (P 1775). Nature's melodies are not necessarily pleasant, and at times they seem oppressive, like the birds figured metonymically in "I dreaded that first Robin, so" (P 348) as "Pianos" with the "power to mangle" an unwilling listener. Moreover, although natural sounds as she describes them may be potent, they are not always accessible to human interpretation. It is interesting that she thought of even the bat as having a "song," one beyond the range of human hearing:

> . . . not a song pervade his Lips –
> Or none perceptible
>
> (P 1575)

What intrigues her in this poem, as the subsequent lines show, is the inscrutability of the universe's unheard music—malign or benign one cannot tell.

In a chapter entitled "Sounds" in *Walden*, Thoreau recounts the noises he could hear during the course of a day in the woods, but the sounds are less significant in themselves than in the stimulus they provide for meditation on the meaning of human activity in relation to deep and permanent truths accessible not to ear or eye but only to intuition. Typically, Dickinson too reaches beyond the sounds of nature, for the "nature" in which she is most interested finally does not consist of physical phenomena. The reality that matters most, she insists in Romantic fashion, is incorporeal, embracing and transcending all individual natural manifestations.

> "Nature" is what we see –
> The Hill – the Afternoon –
> Squirrel – Eclipse – the Bumble bee –
> Nay – Nature is Heaven –
> Nature is what we hear –
> The Bobolink – the Sea –
> Thunder – the Cricket –
> Nay – Nature is Harmony –
> Nature is what we know –
> Yet have no art to say –
> So impotent Our Wisdom is
> To her Simplicity
>
> (P 668)

Her abiding aim is to know and to evoke in words the experience of that unseen "Heaven," that unheard "Harmony," which is the object of "impotent" human longing. Recurrent as theme and image in her poetry, consequently, are sounds beyond hearing, metaphysical sounds heard by an incorporeal ear, felt intuitively rather than received by the bodily senses. In "The Spirit is the Conscious Ear" she writes that "actual," though metaphorical, hearing is intrinsic to the central self, while a lesser, bodily ear "Outside" serves for "other Services" such "as Sound" (P 733); thus, she establishes a hierarchy that overturns conventional assumptions by valorizing spiritual-imaginative hearing above mere sensory hearing.[21] Elsewhere, a robin drawn by an artist can be heard singing in a timeless world of dream (P 188); or "Hope," objectified as a "thing with feathers," can be heard singing tunes amid the gales and cold, remote lands of the soul (P 254). The overwhelming psychic experience described in "He fumbles at your Soul," though vague in its external reference (is "He" a preacher? a poet? a lover? the wind? God?), acquires dramatic, immediate definition in vivid auditory imagery: the preliminary fumbling music of a pianist gives way to hammers heard in crescendo until the process is consummated by "One – imperial – Thunderbolt" (P 315).

Several poems describe the yearning for heaven's elusive harmony in aural terms. A simile in an early meditative verse, for example, uses the "ear" as a metalepsis for the thirsting soul:

> As brooks in deserts babble sweet
> On ear too far for the delight,
> Heaven beguiles the tired
>
> (P 121)

A darker version of the theme appears in a poem that ponders the cruel torture of leading "One denied to drink" to the well so that he can hear the forbidden water drip (P 490). Ethereal music of stars and spheres is heard in "Musicians wrestle everywhere" (P 157), music that "Some – think" comes from "the place / Where we – with late – celestial face – / Please God – shall Ascertain!" In a poem partly comic in its reversal of perspective, one finds a fantastic vision of Charlotte Brontë, newly arrived in heaven, listening with unaccustomed, "puzzled ear" to Edenic sounds, which after a lifetime of anguish bewilder her (P 148). Here, as so often in Dickinson's poetry, music suggests both a universal order and a sense of separation.[22] The supernal harmony is powerfully felt even when it is experienced negatively, as deprivation, like

> Far Psalteries of Summer –
> Enamoring the Ear
> They never yet did satisfy –
> Remotest – when most fair
>
> (P 606)

Music, again, becomes a metaphor for ineffable beauty. The enamored, unsatisfied ear might serve as an emblem of the poet herself in what is perhaps her most characteristic posture —hearkening after a world from which she is shut out.

The plainest aesthetic statement Dickinson ever made appears in a letter of 1876 to Higginson (L 459a): "Nature is a Haunted House – but Art – a House that tries to be haunted." She is not interested in Gothic specters, of course, but in the mysteries of the inner self. Jane Eberwein's comment is apt: "Like most American writers, Dickinson stressed the interior, psychological aspect of gothicism rather than its exterior trappings of haunted abbeys, spectral apparitions, and mad monks" (120). Even more, Dickinson is absorbed by the enigma of a world characterized by its blank refusal to answer humanity's most urgent questions—chief of which is the meaning of death. Her world looms with ambiguities, and she lacks not only steady faith in traditional Christian verities such as the goodness of God and his universal plan but also that confidence in the mutuality of the human mind and nature that sustained Wordsworth and, sometimes, Emerson. Epistemological uncertainty is central to her poetry.

The aesthetic parallel to uncertainty is instability, and instability is a central principle of her poetics. Her art "tries to be haunted." On the one hand, her stance is that of a romantic quester after ultimate Truth and Beauty. "Eternity is the goal of the journey" nearly always in Dickinson, as Suzanne Juhasz contends (133), although heaven is beyond reach (P 121, P 239, P 319) and beauty infinitely receding (P 516). Habitually, Dickinson reaches for the outermost limits of experience, leaping for "Circumference," for "Awe." On the other hand, however, with an almost modernist awareness of irony she perceives that the certainty she seeks would be a disappointment. She savors the bitter sweets of skepticism. "The Risks of Immortality," she wrote, "are perhaps its' charm – A secure Delight suffers in enchantment – " (L 353). Hence, she revels in the fascination of riddles and risks and surprises. Repeatedly, she urges the paradox that unfulfillment is essential to the highest joy:

> Satisfaction – is the Agent
> Of Satiety –
> Want – a quiet Comissary
> For Infinity.
>
> To possess, is past the instant
> We achieve the Joy –
> Immortality contented
> Were Anomaly.
>
> (P 1036)

Comparable passages are legion in her verse, and their tone leaves no doubt as to their significance for the poet. "Impossibility," she says, "Exhilirates" while mere "Possibility / Is flavorless" (P 838). Pleasure cannot be pleasure in fact unless it includes some lack, some anxiety: "Good, without alarm / Is a too established Fortune – / Danger – deepens Sum – " (P 807). For not only is loss a gain in her poetry, as in the time-honored paradox, but gain promises corresponding loss, because anyone who wins riches—literal or metaphorical—cannot "Esteem the Opulence" as the impoverished can; therefore, she says, "I know not which, Desire, or Grant – / Be wholly beautiful" (P 801). We want what we cannot have, and what we *can* have becomes banal with distressing rapidity. As Roland Hagenbüchle observes, "ecstatic experience for Dickinson is precisely a function of evanescence or transitoriness" ("Precision and Indeterminacy" 38). It *cannot* last because "Delight is as the flight," and the "magic" of the rainbow or the butterfly is inseparable from the perceiver's frightened consciousness of their elusiveness (P 257). The "Zest of sweetness," as she writes elsewhere, is "Dismay" (P 1558).

All of this, I suggest, is related generally to the aesthetic function of Dickinson's rhyme. Juhasz has explained that "Dickinson uses a poetic language and a formal structure that may be viewed as responses to the epistemological problems set by her subject matter" (28). Juhasz offers the examples of Dickinson's vocabulary, figures of speech, and structures of thought. One can add to these the phonetic structure of the poems, especially the mixture of partial rhymes and full rhymes that contributes an auditory instability to her art. As banality is the enemy of pleasure, a steady supply of expected rhymes is bound to produce satiety; the risks she takes with rhyme are part of a strategy to alarm and to exhilarate. Important in this regard is Dickinson's recurrent theme that pleasure and pain are scarcely extricable. The theme is stated plainly in these lines:

> . . . Grief and Joy are done
> So similar – An Optizan
> Could not decide between –
>
> (P 329)

This Keatsian theme is one with significant implications for that appealing theory, discussed in the previous chapter, that full rhymes accompany moods of happy confidence and partial rhymes accompany moods of uncertainty and despair. The dichotomy is so logical it seems it *ought* to work, but the reason that it does not work and *could not* work lies in Dickinson's own conviction that there "Must be a Wo" to enable the perception of beauty or the experience of bliss (P 571), that any certainty without skepticism or any "transport" without the thrill of "Fear" is doomed to be barren, "sere" (P 1413). As it is not possible to divide her poems, or even her lines, into happy ones and sad ones or certain ones and uncertain ones, so she could hardly have used full rhymes and partial rhymes according to any such mechanically systematic pattern. She regularly thinks in oxymoronic terms—of "piercing Comfort" (P 561), "sweet . . . Torment" and "sumptuous – despair" (P 505), "sumptuous Destitution" (P 1382), "Confident Despair" (P 522), "beautiful but bleak" wonder (P 1331), "Joy of so much anguish" (P 1420), ecstasy that is "Half a transport – half a trouble" (P 137), or glory that is "bright tragic" momentary power (P 1660). The instability lent by a large proportion of partial rhymes intermixed with full rhymes is fitting, broadly, to a poetic based on the precarious admixture of joy and pain in all the highest experience, on the impossibility of grasping all we most long for. Thus, her rhymes contribute aurally to the search for "hauntedness" of her art.

Strong as the power of sound may be, the meaning of sound is indefinite. As the tangible and the visible are more immediately present than the merely audible, hearing is one of the remoter senses, apprehending the more elusive and indefinite aspects of experience. John Hollander has argued that in Romantic poetry a new emphasis is given to the auditory and that "we observe, for example, the frequent event of the eye giving way to the ear at a particular kind of heightened moment" (*Vision and Resonance* 24).[23] A simple illustration of this phenomenon in Dickinson's verse is in "I Years had been from Home," where the persona, returning home in a strange panic, hears "The Second like an Ocean" roll and break against his ear, then flees holding his ears in terror (P 609). Or one may recall "A Route of Evanescence," where the hummingbird's emerald wings, ruby throat, and rapid flight are absorbed into a synesthetic merging of sound and vision:

> A Resonance of Emerald –
> A Rush of Cochineal –
> (P 1463)[24]

Similarly, in "I heard a Fly buzz – when I died – " (P 465) the synesthetic "Blue . . . Buzz" provides the anticlimactic climax, imaginatively suggesting the loss of physical vision ("the Windows failed") and the access of something still sensory yet more remote and mysterious as the auditory subsumes the visual function at the moment of death. Agnieszka Salska comments on this poem, "her vision grows narrower and narrower until the eyes fix on the fly alone" (128). Salska's inattentiveness to the strong auditory element here and elsewhere in Dickinson's poetry is perhaps not unrepresentative of Dickinson criticism generally, for other readers persistently

visualize the fly as a blue fly, when the poem refers that epi-
thet only to the "Buzz." While the suggestion of a blue fly is
dimly present, to restrict the meaning in that way distorts the
poem and its emphasis on a *sound* that is "Blue" as well as
"uncertain" and "stumbling." The fly *interposes;* the speaker
hears it but does not necessarily *see* it. Significant in clarifying
the meaning of this poem is Dickinson's statement to Higginson in a letter of 1874, written after his departure from a visit
to Amherst: "The Ear is the last Face. We hear after we see"
(L 405). Since she speaks of him as "vanishing in Music," she
is telling him that his voice has continued to echo in her mind
after he has gone. But the statement also refers to the persistence of the faculty of hearing after the dying body loses the
power of sight. In both ways, the poet emphasizes the power
of sound to transcend or supersede physical presence. She
herself planned to be "in sound" long after she was "out of
sight" (P 326).

Another famous poem where the ear perceives what the eye
cannot is "Further in Summer than the Birds" (P 1068). There
the "Glow" of summer light is undiminished, and no change
in the fullness of the season is visible. Proof of an imminent
fall, however, is audible—in the songs of the crickets, which
herald the death of the year.[25] The interplay of visual and aural
images is similar to that in Matthew Arnold's "Dover Beach,"
where the moonlit scene of cliffs and sea is purely beautiful
and only the roar and grating of pebbles in the surf betrays
the melancholy truth of human cruelty. The dark truth in both
poems is not seen but heard.

Because the meanings of sound evade logic, it held a particular appeal for this poet, who was deeply impressed with
the incapacity of language to contain the deepest thoughts
and most intense feelings. As she was aware of a gap between what there *is* and what one *knows,* she was aware of
another gap between what one knows and what one can *say.*
Shira Wolosky has discussed Dickinson's rupture from the
Augustinian framework whereby through "a series of grada-

tions" the articulated word "reaches to the divine" *Logos*; "For Dickinson," she shows, "the links in this series have grown tenuous" (166). Nature has no need for the paltry "Terms" by which men label her (P 811), and death is of a "Sublimer sort – than Speech – " (P 310). A thought may be "somewhere – in [the] Soul" quite positively and yet be inexpressible in language (P 701). What the heart knows may "stoop to speech," as she phrases it in one poem (P 643), but there are feelings that surpass the narrow constriction of a "syllable." Suspicion of the constricting "Word" for her is corollary to admiration for sublimity (P 1668), for the indefinability of beauty (P 988), and of melody (P 797). The "Ultimate of Talk," she insists, is "The Impotence to Tell" (P 407).

> To tell the Beauty would decrease
> To state the Spell demean
> There is a syllable-less Sea
> Of which it is the sign
> My will endeavors for it's word
> And fails, but entertains
> A Rapture as of Legacies –
> Of introspective Mines –
>
> (P 1700)

The failure to find the "word" here is not defeat, or not purely so, because to "state the Spell" by reducing it to syllables (in a latent pun, to "spell" it) would be to deprive it of its magic; paradoxically, this rather prosaic passage does "tell" in words that with the "endeavor," the incompleted quest, the "Rapture" and the "introspective" riches come.

Convinced that truth cannot be uttered except in circuit, Dickinson envisions an ideal poetry that would be grand and awe-inducing like "Thunder" (P 1247),[26] an Orphic poetry that wields music's lyric enchantment (P 1545). Music offered the unstable blend of invitation to ecstasy and painful elusiveness that she associated with awe. Transcending the boundaries of worldly philosophy, "It beckons, and it baffles" (P 501). And this effect is what she is after in her poetry much of the time, to render the ambiguous experience of harrowing delight that is the best life has to offer:

> The Love a Life can show Below
> Is but a filament, I know,
> Of that diviner thing
> That faints upon the face of Noon –
> And smites the Tinder in the Sun –
> And hinders Gabriel's Wing –
>
> 'Tis this – in Music – hints and sways –
> And far abroad on Summer days –
> Distils uncertain pain –
> 'Tis this enamors in the East –
> And tints the Transit in the West
> With harrowing Iodine –
>
> 'Tis this – invites – appalls – endows –
> Flits – glimmers – proves – dissolves –
> Returns – suggests – convicts – enchants –
> Then – flings in Paradise –
>
> (P 673)

Deeply skeptical of the adequacy of literal words, Dickinson looks to music as a means of touching the volatile, glimmering, appalling, inviting, enchanting truth.

Of course, words are a poet's medium, and there can be little doubt that despite everything Dickinson writes in praise of silence and of thoughts too deep for words, her persistent endeavor was to get her words to express the inexpressible. Since the truth of necessity must be told "slant," indirection is her poetic method. Lacking an Emersonian or Coleridgean faith in the symbolic capacity of language to link the phenomenal with the divine, Dickinson inclines less towards concrete language tied to natural objects than towards abstract words with suggestive power (Hagenbüchle, "Sign and

Process" 139–41).[27] Further, moving beyond literal referential language, she exploits the suggestive power of word-sounds. Joanne Feit Diehl discusses the linguistic process whereby Dickinson "converts her estrangement into verbal power" by pushing ever closer to indecipherability" ("Ransom" 156). She somewhat overstates the case when she claims that the revisionary tactics embodied in Dickinson's poetry aim "to rid her words of their literal meaning" in "an act of liberation that would free her from a confining tradition, a gesture that would allow her access to a new mode of signification" (160); Dickinson remains concerned with literal meanings—in fact she often insists on the multivalence of the literal (as Diehl realizes), but her experiments certainly do thrust beyond the literal, searching for more complex modes of signification. She determined to write poetry that would escape definition, like music, like an elusive fragrance:

> They have a little Odor – that to me
> Is metre – nay – 'tis melody –
> And spiciest at fading – indicate –
> A Habit – of a Laureate –
>
> (P 785)

And she finds means to reach beyond compartmentalized words and syllables in several ways. One of these is the pun. The word "Laureate" here involves a pun on the plant name *Laurus nobilis*, the bay laurel, of which the aromatic leaves are spicier when dried. Laurels, traditionally used for wreaths of honor, the verse also suggests, belong to the poetic "melody" that fades beautifully. The synesthetic equation (of "Odor" and "metre" and "melody") is another way of transcending the literal. The actual "melody" of the words is another. As the quatrain shifts twice from a pentameter line to a tetrameter line rhymed with it, the "fading" of the rhymes, from *me* to the less-stressed last syllable of *melody*, and again from the last syllable of *indicate* to the less-stressed last syllable of *Laureate*, as well as the alliterative and assonantal echoes within the lines, is part of the musical "spice" of this poem. Incorporating the music of the phonetic patterns of language into the meaning of her poetry is a significant part of her artistry.

Though Dickinson had serious reservations about language as a purveyor of ultimate truth, still she cherished language as a real and palpable thing; an avowed lover of "Philology," she supposed that everyone must sometimes in quiet ecstasy partake of "A Word made Flesh" (P 1651). One of her chief means of heightening the materiality, the fleshly presence of words, making us aware of them as words and not as mere transparent signifiers, is emphasis on the sheer *sound* of the words and their interplay in a texture of poetic language. All poets use words so, more or less, but we have hardly realized the extent to which she relies on phonology for poetic effects. Part of her strategy is to reduce the logical element of her verse and to emphasize the mysteriously suggestive elements including sound. Thoreau's rumination about poetry in *A Week on the Concord and Merrimack Rivers* expresses an attitude towards language much like Dickinson's: "There are indeed no *words* quite worthy to be set to [the poet's] music. But what matter if we do not hear the words always, if we hear the music?" (268). To read Dickinson aright we need to attend to the sound of her verse.

Several poems with an explicit musical vocabulary indicate that Dickinson thought consciously about modifying the phonic pattern of conventional poetry, or—as she might have said—about modulating its music. In "The Morning after Wo-," she discusses that ironic circumstance that often is inflicted on persons newly bereaved or suffering from some other raw anguish—the morning when all nature seems bursting with jubilation:

> The Birds declaim their Tunes –
> Pronouncing every word
> Like Hammers – Did they know they fell
> Like Litanies of Lead –

On here and there – a creature –
They'd modify the Glee
To fit some Crucifixal Clef –
Some Key of Calvary –

(P 364)

The "Glee" (meaning both "joy" and "song") needs to be muted so that it does not drop down so painfully on the afflicted. Without making any too-neat equation between a "Key of Calvary" and a poetry laden with partial rhymes, we may surmise that a music-conscious poet who could en-vision herself as "Empress of Calvary" (P 1072) sometimes thought she might "modify" the too-merry chimes of con-ventional poetry into a more somber "Key." In this poem, the consonantal rhyme *word/Lead,* under the influence of the sense of those words, sounds with a leaden dullness instead of a chime; and possibly the light rhyme between *Glee* and the normally unstressed final syllable of *Calvary* has a befitting delicacy (unless one pronounces it "Like Hammers," with a beat unnatural to speech). Alliteration adds to the effect in "Like Litanies of Lead" and in the extended sequence "Cru-cifixal Clef" and "Key of Calvary," which, since "clef" is the French word for "key," also make a metathesis pun.

Elsewhere, she writes with fervent admiration of a poetry that is uncontained and "Keyless":

Better – than Music! For I – who heard it –
I was used – to the Birds – before –
This – was different – 'Twas Translation –
Of all tunes I knew – and more –

'Twas'nt contained – like other stanza –
No one could play it – the second time –
But the Composer – perfect Mozart –
Perish with him – that Keyless Rhyme!

So – Children – told how Brooks in Eden –
Bubbled a better – Melody –

Quaintly infer – Eve's great surrender –
Urging the feet – that would – not – fly –

Children – matured – are wiser – mostly –
Eden – a legend – dimly told –
Eve – and the Anguish – Grandame's story –
But – I was telling a tune – I heard –

Not such a strain – the Church – baptizes –
When the last Saint – goes up the Aisles –
Not such a stanza splits the silence –
When the Redemption strikes her Bells –

Let me not spill – it's smallest cadence –
Humming – for promise – when alone –
Humming – until my faint Rehearsal –
Drop into tune – around the Throne –

(P 503)

Probably, by "Rhyme" here (line 8) she meant verse generally
rather than a device of versification. Still, in speaking of a
"Keyless Rhyme" she is drawing an analogy between liberation from the constrictions of conventional poetic form and
liberation from musical tonality. The poem she admires has
transcended the boundaries of conventional, compartmentalized "keys": it is a "Translation – / Of all tunes" and all keys
into a higher music, better even than the bells of "Redemption." The comparison of this "Keyless Rhyme" to legendary
Eden's melodic brooks suggests its equivalence to a purer,
paradisal music that has been surrendered. Further, the implication is that we have been locked out of paradise by keys;
to recover paradise is to regain something uncontained and
"keyless." She is careful to differentiate the fulfillment figured
in the last stanza from church music and from the songs of
the redeemed around God's throne; it is a poetic fulfillment,
and the throne is that of artistic immortality. [28]

These two poems indicate two directions in which Dickinson's departures from rhyme conventions might move—to

correspond with woe (a "Key of Calvary") and to correspond with paradisal liberty ("Keyless"). Since she sees *both* apparently opposite emotional states as congruent with departures from customary keys, the logic seems a little confused. But since Dickinson clearly believed that bliss and woe are not separable and that the experience of sublimity partakes of both, the difficulty is more apparent than real. In the context of any one poem, correlations between rhyme and emotional meaning may operate in various ways, but it is evident that she was aware of manipulating the acoustic effects of her rhymes to aesthetic purpose, suggesting, hinting, baffling, appalling, enamoring, delighting, and enchanting readers with her "weird and beautiful melodies." [29]

In Wimsatt's terms, Dickinson's rhymes "impose upon the logical pattern of expressed argument a kind of fixative counterpattern of alogical implication" (153). The rhyme *word/Lead* in "The Birds declaim their Tunes" even makes a verbal icon of the sort that he points out in Pope's poems, like the rhyme *Queen/screen* discussed previously. The rhymes of Dickinson's "Better – than Music!" operate in a broader way, however, and the link there between a "Keyless" music and the unconventional rhymes is less a matter of the intellectual import of specific words paired in rhymes than of something evoked by the different sound of the rhymes, something "dimly told" and then "heard"—overheard, almost—in the music of the language. Actually, in both of Dickinson's poems (though not in Pope's) the sheer sound of the rhymes is crucial to the alogical implications that interact with the stated ideas of the poem.

Acknowledging the semantic value of such alogical implications, particularly those deriving from acoustic suggestiveness, may come hard to critics who, fearful of impressionistic subjectivity, want to see language as a strictly determinate system of meaning. One should recall, though, that Dickinson, as a lyric poet, took subjectivity as a starting point. Moreover, the instability she associated with music she saw as appropriate not only for the stance of the artist trying to articulate in frail, inadequate words her intense but uncertain experience of life in a gloriously agonizing world but also for the stance of the reader, equipped with a different experience of life's uncertainties, trying to understand the meaning of a poem written by another person far away in time or space by ciphering at those written words. There are variables at every turn, and a sliding beyond objectivity is a fact of perception of the world and of perception of poetry, as Dickinson fully recognized. In a much-discussed poem, she argues that "Perception of an object costs / Precise the Object's loss . . . / The Object Absolute – is nought – " (P 1071).

Remarkably modern in her understanding of the relation of author, text, and audience, she acknowledges that whatever light a poem sheds is understood a little differently by different ages, and enlarged in meaning thereby:

> The Poets light but Lamps –
> Themselves – go out –
> The Wicks they stimulate –
> If vital Light
>
> Inhere as do the Suns –
> Each Age a Lens
> Disseminating their
> Circumference –
>
> (P 883)

This poem adopts two favorite romantic metaphors for poetic activity—the lamp, projecting radiance, and the seed, living and growing. Ordinarily, these figures are applied with reference to the creative activity of the poet's mind. Here, though, Dickinson extends the creative activity to *readers*, who, stimulated by the life embodied in the poetic text, in turn participate in "Disseminating" its "Circumference," scattering the light and scattering the seed abroad. The mechanical action of the "Lens" and the organic activity of the sower join in the word

"Disseminating" to suggest a dynamic process of historical evolution that operates through the germinal activity of generations of readers. The pluralistic implications of the poem coincide in an interesting way with Jacques Derrida's use of the word "Dissemination"; here, too, the non-presence of the writer in the text entails the substitution, for the progenitor's (Sun's) light, of the seminal/semiotic activity of the sons (agents of "each Age," who—the word "Inhere" indicates— are inherent in and inheritors of the Sun), which perpetually spreads the boundaries ("Circumference") of the original light (or text) into indeterminacy. Dickinson, as reader and writer, accepted gladly the variability and vitality of the interpretive process.

There is an undeniable gap, but not necessarily a lamentable one, between what a poet says and what any given reader understands the poet to say. The understanding of the perceiver unavoidably is affected by his angle of vision, or as she puts it—in aural terms—by the "Fashion" of his "Ear":

> To hear an Oriole sing
> May be a common thing –
> Or only a divine.
>
> It is not of the Bird
> Who sings the same, unheard,
> As unto Crowd –
>
> The Fashion of the Ear
> Attireth that it hear
> In Dun, or fair –
>
> So whether it be Rune,
> Or whether it be none
> Is of within.
>
> The "Tune is in the Tree – "
> The Skeptic – showeth me –
> "No Sir! In thee!"
>
> (P 526)

In her manuscript, Dickinson wrote "din – " as a variant for the word "none" in line eleven; as a term denoting discordant sound, it functions in nice opposition to "Tune." It also sounds an interesting discord with "Dun" in the previous stanza, whereas "Rune" chimes prettily with "Tune" in the following stanza. The idea of the poem, clearly, is to emphasize the receiver's role in making meaning. Sound does not become a "Tune" until it is heard and attired with significant meaning by the hearing ear. The tune acquires reality in the listener.[30] Whether what one hears is ordinary or splendidly melodious, dull or hinting of profound and magical secrets, depends in large part on how one's ears are attuned.

An ear may be closed to what it hears, as when the speaker of "The Birds reported from the South – " says she cannot heed the birds because "I am deaf – Today – " (P 743). Or the ear may be open and receptive, thus stimulated to participate in the attempt to grasp a meaning that escapes the power of words to contain and report:

> Reportless Subjects, to the Quick
> Continual addressed –
> But foreign as the Dialect
> Of Danes, unto the rest.
>
> Reportless Measures, to the Ear
> Susceptive – stimulus –
> But like an Oriental Tale
> To others, fabulous –
>
> (P 1048)

There can be little doubt that the "Ear" in these poems is not only a literal ear listening to natural sounds but also a metonymy for the recipient of poetry, whose "Conscious Ear" (P 733) either apprehends or is deaf to the "Reportless Measures" the written word indicates.

Since she acknowledges the importance of the incommunicable, Dickinson accepts as an inevitable consequence that interpretation of any poetic statement is partially a creative act.[31]

The poetic process includes the reader's completion, which Dickinson overtly and comically demands in one poem:

> As if some little Arctic flower
> Upon the polar hem –
> Went wandering down the Latitudes
> Until it puzzled came
> To continents of summer –
> To firmaments of sun –
> To strange, bright crowds of flowers –
> And birds, of foreign tongue!
> I say, As if this little flower
> To Eden, wandered in –
> What then? Why nothing,
> Only, your inference therefrom!
>
> (P 180)

While she accepts the instability of meaning as it goes from world to poet to poem to reader, she invites not a wild delirium of self-indulgent personal "readings" but a responsible attempt to get at, or near, what the poet tried to say. She did not want to be *easy* to understand, but she did want to be understood, even when part of what she had to say was that meanings are not easily or precisely communicable:

> Good to know, and not tell,
> Best, to know and tell,
> Can one find the rare Ear
> Not too dull –
>
> (P 842)

The audience she imagined for her poetry, too, had an ear lively enough to appreciate her "fuller tune" (P 250).

The music of poetry is elusive, to be sure. Especially because Dickinson's linguistic music differs from common poetic practice, our ears must be attuned to hear it. But it is time to recognize that music is an essential part of the architectonics of her poetry. She was not only a songbird but also a "Carpenter" (P 488).

T W O

Structural Strategies

Rhyme is not only a phonic repetition, a pleasant musical chime. It is also an indicator of poetic structure, a marker of units and patterns of verse. Rhyme shapes a poem in a reader's ear.

The effect of any rhyme depends on how it interacts with a reader's expectations, which in turn are conditioned by conventional stylistic norms and by the way those norms are reorganized in the rhyme pattern of an individual poem. Expectations for rhyme are associated with stanzaic arrangement and with the position of a rhyme in relation to other rhymes in a poem. Since what happens acoustically in a poem takes place as part of a larger process by which a reader experiences and understands the poem, the effect of a rhyme lies ultimately in the reader's apprehension of the relationship between the sound of the rhyme and the semantic content of the poem.

In trying to account analytically for a partial rhyme where a full rhyme has been expected, one searches for clues in the discursive sense of the poem. In Blake's "The Tyger," for example, the word "symmetry" comes as a surprise at the end of the first stanza:

> Tyger Tyger, burning bright,
> In the forests of the night;
> What immortal hand or eye,
> Could frame thy fearful symmetry?

The first couplet closes with a ringing full rhyme, and as the insistent rhythm continues, the reader is led to expect another. Unaccented rhymes such as *eye/symmetry* are within the bounds of usual poetic practice, and in a setting of longer verse lines, or in the middle of a long stanza, or separated by intermittent lines, the rhyme might be hardly noticeable. But here (and again at the end of the poem) it does carry a little shock—especially in conjunction with the word *symmetry*, for the rhyme is acoustically asymmetrical. It poses something of a conundrum, resolvable perhaps in the conjecture that the sound constitutes an ironic gesture congruent with the oxymoron "fearful symmetry," the fearsomeness of the tiger, and the paradox of immortal benevolence forging dreadful predators according to some inscrutable plan. If one could not in some such way see the rhyme as appropriately consistent with other elements of integrity in the poem, it would seem a lapse on Blake's part.

The interpretive problem with Dickinson's poetry is that critical efforts to correlate partial rhymes with themes of sadness or uncertainty do not always succeed—but often do. Consideration of the effects of rhyme keeps returning, as if inevitably, to that old theory that full rhymes are happy and confident while partial rhymes are sad and mysterious, a theory I have been at some pains to point out could not work for interpreting Dickinson's poetry because she does not see experience in such dichotomous terms. What, then, is the attraction of this theory? *Something* must inhere in it. Some sort of truth must be responsible for its common-sense appeal, an appeal so strong that some readers have concluded that Dickinson's rhymes represent an eccentric technical deficiency. The explanation, I believe, lies in the fact that we have confusedly equated the instability of partial rhymes with negative emotions (despair, frustration, anxiety, and the like). It is clear enough that full rhymes have served well in poems that express a complete range of emotions, from joy to rage to anguish. The assumption that partial rhymes ought to be restricted to one end of the emotional range, then, is un-reasonable, even considered apart from Dickinson's idea that emotional extremes tend to meet. It is true that full rhyme affords "the ring of authority and conclusiveness" (Wesling, *Chances* 129) and that, given the conventional background of a poetry centered on full rhyme, partial rhyme is more unstable, more ambiguous in effect; but it is not necessarily sad.

Wells's suggestion that full rhyme is comparable to the major mode and partial rhyme to the minor mode has some merit (267). Though I believe he is mistaken in assuming that partial rhymes (and the minor keys) inevitably possess "un-happy connotations" (270), there are a considerable number of Dickinson's poems—and of musical compositions—in which such a relationship does hold. Musicologists have long strug-gled to account for the affective power of the minor mode, and it seems to me that Leonard Meyer's discussion of the issue sheds light on the affective possibilities of partial rhyme as well. The minor mode, he points out, "is quasi-chromatic and changeable, appearing in several different versions, while other modes . . . are essentially diatonic" (224); as a result, it is "more ambiguous and less stable than the major mode . . . because the repertory of possible vertical combinations is much greater in minor than in major, and, consequently, the possibility of any particular progression of harmonies is smaller" (226). The affective power of the minor is related to the power of chromaticism in general, which, as a deviation from the fundamental diatonic organization of Western music, "may delay or alter the expected diatonic progressions which are the norms of tonal harmony" and thus "tends to create ambiguity and uncertainty as to harmonic direction" and to "obscure the feeling of tonal center" (220). Similarly, I believe, partial rhyme is more ambiguous than full rhyme because the possibility of combinations of partly rhyming words and sounds is much greater; the affective power of partial rhyme, then, is attributable to the fact that, as a deviation from nor-mative full rhyme, it obscures the reader's "feeling of tonal center," creates ambiguity of expectation, disrupts a secure sense of acoustic progression, and thus arouses suspense and tension.

Dickinson's own sensitivity to the minor mode is indicated in the opening lines of P 248:

> Why – do they shut Me out of Heaven?
> Did I sing – too loud?
> But – I can say a little "Minor"
> Timid as a Bird!

It is tempting to speculate about connections she might have made between partial rhyme and the "Minor." Did partial rhyme seem to her more "Timid," more hesitant and tentative, than full rhyme? Probably. In "Further in Summer than the Birds" (P 1068) her reference to the crickets as "A minor Nation" surely includes the musical sense of the term "minor"; that term introduces an analogy between the mysterious (if not exactly "Druidic") "Difference" one feels between the minor and the major keys and the difference between the pensive, elegiac cricket songs of late summer and the songs of the birds earlier in the season. Evidence that she intended a reference to musical keys is given by two stanzas in a variant version of this poem; these stanzas, included in the Johnson edition as P 1775, begin "The earth has many *keys*" (emphasis added).[1] Is it not significant that except in the first stanza, the rhymes in "Further in Summer" are partial rhymes? Are we not supposed to hear some lovely and pathetic difference, for example, as *Grass/Mass* is transmuted to *Grace/Loneliness?*[2]

Neither the ambiguity of the minor mode nor the ambiguity of partial rhyme, however, inevitably produces a mood of sorrow or despair. Meyer explains the perennial association of the minor mode with sadness as an outgrowth of a general assumption that contentment is normative, but he remarks the numerous instances of minor music that is not sad (227–28). The fact, of course, is that ambiguity or suspenseful tension can be wrenchingly painful, or quietly uncertain, or

delightfully thrilling, or humorous. Contentment—and bore-
dom—are unambiguous. We may consider Northrop Frye's
comment, "A musical discord is not an unpleasant sound; it
is a sound which throws the ear forward to the next beat;
it is a sign of musical energy . . ." (xiii). Frye's statement
needs modification: a discord is not inherently unpleasant,
but it may seem unpleasant, or not, depending on its context. Chromatic musical passages depend on a musical context
for their specific effect. Passages of partial rhyme too—*generally* unstable and ambiguous—depend on a poetic context for
their *specific* effect. As a consequence of its instability, partial
rhyme lends itself well to the ironic gesture, the "sour note" of
despair or perplexity, or to contexts of thematic uncertainty,
but it is considerably more versatile than that, as Dickinson's
practice shows.

I suggested earlier that her use of a mixture of partial and
full rhymes is related to her desire for an art that is—to use
her term—"haunted" and hence imbued with the finer zest of
pleasure that instability offers. This principle works in a broad
way to explain her general aesthetic approach, but its application varies considerably when viewed in relation to different
structural arrangements in individual poems. In poems without any pre-established stanza structure, rhyme (both full and
partial) can function as a kind of free acoustic word play that
is almost an end in itself. In poems with identifiable stanza
patterns, however, where rhyme interacts with more specific
expectations set in motion by conventional norms, its effect
alters in relation to the context. A partial rhyme appearing
after a long series of full rhymes has a markedly different effect from a partial rhyme at the beginning of a poem. One
partial rhyme has a different effect from an extended sequence
of such rhymes. The same principles apply, of course, to full
rhyme. Always the discursive sense of the poem is a major
determining force guiding the reader's interpretation of the
meaning of a rhyme, even at a subliminal level.

Because rhymes operative within familiar stanza patterns

arouse expectations for recurrence, shifts from one type of rhyme to another within a stanzaic arrangement are particularly noticeable. Dickinson's peculiar sensitivity to such acoustic shifts is suggested by a passage in an 1872 letter to Higginson, where she wrote:

> When I saw you last, it was Mighty Summer – Now the Grass is Glass and the Meadow Stucco, and "Still Waters" in the Pool where the Frog drinks.
> These Behaviors of the Year hurt almost like Music – shifting when it ease us most.
>
> (L 381)

Her idea that a musical shift or modulation might "hurt"— or, on the other hand, "ease"—hardly provides a full-fledged rationale for the phonic shifts of her rhymes, but it does indicate at least her intuitive grasp of their affective value. Even the poetic prose of this letter caresses the syllables as the modulation of the word-sounds themselves suggestively imitates the transformation of *Grass* to *Glass* in a winter freeze, and the unstressed endings of *Meadow* and *Stucco* provide a faint echo that seems to fit the wistful tone.

That she purposely introduced such phonic shifts into her poetry is indicated in a poem where she depicts herself as a skilled craftsman, a carpenter:

> Myself was formed – a Carpenter –
> An unpretending time
> My Plane – and I, together wrought
> Before a Builder came –
>
> To measure our attainments –
> Had we the Art of Boards
> Sufficiently developed – He'd hire us
> At Halves –
>
> My Tools took Human – Faces –
> The Bench, where we had toiled –

Against the Man – persuaded –
We – Temples build – I said –

(p 488)

In stanza one, the rhythmic flow is perfectly smooth; that stanza describes the peaceful time "Before a builder came" to interrupt her work, to evaluate it, and to demean her by offering a substandard wage. The entrance of the entrepreneurial builder into the poem coincides with an unsettling enjambment across the stanzaic boundary and with acute rhythmic disruption in lines seven and eight, which, even more than the literal meaning of the words, conveys the agitation and anger of the speaker, whose recovery of composure is indicated by the return of rhythmic normalcy in stanza three as well as by the supreme self-assurance of her reply. The content of the poem conveys both the speaker's defiance of "the Man" who would exploit her and her unswerving confidence in her own skill. Meanwhile, the structural craft of the poem *demonstrates* the expertise of its artisan.

While in this instance, rhythmic shifts are prominent among the "Tools" Dickinson wields, rhyme shifts are more fundamental to her poetic constructions. Setting up a certain pattern of rhyme, she arouses expectations. Defeating those expectations can "hurt" like shifting music, but her practice shows that many kinds of deviations from "normal" rhyme schemes can achieve a wide variety of effects, enhancing poetic affect, supporting poetic movement, and contributing to poetic meaning in complex ways.

Dickinson often begins a poem with full rhymes and then switches over to partial rhymes. Three poems structured with that kind of rhyme arrangement may illustrate the diverse but powerful effects of such rhyme-shifts in her hands.

The first Day's Night had come –
And grateful that a thing
So terrible – had been endured –
I told my Soul to sing –

> She said her Strings were snapt –
> Her Bow – to Atoms blown –
> And so to mend her – gave me work
> Until another Morn –
>
> And then – a Day as huge
> As Yesterdays in pairs,
> Unrolled it's horror in my face –
> Until it blocked my eyes –
>
> My Brain – begun to laugh –
> I mumbled – like a fool –
> And tho' 'tis Years ago – that Day –
> My Brain keeps giggling – still.
>
> And Something's odd – within –
> That person that I was –
> And this One – do not feel the same –
> Could it be Madness – this?

(P 410)

In this instance, the reader experiences the security of conventional, full rhymes in the first stanza (*thing/sing*). After that, and by contrast to it, the intervention of consonantal rhyme —persistent throughout the remainder of the poem and thinning out in the final stanza to a semi-consonance (between a voiced and an voiceless sibilant)—seems a disharmony correlative with the snapped strings and shattered bow that represent the speaker's distraught "Soul" and hysterical "Brain." The explicit musical references point to an interpretation of the partial rhymes as dissonant, disoriented, and disorienting, echoing despair. [3]

The effect of a shift to partial rhyme is very nearly the opposite, however, in this famous poem:

> A Bird came down the Walk –
> He did not know I saw –
> He bit an Angleworm in halves
> And ate the fellow, raw,

And then he drank a Dew
From a convenient Grass –
And then hopped sidewise to the Wall
To let a Beetle pass –

He glanced with rapid eyes
That hurried all around –
They looked like frightened Beads, I thought –
He stirred his Velvet Head

Like one in danger, Cautious,
I offered him a Crumb
And he unrolled his feathers
And rowed him softer home –

Than Oars divide the Ocean,
Too silver for a seam –
Or Butterflies, off Banks of Noon
Leap, plashless as they swim.

(P 328)

The metrical pattern here is the same as in "The first Day's
Night had come" (short meter), but the initial impression is
strikingly different. End-stopped lines, elementary diction,
ultra-commonplace subject matter, rhyme, and rhythm in the
first two stanzas are obliquely suggestive of the genre of children's verse, so that the stanzas seem comparable with such
a poem as this one from Robert Louis Stevenson's *A Child's
Garden of Verses:*

A birdie with a yellow bill
Hopped upon the window-sill,
Cocked his shining eye and said:
"Ain't you 'shamed, you sleepy-head!"

(26)

Dickinson's opening stanzas suggest an ingenuous persona,
with a childlike wonder at the ordinary, and the adult reader
almost automatically adopts a stance of some superiority to-

ward the simple vignette of one of nature's creatures. All rather mundane, it seems, except for the artful shock provided by the bird's eating the worm "raw," a surprise magnified by its unexpectedness as a rhyme for the unremarkable "saw." The shock is but a pleasant tremor, really, as one smugly chuckles, "well, of course, raw," readjusting one's sensibilities for more of this clever but perhaps trivial verse. But the poem then is transmuted into something rich and strange. As the bird becomes frightened and the persona tries unsuccessfully to cross the gap separating humans and nature, full rhymes are replaced by partial rhymes. The word "Head" is unsettling; acoustically, it does not fit; the rhymes that follow are similarly ambiguous. As Carpenter has seen, these rhymes suggest "a gradual feeling of alienation between poet and bird" and are part of a rhetorical pattern of increasing disruption as "the last six lines suddenly mix their metaphors, flout the rules of grammar, fly off at tangents to reality, and end with triumphantly strange images" (119). To that list can be added metrical irregularities and enjambment. Here, such stylistic dislocations indicate not disharmony but some breathtaking higher harmony just glimpsed in the flight of a bird; as Carpenter puts it, the technical strategies correlate with a "psychological movement from a world of common sense to a world of pure aesthetic and religious experience" (120). The perspective widens at the end as the bird glides softly to a home that seems mysteriously far away across a "seamless" world, neither water nor air but, miraculously, both. Hecht, who sees in the bird's flight an ascension whereby "a carnivore is translated to a species of angel," views the poem as a liberating "allegory of human possibility" (5). While the poem suggests that chance, though, his interpretation is rather too restrictive, for the poem leaves as an equal likelihood the permanent exclusion of humankind from such transcendent flights. The final mood is ambiguous—delight touched by disappointment. More important, the mood here is one of transport from the ordinary, with which partial rhymes are clearly associated. Along with the images, the partial rhymes support the tone of quiet awe at a splendidly appealing but elusive creature. The final four rhyme-words, softly modulated on the consonant *m*, *crumb/home/seam/swim*, bring the poem to a delicate close while leaving a faint hum of something elusive, not quite resolved.

In this brief poem, a shift from full to partial rhyme works still differently:

> A Spider sewed at Night
> Without a Light
> Upon an Arc of White.
>
> If Ruff it was of Dame
> Or Shroud of Gnome
> Himself himself inform.
>
> Of Immortality
> His Strategy
> Was Physiognomy.
>
> (P 1138)

The first triplet, a simple sentence utterly straightforward in its statement, employs the most obvious kind of rhyme available (fully rhyming nouns, commonly used, and linked by clear semantic associations as well as phonetic similarity). The next triplet, grouped around a consonant rhyme, is convoluted in its syntax and intricate in its meaning. It expresses uncertainty about the purpose of the spider's endeavor—is his web creative or destructive, an ornament for the living to admire or a burial cloth fashioned to trap prey in a gossamer death? These lines deny access to the spider's knowledge, which he earns as he forms himself and his web in one ambiguous process. The pun on "inform" makes understanding of these lines tricky, but possible; what we comprehend, though, when we decipher it, is that our comprehension of the spider's art is inevitably limited. The final triplet, with unmatching unaccented rhymes, has a meaning that is un-fathomable. Is the spider being satirized as a fool for aiming at immortality by physical means? Isn't physiognomy a discred-ited pseudo-science, unlikely to achieve any spiritual truth? Or, on the other hand, is everyone inescapably in the spider's predicament, spinning webs of thought and act and dream and casting them toward immortality? Barton St. Armand ob-serves that *physiognomy* is "a word that itself encapsulates the root for 'gnome' and 'gnomic'" and thus perhaps "indicates that there are other strategies, other methods, other illumi-nations than those given solely by the light of reason" (37); that is true, but the ultimate success of any strategy remains dubious. *Physiognomy* also encapsulates the root for 'gnomon,' the index of a sundial, useless at night; and are we not all, like the spider, in the dark? The spider is an artist figure, as Albert Gelpi argues, spinning out his own substance to outwit night and death (*Mind* 151–52), and one wonders, as Sewall does, what this poem meant to Dickinson herself, writing at night the poems that were her hope for literary immortality (398–99n). *Is* there any art that can apprehend the truth of im-mortality? Is any art more than a splendid shroud? These are questions the poem raises without answering, and ultimately the poem leads, as Charles Anderson has said, to a "paradox of whatever may be one's attitude towards . . . 'Physiog-nomy'" (128).[4] As the poem moves from clarity to an abyss of unknowing, the rhymes move from the plain to the bizarre.

The matter of unaccented rhymes is a particularly difficult one. When these endings receive a metrical promotion stress, as they usually do (including the ones at the end of this spider poem), they can sometimes be absorbed very easily, without drawing attention to themselves. Such rhymes are least con-spicuous where the unaccented and promoted syllable ending in -*y* follows a stressed syllable ending in -*ē*, as in *thee/Eternity*. They are somewhat more conspicuous if the -*y* is rhymed with -*ī*, as in *by/misery*, and still more so if -*y* is rhymed with -*ā*, as in *say/simplicity*. The greater the difference in pronunciation, the less stable an unaccented rhyme becomes (for instance, we may note *Drawer/Rosemary*). If the order is reversed and the unaccented rhyme precedes the stressed syllable, the result is also less stable, and Dickinson rarely creates such rhymes. (Keats's *loitering/sing* is an effective use of this kind of rhyme.) Unaccented rhymes are less disturbing in certain positions, least of all perhaps in the middle of a long poem not divided into stanzas. At the end of a stanza or, especially, at the end of an entire poem, their instability is palpable. In this poem, where the rhymes involve three grandly polysyllabic words in uncomfortably close proximity to each other at the end of a poem, they seem part of the movement away from clarity which is the poem's cognitive as well as acoustic shape.

In these three poems, then, partial rhyme supports tones of despairing madness, of rapturous wonder, and of subtle mystery. In none of the poems is the emotion unmixed— giggles are inseparable from horror in "The first Day's Night had come," estrangement from ecstasy in "A Bird came down the Walk," and affirmation from doubt in "A Spider sewed at Night." If partial rhymes sound very nearly like a "Key of Calvary" (P 364) in the first, they seem a delightful flight from the ordinary into liberty in the second, and in the third they strike a note of futility or promise according to the "fashion" of the listening ear:

> The Fashion of the Ear
> Attireth that it hear
> In Dun, or Fair –
>
> So whether it be Rune,
> Or whether it be none
> Is of within.
>
> (P 526)

In a poetic tradition based on full rhyme, full rhyme is more stable than partial rhyme. That is a poetic fact. Partial rhyme is more ambiguous in effect; that too is a fact. The remarkable thing is that Dickinson's experiments show she understood that the stability of full rhyme can signal pleasant

security or stultifying ordinariness and that the instability of
partial rhyme can indicate painful uncertainty or the sublime
transport of freedom. And more.

Some poems move in the opposite direction, beginning with
a series of partial rhymes and then shifting to full rhymes.
This pattern of progression, too, Dickinson uses to more than
one end. It may, for example, support the idea of a contorted
pain out of which a note of harmony can emerge:

> Sang from the Heart, Sire,
> Dipped my Beak in it,
> If the Tune drip too much
> Have a tint too Red
>
> Pardon the Cochineal –
> Suffer the Vermillion –
> Death is the Wealth
> Of the Poorest Bird.
>
> Bear with the Ballad –
> Awkward – faltering –
> Death twists the strings –
> 'Twas'nt my blame –
>
> Pause in your Liturgies –
> Wait your Chorals –
> While I repeat your
> Hallowed name –
>
> (P 1059)

Literalizing the cliché with which it opens, the poem gives
a bloody picture of a bird—ambiguously vulture ("the Poor-
est Bird") or swan (singing as it dies)—ripping a song "from
the Heart." No common songbird this! The jerky, irregular
rhythms and the consonantal rhyme (*Red/Bird*) work well to
make an "Awkward – faltering" tune, which the bird apolo-
getically explains as resulting from the agony it suffers. But
the last word of the poem unexpectedly makes a full rhyme
on "your Hallowed *name*," with the implication that it sounds

the clear, sweet note of loyal love, the "Wealth" retrieved from a ghastly death.

Charles Anderson explains this poem as Dickinson's own confession of "the inadequacy of her form to the overmastering power of [her] emotions" (72). The protestation of inadequacy, however, is an old, old rhetorical device, and it is a mistake to equate the speaker's rhetoric with Dickinson's own voice pouring out sincere confessions. The sanguinary cleverness of the central conceit and the histrionics of the expiring apologist suggest a tone that is not desperately earnest. Even that final harmony sweetly but slyly connects the *blame* (which the bird has said is not her own) with the *name* of the man she refers to as "Sire." (Ironically, then, it intimates that *he* is to blame and thus faintly recalls the story of Philomela, who was transformed into a nightingale that sang the name of her ravisher, "Tereu, tereu.") Only apparently do the emotions overpower the considerable technical mastery the form of the poem demonstrates.

A similar progression, from uncertainty to triumph, is accompanied by a shift from partial to full rhyme in this poem:

> I am ashamed – I hide –
> What right have I – to be a Bride –
> So late a Dowerless Girl –
> Nowhere to hide my dazzled Face –
> No one to teach me that new Grace –
> Nor introduce – my Soul –
>
> Me to adorn – How – tell –
> Trinket – to make Me beautiful –
> Fabrics of Cashmere –
> Never a Gown of Dun – more –
> Raiment instead – of Pompadour –
> For Me – My soul – to wear –
>
> Fingers – to frame my Round Hair
> Oval – as Feudal Ladies wore –
> Far Fashions – Fair –

Skill – to hold my Brow like an Earl –
Plead – like a Whippowil –
Prove – like a Pearl –
Then, for Character –

Fashion My Spirit quaint – white –
Quick – like a Liquor –
Gay – like Light –
Bring Me my best Pride –
No more ashamed –
No more to hide –
Meek – let it be – too proud – for Pride –
Baptized – this Day – A Bride –

(P 473)

The first stanza establishes the pattern of common particular meter (rhyming *aabccb*), with two deviations—a metrical deficiency of two syllables in line one, and a consonantal rhyme in line six—that seem to parallel the shy, shrinking hesitation of the bride. Two partial rhymes in the second stanza (*tell/beautiful* and *Cashmere/wear*) continue the suggestion of uncertainty. Stanza three, where the speaker strives to acquire the grace and presence of her new estate, also contains two partial end-rhymes (*Hair/wore*) and (*Fair/Character*). At the same time, metrical disruption reflects the agitation of the speaker as she readies herself to emerge from girlhood. The rhymes, though, are less deficient than they seem, for the first b-rhyme (*Fair*) chimes perfectly with the first a-rhyme (*Hair*) and with the final b-rhyme of the previous stanza (*wear*). *Far* and *Fair* sound a rich consonance, *Skill* rhymes lightly with *Whippowil*, and *Earl/Pearl* rhymes at a distance with *Girl* in stanza one. Alliteration too is abundant here. Amid the apparent chaos, then, is perceivable an acoustic thrust toward a fuller harmony. That harmony is manifest in the final stanza, which rings with a surprising accord of rhyme-sounds: *white/Light/hide/Pride/Pride/Bride*. The b-rhymes and the c-rhymes become one, and they are closely allied phonologically with the a-rhymes; all of them sound bright and confident. Shameful shrinking is gone as the speaker arrives at a fulfillment that transcends even pride. The excited rhythms of the early part of the stanza subside to a stately pace as she steps forth at last into her promised role as bride. And the poem ends grandly on the same rhyme-sound with which it so tentatively began. Porter cites this poem as evidence of Dickinson's "inability to sustain a rather intricate rhyme scheme"; "Under her pen," he says, "it unraveled, came apart in the last stanza" (*Idiom* 100). On the contrary, in that stanza the rhyme scheme brilliantly *knits*.[5]

Whereas in both these instances the movement from partial to full rhyme supports a progression from perplexity to affirmation, elsewhere it may be seen as working in more complex ways. In the following poem, the initial structural irregularities parallel the desperate plight of the sinking ship:

> It tossed – and tossed –
> A little Brig I knew – o'ertook by Blast –
> It spun – and spun –
> And groped delirious, for Morn –
>
> It slipped – and slipped –
> As One that drunken – stept –
> It's white foot tripped –
> Then dropped from sight –
>
> Ah, Brig – Good Night
> To Crew and You –
> The Ocean's Heart too smooth – too Blue –
> To break for You –
>
> (P 723)

The stanzaic structure is vague, and the consonantal rhymes *tossed/Blast* and *spun/Morn* appear in context like mere shreds of rhyme at which one gropes in pursuit of a pattern; the rhymes suggest a couplet structure, but metrically these lines are fairly distant from conventional couplets.[6] In the next stanza, one keeps on groping for secure ground; at first *slipped/*

stept reinforces the pattern of consonantal rhymed couplets
suggested in the first strophe, but *tripped,* by making a full
rhyme, readjusts readers' expectations for another full rhyme
in the next line answering *stept* (which would thus complete
a familiar *abab* pattern). That expectation too is thwarted,
though, when *sight* ends the strophe on another consonantal rhyme—a consonantal rhyme for *stept,* that is—or is it for
tripped?—and it is also a full rhyme for *white* internally in
the previous line. Meanwhile *dropped* makes another (internal)
consonantal rhyme, actually closer in sound (by its shared
consonant cluster) to *slipped, stept,* and *tripped* than *sight* is.
The entire series reaches back to *groped* in the first stanza.
The effect of all this erratic play of rhyme and off-rhyme is
to put the reader off balance, to give a sense of "drunken,"
"delirious" tossing mimetic of the ship's experience. Additionally, because the downward vowel gradation in *slipped/stept/
dropped* is akin to that in the English irregular verb paradigm,
it suggests, however slightly, an action sliding into past history—as does this little ship. If the formal irregularities of the
first two strophes parallel the chaos of a shipwreck, the final
strophe reasserts equilibrium with a series of full rhymes and
assonances centered on oo-sounds: the placidity of the ocean
after the brig sinks is emphasized by the sequence of long,
round vowels (in *To Crew—You—too smooth—too Blue—To—
You*), the obtrusive smoothness of which ironically resembles
the serene indifference of the universe to human tragedy.

Interestingly, the poem placed immediately after this one in
Dickinson's fascicle number 36 uses a similar rhyme strategy to
support a similarly ironic point. Here too the appearance of full
rhyme for the first time in the final stanza corresponds with
the imperturbability of providence in the face of human loss:

> It's easy to invent a Life –
> God does it – every Day –
> Creation – but the Gambol
> Of His Authority –

It's easy to efface it –
The thrifty Deity
Could scarce afford Eternity
To Spontaneity –

The Perished Patterns murmur –
But His Perturbless Plan
Proceed – inserting Here – a Sun –
There – leaving out a Man –

(P 724)

The transition to full rhyme is less striking here than in the previous poem, as there is less prosodic disruption in the early stanzas; the viewpoint is detached, the stanzaic pattern is a swinging common meter, and the unaccented rhymes (with stress promotion) are only slightly deviant from the norm. In fact, such unaccented rhymes have sometimes been called "light rhymes" (Malof 194), a term that fits very well their use in this context, where they accord with the careless ease with which a gamboling God asserts his power. Beneath the song-like ease of these lines, though, is a black humor reminiscent of Hamlet's bitter jest at his widowed mother's hasty remarriage: "Thrift, thrift, Horatio. The funeral baked meats did coldly furnish forth the marriage tables." The "thrift" of this Deity is callous cruelty to the suffering mortals he so casually "invents" and "effaces." The joking tone subsides in the final stanza, however, where tripping rhythms yield to the slow pace of ponderous lines heavily alliterated; serenely "normal" full rhyme seems part of an ironically relentless "harmony" in which the final word, "Man," is as inevitable as death.

While in general terms it is partial rhyme that is a deviation from the norm of rhymed verse, in poems that set forth an unbroken series of partial rhymes a full rhyme is a deviation from that pattern and hence can come with a surprising force —the longer the preceding series, the greater the force. That is part of the rhetorical strategy of this very famous poem:

A narrow Fellow in the Grass
Occasionally rides –
You may have met Him – did you not
His notice sudden is –

The Grass divides as with a Comb –
A spotted shaft is seen –
And then it closes at your feet
And opens further on –

He likes a Boggy Acre
A Floor too cool for Corn –
Yet when a Boy, and Barefoot –
I more than once at Noon
Have passed, I thought, a Whip lash
Unbraiding in the Sun
When stooping to secure it
It wrinkled, and was gone –

Several of Nature's People
I know, and they know me –
I feel for them a transport
Of cordiality –

But never met this Fellow
Attended, or alone
Without a tighter breathing
And Zero at the Bone –

(P 986)

The startling effect of those last lines, of course, derives largely from its idea (and the fear of snakes nearly everyone shares), but the first full rhyme in the poem also commands a "notice sudden."[7] The first line of the poem introduces a peculiar repetition of sound in "narro*w* Fell*ow*" (like Mead*ow* and Stuc*co* in the letter quoted above), and a faint hissing of sibilants is detectable in the first three stanzas. Otherwise, the sounds are fairly muted, in the absence of any recurring chime of full rhyme. The long succession of consonantal rhymes sharing an n-sound (in alternate lines from 6 to 16) contributes to the quiet ambiguity of this portion of the poem, and it establishes a pattern into which the first word of the final rhyme-pair (*alone*) fits; probably, then, it helps to intensify the piercing effect of that final unexpected full rhyme, which contributes to the reader's sensation of "Zero at the Bone."

Equally striking, but quite different in effect, is a similar pattern in "I am alive – I guess" (P 470), where partial rhymes turn to full rhymes in the final stanza with a droll musical pun. At the same moment, the bizarre ruminations of one who is uncertain whether she is alive or dead shift to blissful clarity.

> I am alive – I guess –
> The Branches on my Hand
> Are full of Morning Glory –
> And at my finger's end –
>
> The Carmine – tingles warm –
> And if I hold a Glass
> Across my Mouth – it blurs it –
> Physician's – proof of Breath –
>
> I am alive – because
> I am not in a Room –
> The Parlor – Commonly – it is –
> So Visitors may come –
>
> And lean – and view it sidewise –
> And add "How cold – it grew" –
> And "Was it conscious – when it stepped
> In Immortality?"
>
> I am alive – because
> I do not own a House –
> Entitled to myself – precise –
> And fitting no one else –

And marked my Girlhood's name –
So Visitors may know
Which Door is mine – and not mistake –
And try another Key –

How good – to be alive!
How infinite – to be
Alive – two-fold – The Birth I had –
And this – besides, in – Thee!

Morbidly uncertain, the speaker scrutinizes evidence that she is not a corpse laid out in parlor or grave, while the ambiguous rhymes ring an undertone. She entirely relinquishes her fears, though, in the dramatic tonal shift of the last stanza. There is a witty *double entendre* in the word "Key"; first it means an implement to unlock a door (the door of the grave, luckily not yet occupied), and then, as the speaker proclaims delight in life and love, comes to mean a new—and joyous— musical tonality. The final rhyme *be/Thee* makes a full rhyme with *Key*, too. In effect, then, *Key* is a pivotal note, dissonant or chromatic in the setting of stanza six, but modulated into something like a sustained diatonic harmony in the final stanza. Retrospectively, the speaker's preceding uncertainties are revealed as results of the newness of her experience of rebirth in love, and the tensions, thematic and acoustic, are resolved in a happy surprise.

Another structural strategy in Dickinson's poetry is to open with one kind of rhyme, move to another, and return at last to the original kind (in what can be called an ABA structure). This pattern is a significant feature of a poem I quoted in the previous chapter, discussing it in relation to Dickinson's idea of poetry as a kind of music that she wanted to modify, to "translate" into a better music:

Better – than Music! For I – who heard it –
I was used – to the Birds – before –
This – was different – 'Twas Translation –
Of all tunes I knew – and more –

'Twas'nt contained – like other stanza –
No one could play it – the second time –
But the Composer – perfect Mozart –
Perish with him – that Keyless Rhyme!

So – Children – told how Brooks in Eden –
Bubbled a better – Melody –
Quaintly infer – Eve's great surrender –
Urging the feet – that would – not – fly –

Children – matured – are wiser – mostly –
Eden – a legend – dimly told –
Eve – and the Anguish – Grandame's story –
But – I was telling a tune – I heard –

Not such a strain – the Church – baptizes –
When the last Saint – goes up the Aisles –
Not such a stanza splits the silence –
When the Redemption strikes her Bells –

Let me not spill – it's smallest cadence –
Humming – for promise – when alone –
Humming – until my faint Rehearsal –
Drop into tune – around the Throne –

(P 503)

As in "I am alive – I guess," Dickinson here exploits the parallel between music and poetry. The first two stanzas contain
full rhymes, the next three only partial rhymes, and the final
one full rhymes. This arrangement reflects the pattern of lyric
narration in the poem, rhapsodizing first about a wonderful
"strain" the speaker has heard, then wandering off to a consideration of legends about Eden and its "better – Melody,"
and at last returning to the wonderful "tune." The digression is
apparently triggered by an association between this "Keyless
Rhyme" and a lost paradisal music now only dimly perceived;
Eve's surrender of paradise is portrayed in terms of "feet –
that would – not – fly," a phrase that applies both literally to
her unwilling feet and metaphorically to plodding, recalci-

trant metrical feet, onomatopoeically suggested by a series of monosyllables interspersed with dashes. Children, "mostly," outgrow legends of Eden and the fall as they mature; the parallel implication is that "Church" music and the "Bells" of "Redemption" (explicitly rejected as identical with this tune) will also be outgrown as the race, or the individual mind, progresses beyond its present infantile beliefs and tastes. A faint intimation of a better melody may be retained, however; one of the variant words for "told"—"crooned"—specifically stresses the musical nature of an adult's dim recollections of paradise. These recollections link the tune the speaker has heard not only to a legendary past but also to a promised future, for which she now rehearses, humming, anticipating the time when her music will attend the throne of immortality—not that throne of a patriarchal God in legends told to children, but a throne truer and more deserving of aspiration. In part, it seems to be the throne of poetic immortality. The pattern of the rhyme scheme is well suited to the theme of paradise, exile, and return. We can hear the conclusion "Drop into tune," on the rhyme *alone/Throne,* just as the words say it will; hence, we as readers are given a small aesthetic experience of exile and return that approximates the larger experience the poem is about. [8]

Similarly, partial rhyme separates the more ordinary experiences of the central stanzas in this poem from the exaltation of the first and last sections:

> Again – his voice is at the door –
> I feel the old *Degree* –
> I hear him ask the servant
> For such an one – as me –
>
> I take a *flower* – as I go –
> My face to *justify* –
> He never *saw* me – *in this life* –
> I might *surprise* his eye!

I cross the Hall with *mingled* steps –
I – silent – pass the door –
I look on all this world *contains* –
Just his face – nothing more!

We talk in *careless* – and in *toss* –
A kind of *plummet* strain –
Each – sounding – shily –
Just – how – deep –
The *other's* one – had been –

We *walk* – I leave my Dog – at home –
A *tender – thoughtful* Moon
Goes with us – just a little way –
And – then – we are *alone* –

Alone – if *Angels* are "alone" –
First time they *try* the *sky!*
Alone – if those "vailed faces" – be –
We cannot *count* – on High!

I'd give – to live that hour – *again* –
The *purple – in my Vein* –
But *He* must *count the drops – himself* –
My price for *every stain!*

(P 663)

Full rhyme supports the tone of excitement in the three stanzas leading up to the meeting. The emotional pitch relaxes as the speaker's anticipation gives way to the mundane reality of tentative, shy conversation, and the unobtrusive consonantal rhymes in stanzas four and five, linked by a soft nasal sound, seem accordingly "careless" and—by contrast with the earlier full rhymes and by association with the sense of the words—sound a somewhat subdued music, "A kind of plummet strain" (a phrase that also functions in relation to the couple's shy "sounding" of each other's hidden depths). With the repeated word *alone*, however, the poem returns to rapture, now even more intense as the two, alone and together, are transported to angelic ecstasy. The trick of repeating the final word of the stanza as the first word of the succeeding stanza, where it acquires a different sense and participates in an altered mood, recalls Keats's use of the word "forlorn" in "Ode to A Nightingale," which functions in a similarly pivotal way. With full end rhymes and additional internal rhymes (*try/sky, be/We, give/live*), the poem is transposed, as it were, into a brighter key. Thus, technical adjustments of rhyme reinforce the poetic pattern of expectation, delay, and ultimate fulfillment.

Contrasting rhyme groups in an ABA arrangement may work, though, in conjunction with considerable variations of tone and mood. A frame of full rhyme serves in "My Life had stood – a Loaded Gun" (P 754) to set off the four middle stanzas, which describe the activities of the present, from the first, which tells of the purposeless idleness of the speaker's past life before the "Owner" came, and from the last, which foretells the purposelessness of any future life should the owner die. In "Publication – is the Auction" partial rhymes separate the high disdain of the first and last stanzas from the calmer middle section:

> Publication – is the Auction
> Of the Mind of Man –
> Poverty – be justifying
> For so foul a thing
>
> Possibly – but We – would rather
> From Our Garret go
> White – Unto the White Creator –
> Than invest – Our Snow –
>
> Thought belong to Him who gave it –
> Then – to Him Who bear
> It's Corporeal illustration – Sell
> The Royal Air –

In the Parcel – Be the Merchant
Of the Heavenly Grace –
But reduce no Human Spirit
To Disgrace of Price –

(P 709)[9]

In another poem, informed by the grisly facts of Civil War battles, full rhyme sets off a contrasting central section from a beginning and end that are comparatively wistful and pensive:

My Portion is Defeat – today –
A paler luck than Victory –
Less Paeans – fewer Bells –
The Drums dont follow Me – with tunes –
Defeat – a somewhat slower – means –
More Arduous than Balls –

Tis populous with Bone and stain –
And Men too straight to stoop again,
And Piles of solid Moan –
And Chips of Blank – in Boyish Eyes –
And scraps of Prayer –
And Death's surprise,
Stamped visible – in Stone –

There's somewhat prouder, over there –
The Trumpets tell it to the Air –
How different Victory
To Him who has it – and the One
Who to have had it, would have been
Contenteder – to die –

(P 639)

The first and last stanzas, partially rhymed, seem quiet against the graphic horrors between, and the full rhymes there seem clangorous when rigor mortis stops young *Eyes* in "Blank" *surprise* and provides a sinister link between *Moan* and *Stone*. Here is a notable exception to the supposed rule that partial rhymes belong in settings of anguish. An experiment without any close parallel in Dickinson's verse, it is an instructive example of what rhyme-shifts can accomplish; whereas an effective poem of a similar nature might have been written with full rhymes at beginning and end and "dissonant" partial rhymes between, this poem, effective in a different way, proves that contrasting rhymes can make one portion of a poem stand out from the rest and intensify it.

The structures outlined in these examples are typical of Dickinson's poetry. Shifting emotional and psychological currents characteristically are allied with patterned shifts of rhyme. The structural patterns represented above, however, by no means exhaust the patterns one can locate in her verse, where the proliferation of types of verse patterns reflects her formal flexibility. The structure of this monologue, for instance, might be classified as ABA plus a coda:

> Let Us play Yesterday –
> I – the Girl at school –
> You – and Eternity – the
> Untold Tale –
>
> Easing my famine
> At my Lexicon –
> Logarithm – had I – for Drink –
> 'Twas a dry Wine –
>
> Somewhat different – must be –
> Dreams tint the Sleep –
> Cunning Reds of Morning
> Make the Blind – leap –
>
> Still at the Egg-life –
> Chafing the Shell –
> When you troubled the Ellipse –
> And the Bird fell –
>
> Manacles be dim – they say –
> To the new Free –

Liberty – Commoner –
Never could – to me –

'Twas my last gratitude
When I slept – at night –
'Twas the first Miracle
Let in – with Light –

Can the Lark resume the Shell –
Easier – for the Sky –
Would'nt Bonds hurt more
Than Yesterday?

Would'nt Dungeons sorer grate
On the Man – free –
Just long enough to taste –
Then – doomed new –

God of the Manacle
As of the Free –
Take not my Liberty
Away from Me –

(P 728)

The first two stanzas recall the speaker's famished life before
the miracle of "You – and Eternity"; the partial rhymes here
may seem a deprivation, the acoustic equivalent of "a dry
Wine." The next four stanzas, with full rhymes, describe the
"Miracle." In the third stanza, the first full rhyme of the poem
falls on the verb "leap," and it gives a surprise consistent with
the meaning. The speaker's narration of her breakthrough to
liberty in the next stanza, similarly, comes with a full rhyme
on the verb "fell," an acoustic as well as a cognitive stimulant
(a fall to freedom being a tantalizing and familiar paradox imaged here in the bird's fall from the confinement of the nest).
The rhymes continue to chime (merrily?) for two more stanzas,
but an ominous element is introduced by the use of the past
tense as the speaker expresses her gratitude: " 'Twas my last
gratitude . . . 'Twas the first Miracle"—is it *over?* we must won-

der. The partial rhymes in the next two stanzas accompany a transposition to a new key, worried and questioning; the speaker's freedom is clearly in some danger. The last stanza, a prayer against threatening loss to a "God of the Manacle" who circumscribes human liberty—giving it and taking it away, serves as a sort of coda to the story. Full rhymes (*Free/Me* and an additional light rhyme on *Liberty*) echo the same rhymes at the midpoint of the poem; they also mark the section off as separate, support a sense of closure, and strengthen the urgent tone of the plea.

The uncertainties of experience, the long protractions of desire, and the brevity of its fulfillments are Dickinson's great subjects. Disjuncture and deferral and surprise, accordingly, are chief among her artistic tools. Shifts of rhyme and rhythm that move along with subtle fluctuations of thought and feeling provide a dynamic means of stirring, shaping, and guiding responsive currents of lyric emotion. Absence of a predictable rhyme pattern leaves the reader a little off balance, dislocated, and thus draws the reader into active participation in the poetic process. Whether a formal configuration constitutes a "Rune" or a "din" may depend on how each reader's ear cooperates in the process of discovering and creating meaning (P 526). But it is clear that Higginson's willingness to overlook "faulty" rhymes when a thought took his breath away misses one of the secrets of her art: often it is the rhymes themselves that take one's breath away.

Ultimately, attempts to classify Dickinson's structural arrangements must yield to a diversity of formal structures that exceeds taxonomical ambitions. But her technical daring is in evidence everywhere, and even more dramatic structural disjunctures than those rhyme modulations I have been describing make up a prominent strategy. Not infrequently, she wrenches one portion of a poem into a new shape for special prosodic and semantic purpose. The third stanza of this poem (otherwise in common meter) is an example:

I prayed, at first, a little Girl,
Because they told me to –
But stopped, when qualified to guess
How prayer would feel – to me –

If I believed God looked around,
Each time my Childish eye
Fixed full, and steady, on his own
In Childish honesty –

And told him what I'd like, today,
And parts of his far plan
That baffled me –
The mingled side
Of his Divinity –

And often since, in Danger,
I count the force 'twould be
To have a God so strong as that
To hold my life for me

Till I could take the Balance
That tips so frequent, now,
It takes me all the while to poise –
And then – it doesn't stay –

(P 576)

Lindberg-Seyersted has explained the prosodic deviation of the third stanza in relation to the adult's ironic recognition of all that is "mingled" about divine doings: "This pivotal stanza changes the regular metric and stanzaic pattern established in the first two stanzas of alternating iambs in Eights and Sixes. The division of 'That baffled me – / The mingled side' into two lines—which alters the line pattern—is most certainly intentional: 'me' rhymes with the end word of the last line, 'Divinity', breaking up the rhyming pattern, which in the first two stanzas is *xaya* . . ." (41). One anticipates some rhyme-word for *plan*, but none comes; instead, another rhyme comes in the wrong place, throwing things out of kilter. The only full rhyme in the entire poem comes in the fourth stanza along with the speaker's nostalgic vision of a God who could "hold my life" in perfect poise. In a sense, this is the climactic stanza, the one toward which all the earlier stanzas and all those partial vowel rhymes (zero-consonance and unaccented rhymes) *to/me/eye/honesty/me/Divinity* move and at last arrive: *be/me* sounds, just briefly, a secure harmony consistent with the imagined fulfillment. Then "the Balance" slips crooked again, dropping back to partial rhymes, *now* and *stay*. Lindberg-Seyersted comments on the poem, "there is no status quo, no resting position, no final happiness or unhappiness; loss and gain, pain and ecstasy, life and death—both weights are in the Balance, and the scales are never at perfect equilibrium" (42). Oddly, though, for a critic so sensitive, she misses the acoustic significance of the rhyme progression and complains that the poem fails because it "peters out in the flatness of the final line" (41), because "the nerveless last two lines . . . only serve to weaken the promising image of the Balance" (42). Precisely. Or almost so. The nervelessness of that last line and the out-of-balanceness of that last rhyme are exactly *right* for the meaning of the poem; they contribute to its success. Lindberg-Seyersted cites Dickinson's variant last line as evidence that the poet was not satisfied with the weak ending, but the alternate line is equally weak: "It isn't steady – tho' – ." This variant ends with a partial rhyme and the same idea of failure. The flaccidity of *both* lines is indicative of the poet's deliberate aim.

Similarly, Eberwein, arguing Dickinson's lack of craftsmanship, identifies as "organizational collapse" (129) a prosodic disarray that is almost certainly deliberate:

> I got so I could hear his name –
> Without – Tremendous gain –
> That Stop-Sensation – on my Soul –
> And Thunder – in the Room –

I got so I could walk across
That Angle in the floor,
Where he turned so, and I turned – how –
And all our Sinew tore –

I got so I could stir the Box –
In which his letters grew
Without that forcing, in my breath –
As Staples – driven through –

Could dimly recollect a Grace –
I think, they call it "God" –
Renowned to ease Extremity –
When Formula, had failed –

And shape my Hands –
Petition's way,
Tho' ignorant of a word
That Ordination – utters –

My Business, with the Cloud,
If any Power behind it, be,
Not subject to Despair –
It care, in some remoter way,
For so minute affair
As Misery –
Itself, too great, for interrupting – more –

(P 293)

The speaker tells how she (or, maybe, he) gradually regained equilibrium after a dreadful trauma; appropriately, the poem starts in common meter, almost regular except for a consonantal rhyme, and then progresses to two stanzas completely regular and fully rhymed. As Eberwein correctly notes, "the tight parallel construction of the opening three stanzas reinforces the sense of hard-won self-control" (129). Then "Formula" starts to fail again, only a little at first, with a deviant rhyme, but it is a foreboding one: *"God"/failed*. Then the pattern disintegrates further, and what the speaker describes the reader partially experiences; the ear hears *word* where it belongs metrically and then gropes for its anticipated mate, which at first seems to be missing and then turns out to be way down in the next stanza, in *Cloud*. God, it seems, is hidden behind the clouds. Or not there at all. The structure disintegrates as the speaker becomes increasingly uncertain about how to address this rumored God and, "If" He *is* there, about whether "It" could even care about one soul's "minute . . . Misery." *Despair* and *affair* rhyme fully on the right metrical beats (and with *care* internally), but they are obscured by the surrounding words that look shapeless and uncontrolled and ramble on until, abruptly, they stop. The speaker is immersed again in her misery, gigantic to her if "minute" to God, and she is again victimized by the "Stop-sensation" she had thought she had conquered. Actually, the hard-earned control she has bragged of was but a brief interruption of her "Extremity." The rhymes as structural markers, and as acoustic indicators of stability and instability, play a crucial role in underlining the meaning of this poem. The speaker's form has collapsed. The poet's has not.

Calculated disruptions of structure work with great success in the following poem, which is something of a *tour de force:*

No Bobolink – reverse His Singing
When the only Tree
Ever He minded occupying
By the Farmer be –

Clove to the Root –
His Spacious Future –
Best Horizon – gone –
Whose Music be His
Only Anodyne –
Brave Bobolink –

(P 755)

The poem opens in regular rhythm and alternate lines of nine and five syllables (a variation of fourteeners), with full rhymes in lines two and four and, in lines one and three, the repetition of the unstressed final syllable -*ing*. Here's another nice little verse about a singing bird, one unsuspectingly assumes, when suddenly the form is "Clove to the Root." The harsh enjambment throws into focus the break between stanzas as a hiatus that cleaves the poem, as the bird's security is cloven. The rhythmic deviation in the line "Clove to the Root" is likewise jarring. The structure is felt to be tottering. It gradually regains equilibrium in the next lines as the rhythm approaches the original paradigm. The consonantal rhyme of *gone/Anodyne* partly satisfies the anticipation of a restored pattern, but just partly, as "Music" assuages the bird's pain but does not bring back its lost horizon. Then the poem ends with a remote consonance, hardly a rhyme at all, an isolated, onomatopoeic name—"Bobolink." [10] The poem itself, like the bird, trembles on the brink of chaos with a virtuosity that lightens the tone of a meditation otherwise passionately somber. [11]

Knowing that Dickinson at least once referred to herself as a "little Bob o' Lincoln" (L 223) adds a dimension to the poem. The poet wrote with bitter knowledge of personal loss, and she must have thought at times of her poetry, her "Music," as a consolation. But expression of personal feeling is a lyric convention, and the real meaning for readers arises out of their own experiences of catastrophic disappointment, their sense of their own identification with the bobolink. It is not Dickinson's pain that moves us, but the dramatization of that pain in carefully crafted language that organizes images and word-sounds to enhance the emotional resonance of an intellectual statement and so turns it into "Singing."

Another tactic Dickinson employs is the deliberate dislocation of a rhyme for a special semantic effect. In the well known "After great pain, a formal feeling comes" (P 341), the lines are arranged in rhymed couplets, except in the anomalous second stanza:

> After great pain, a formal feeling comes –
> The Nerves sit ceremonious, like Tombs –
> The stiff Heart questions was it He, that bore,
> And Yesterday, or Centuries before?
>
> The Feet, mechanical, go round –
> Of Ground, or Air, or Ought –
> A Wooden Way
> Regardless grown,
> A Quartz contentment, like a stone –
>
> This is the Hour of Lead –
> Remembered, if outlived,
> As Freezing persons, recollect the Snow –
> First – Chill – then Stupor – then the letting go –
>
> (P 341)

In the middle stanza, the unthinking, "Wooden" motion that continues in states of spiritual numbness is suggested not only by the idea of feet functioning mechanically without the guidance of the mind and will but also by the steady iambic movement that proceeds dully without regard to ("Regardless" of) stanzaic shape or placement of rhyme. *Ground* rhymes perfectly with *round,* but not at the end of the line where it would seem orderly and coherent. Instead, it falls almost lost amid two unrhymed lines that move as if randomly, aimlessly, like the body whose soul is stupefied by pain. The word "Feet," then, refers not only to human feet but, in a subsidiary way, to poetic feet.[12] As the poem comments on the feeling of disconnectedness experienced by suffering persons, whose "Nerves" and "Heart" and "Feet" (and perhaps eyes, too, implied in the word "Regardless") continue to function without any sense of unity or purpose, so the poetic feet in the middle stanza continue to move detached not only from the pattern of pentameter couplets established in the first stanza but also from the pattern of tetrameter couplets suggested but withheld (as if lost) in its own structure.[13] The return to the pentameter couplet paradigm at the end of the poem carries with it a suggestion of a recovered stability—in context, though, a frozen, deathlike stability worse even than wooden, mechanical motion.

A dislocated rhyme leaves the ending of another poem slightly, but purposefully, askew:

> We grow accustomed to the Dark –
> When Light is put away –
> As when the Neighbor holds the Lamp
> To witness her Goodbye –
>
> A Moment – We uncertain step
> For newness of the night –
> Then – fit our Vision to the Dark –
> And meet the Road – erect –
>
> And so of larger – Darknesses –
> Those Evenings of the Brain –
> When not a Moon disclose a sign –
> Or Star – come out – within –
>
> The B[r]avest – grope a little –
> And sometimes hit a Tree
> Directly in the Forehead –
> But as they learn to see –
>
> Either the Darkness alters –
> Or something in the sight
> Adjusts itself to Midnight –
> And Life steps almost straight.
>
> (P 419)

The poem is structured around an analogy: as when we step into literal darkness our eyes gradually adjust, so when we step into emotional darkness we gradually become accustomed to it. The first two stanzas, treating the adjustment to literal "Dark," explain that initial uncertainty is followed by the return of stability (meeting "the Road – erect"); hence, when the next stanzas draw the metaphorical parallel, we are led to anticipate an affirmative conclusion. The full rhyme in the fourth stanza, especially *Tree/see* as the first full rhyme in the poem (following as it does the uncertain-sounding partial rhymes preceding), seems to herald a positive climax: "But as they learn to see," chiming fully, prompts our ears to listen for another full rhyme to accompany the expected statement about how firmly and confidently these veterans of psychic darkness will walk through the gloom. The final stanza, however, offers a surprise. The anticipated rhyme is there—almost —as *sight/Midnight*, but in the wrong position and with the stress awry; in the position where we expected a full rhyme, there is a partial rhyme, *sight/straight*, which does not strike the firm note we anticipated at all. The effect of the rhymes is calculated so that a reader's experience of these lines accords precisely with the meaning: "Life steps almost straight."

In another poem, where the shift from full rhyme to partial rhyme in the final stanza reflects the speaker's transition from naive faith to cynicism, there is also a deliberately misplaced rhyme in the penultimate stanza:

> I meant to have but modest needs –
> Such as Content – and Heaven –
> Within my income – these could lie
> And Life and I – keep even –
>
> But since the last – included both –
> It would suffice my Prayer
> But just for One – to stipulate –
> And Grace would grant the Pair –
>
> And so – upon this wise – I prayed –
> Great Spirit – Give to me
> A Heaven not so large as Your's,
> But large enough – for me –
>
> A Smile suffused Jehovah's face –
> The Cherubim – withdrew –

Grave Saints stole out to look at me –
And showed their dimples – too –

I left the Place, with all my might –
I threw my Prayer away –
The Quiet Ages picked it up –
And Judgment – twinkled – too –
That one so honest – be extant –
It take the Tale for true –
That "Whatsoever Ye shall ask –
Itself be given You" –

But I, grown shrewder – scan the Skies
With a suspicious Air –
As Children – swindled for the first
All Swindlers – be – infer –

(P 476)

To make a conventionally "correct" rhyme, Dickinson might easily have written "My Prayer away I threw" in line 18, as in fact did the editors of the 1891 *Poems;* but she clearly wanted to emphasize the casting away of ingenuous prayer by casting away the rhyme. The internal rhyme "threw" emphasizes the absence of the proper rhyme at the line end while the speaker's sharp break from smiling saints and smiling hopes is reflected in the acoustic break between this line and the unusually long sequence of full rhymes surrounding it—*withdrew/too/[away]/too/true/You.*[14] Dickinson draws attention throughout the poem to the speaker's childishness, evidenced both in the naively pious expectations of the opening (where that first consonantal rhyme, *Heaven/even,* so conventional in religious verse, seems particularly apt) and in the exaggeratedly skeptical reaction of the end (where the unconventional consonantal rhyme *Air/infer* is compatible with the new sophisticate's rejection of convention). Thus, in the context of a fairly benign array of divinity—God with cherubs, dimpled saints, and twinkling Judgment—all amused by the speaker's childish honesty, both the action and the misplaced rhyme in line 18 serve as a display of what may best be described as a fit of pique.

Somewhat different in effect is the rhyme submerged in this verse, which arises from the mature wisdom that the ravages of mortality make love and beauty dearer:

> Like Time's insidious wrinkle
> On a beloved Face
> We clutch the Grace the tighter
> Though we resent the crease. . . .
>
> (P 1236)

The consonantal rhyme *Face/crease,* in its acoustic imbalance, suits the idea of the ineluctable dishevelment imposed by time, but the fully rhyming *Grace,* an internal rhyme, suggesting a harmony obscured but real and "clutchable," marks acoustically a beauty that yet endures. [15]

Among the most masterful of Dickinson's formal restructurings is an elaborate arrangement of dislocated full and partial and internal rhymes that provides a conclusion to the poem "I cannot live with You" (P 640). In eleven preceding stanzas of four lines each, the speaker explains the reason why life with the person addressed is impossible, why death together is also impossible, why even resurrection together is out of the question. All the preceding stanzas, except for the eighth, rhyme in an alternate scheme *abcb,* six of them (and the three immediately before the last) fully. Then comes the marvelous conclusion:

> So We must meet apart –
> You there – I – here –
> With just the Door ajar
> That Oceans are – and Prayer –
> And that White Sustenance –
> Despair –

The pattern established earlier leads one to expect a rhyme-word, probably a full rhyme, for *here* at the end of the second line after it. But the acoustic pattern of the stanza throws the reader off balance. What rhymes with what? What is the shape of this six-line stanza? *Here* finds a consonantal rhyme-mate on the right metrical beat, but internally, two lines later, in *are*, and, on the wrong metrical beat in the right position at line-end, another consonantal rhyme-mate, *Prayer*. There are partial rhymes, *apart* and *ajar*, at the ends of the *a* and *c* lines. Moreover, *are* rhymes fully but internally with *ajar*, and *Prayer* at line-end rhymes fully with the internal *there*. All these criss-crossing rhyme-sounds are stimulating and disturbing, correlative perhaps with the paradoxical idea of lovers who must always "meet apart." But the poem closes with a full rhyme; the rhyme is nothing anyone might have anticipated, as there is no precedent for such a stanza structure in this poem or in the body of previous poetry, but when the rhyme comes, it fits perfectly the strange devotion—permanently uniting permanently separated lovers—this poem describes and its strangely uplifting anguish. The rhyme-words themselves make an oxymoron—*Prayer* and *Despair* are virtual antitheses—yet acoustically they provide a resting point, a partial relaxation of ambiguity and tension that feels like a kind of "Sustenance."

While internal rhymes are not abundant in her poetry, there is a marked difference between the thoroughly conventional way they are used in the very early poems and the innovative way they are used in the poems of her middle and late career. In the early verse, internal rhymes are chiefly ornamental, appearing in the medial position and rhyming with the end word of the same line; this is what is sometimes called leonine rhyme (though in stricter usage the term is reserved for pentameters and hexameters). The effect is one of a heightened formality, as, for example, in P 31:

> Summer for thee, grant I may be
> When Summer days are flown!
> Thy music still, when Whippowil
> And Oriole – are done!

> For thee to bloom, I'll skip the tomb
> And row my blossoms o'er!
> Pray gather me –
>   Anemone –
> Thy flower – forevermore!

In the later verse, however, internal rhymes are placed irregularly and are usually aimed at particular expressive effects. See, for instance, the jarring juxtaposition of *poured* (an end word paired in a consonantal rhyme with *Bird*) and *Gored* (the first word of the following line) in the middle of P 1102:

> His Bill is clasped – his Eye forsook –
> His Feathers wilted low –
> The Claws that clung, like lifeless Gloves
> Indifferent hanging now –
> The Joy that in his happy Throat
> Was waiting to be poured
> Gored through and through with Death, to be
> Assassin of a Bird
> Resembles to my outraged mind
> The firing in Heaven,
> On Angels – squandering for you
> Their Miracles of Tune –

The speaker's outrage is underscored by the shock the reader experiences as expectations aroused by the mention of a "Joy . . . waiting to be poured" are followed by a harsh enjambment to a stressed word with painful meaning and an abnormal clash of rhyme where rhyme does not belong. The unanticipated *only* and *lonely* in P 1204, however, lend a poignant effect:

> Whatever it is – she has tried it –
> Awful Father of Love –
> Is not Our's the chastising –
> Do not chastise the Dove –

Not for Ourselves, petition –
Nothing is left to pray –
When a subject is finished –
Words are handed away –

Only lest she be lonely
In thy beautiful House
Give her for her Transgression
License to think of us –

As Cynthia Griffin Wolff comments, this elegy begins with "an eloquent, matter-of-fact directness" and expresses an "acceptance" of the fact of death: "No longer disposed to 'petition' for self . . . , no longer defiantly determined to wrestle for dominion, this speaker is willing to accord final authority to the Lord. It is to *His* 'beautiful House' that the young woman has repaired" (497). There is no use in complaining, so "Words," Dickinson writes, "are handed away." But more words do follow. The denial that there is anything more to be said is interrupted by "Only"—only one request, and the poem concludes with a prayer for the departed, who the speaker fears may be "lonely" removed from those she has loved. A delicate wit underlies the suggestion that in heaven, not to "chastise" her but to requite her for "her Transgression" (a notion alien to standard conceptions of heaven as beyond considerations of trespass and reparation), she might be given "License" to remember the erring mortals she has held dear. The end rhyme of the stanza is consonantal (*House/us*), significantly less stable than the full rhymes of the first two stanzas, and the musical reiteration of the falling double rhyme *Only/lonely* adds a note of plaintive beauty.

Dickinson has other strategies, however, that defy classification. We may remark, for example, the brilliant way rhyme functions in a poem, the rigid structure of which embraces nearly every feature *except* the rhyme:

Behind Me – dips Eternity –
Before Me – Immortality –

Myself – the Term between –
Death but the Drift of Eastern Gray,
Dissolving into Dawn away,
Before the West begin –

'Tis Kingdoms – afterward – they say –
In perfect – pauseless Monarchy –
Whose Prince – is Son of None –
Himself – His Dateless Dynasty –
Himself – Himself diversify –
In Duplicate divine –

'Tis Miracle before Me – then –
'Tis Miracle behind – between –
A Crescent in the Sea –
With Midnight to the North of Her –
And Midnight to the South of Her –
And Maelstrom – in the Sky –

(P 721)

Elizabeth Mills has pointed out that the syntax of this poem
"echoes that of Tennyson's fifth stanza of 'The Charge of
the Light Brigade' (1854), emphasizing the precarious futility
of the trapped position" (75). The glory of Tennyson's bold
heroes and the wonder of their wild encounter amplifies the
sense here of the individual's dramatic confrontation with infinity.[16] Common particular meter works especially well in this
poem, where each three-stress line sets off a significantly different element from the paired four-stress lines preceding it.
The first three lines, for instance, accentuate the existential
situation of "myself" as isolated between twin vastnesses on
either side. The looser rhymes offset the tight structure of the
poem, every line of which is end-stopped, and diversify the
repetitions at the beginnings of lines.

The partial rhymes here are mildly unsettling. It is notable
that the first five lines arouse expectations for full rhyme that
the remainder of the poem does not fulfill.[17] Lines four and

five, which offer the standard religious assurance that death is merely the portal to heaven, are accompanied by a full rhyme that helps to make that assurance seem easy, even glib. The consonantal rhyme that follows (*begin,* answering *between*) comes unexpectedly, diluting the tone of pat certainty; and there are no more smoothly predictable rhymes. The next line undercuts its assertion of kingdoms after death by adding that this information is based on hearsay. (It may be significant also that "they say" rhymes both with itself and with the couplet of easy assurance in the previous stanza.) The unmatching rhyme-sounds lend an element of ambiguity, a slightly unsettling tension to the rest of the poem, which does not sweep on to a vision of heavenly bliss.

An internal rhyme at the mid-point of the poem, however, draws attention to a subject of central importance. "Son of None" in part refers to the Son who is coeval with the Father, according to Christian doctrine; it also, as Peggy Anderson has astutely pointed out, associates Jesus with Joshua, called "Son of Nun" in the Old Testament (32). Joshua is a figure typologically linked with Jesus (whose name is a Late Latin version of the Hebrew word for "Joshua"). As Joshua led the Israelites into the promised land of Canaan, Jesus is to lead the faithful into the promised land of heaven.[18] The pun "Son of None," then, joins Old Testament and New Testament, past and future, in "Duplicate divine," a duplication emanating from the self-diversifications, in time, of a Monarch who is timeless, "Dateless." The "Duplicate divine," then, is simultaneously a perfect unity enfolding the figure "between" into an all-inclusive "Miracle."

The reality the poem describes is not the miracle of reported kingdoms afterward, but the miracle of that trembling point of the here and now, the very nick of time, where the self is encompassed by timeless miracle on all sides. (The syntactic ambiguity of "between" in line fourteen emphasizes the tension between the self as absorbed into the miracle—if the line is understood as "Miracle behind [and] between"

—and as separate from it—if the line is read as "Miracle behind; between [there is] A Crescent. . . ." The arrangement of
the line encourages us to read it both ways.) The final image
is of the persona still partial—*A Crescent*—yet a part of the
boundless whole, amid the dark of *Midnight* yet with the terrifying splendor of *Maelstrom* overhead. These terms also imply
doubleness. "Crescent" suggests both moon and boat, as if
the crescent moon were mirrored in the sea. "Maelstrom" suggests both whirlpool and swirling clouds or aurora borealis,
as if the terror of the deep were reflected by miracle on high.
It is an ecstatic vision of whirling separation and merger. The
unorthodox rhymes, which provide an acoustic instability, a
delicate difference from what one expects and from each other,
do their part to lend an awe to this hauntingly beautiful poem.

Although Dickinson's rhymes are unconventional, then,
a structural logic is perceptible beneath her modulations
and dislocations of conventional rhyme patterns. Rhyme is
a crucial part of her structural arrangements, carrying to the
reader's ear an immediate sense both of fundamental pattern
and of expressive deviations from pattern that strategically
surprise expectations and, interacting with lexical meanings,
yield cognitive significance. Her manipulations of language
reveal that, though she was a lyricist, she was anything but a
simple songbird wantonly pouring forth the throbbing emotions of an overladen heart: with a craftsman's careful attention to structural symmetry and artful irregularity, she planed
and shaped the stanzas that were to be her "Temples." For-
malist analysis of her poetic structures and the function of
rhyme in those structures, consequently, is productive, as I
have demonstrated.

Yet the resistance of her structures to categorization, the impossibility of reducing her rhyming procedures to consistent,
mechanical rule, indicates an aspect of Dickinson's language
that is more spontaneous, experimental, improvisatory. It is
that side of her art she imaged in musical terms, as "Instincts
for Dance – a caper part – / An Aptitude for Bird – " (P 1046).

THREE

Experiments in Sound

Canny artist though she was, Emily Dickinson was closely attuned to the uncanny. The careful construction of her poems is poised against, and indeed includes, a brilliant unruliness. Paradoxically, unruliness is a facet of the structural logic fundamental to her verse. When she wrote, "I had no Monarch in my life, and cannot rule myself," we may be sure that, however much she may have longed for responsiveness, for appreciation, for advice, she did not want to be *ruled*—by Higginson or anyone else. She was to herself sufficient Monarch. The only rigidity in her poetic approach was a strict adherence to her own sense of propriety and a corresponding resistance to other ideas of what a poem should be. Disciplined control and lyrical freedom mingle in her poetic patterns and their daring flights. Exhilarated by risk-taking experiment, Dickinson took her liberties seriously. And playfully. Her art thrives in formal experimentation, in semantic and phonetic play.

Analytic discussion of her rhyming procedures makes the separation between the acoustic and the lexical levels of her poems seem much sharper than it is in the experience of reading them and hearing them in the mind's ear. Beneath and prior to analysis, the phonetic and the intellectual value of words interpenetrate each other, working together on and in the reader's consciousness. In the process of dissecting a poem, gazing at thematic content on the one hand and acoustic content on the other, probing for relationships between the two, one is apt to forget that the dualism ignores or destroys the vital functioning of the poem. The sheer variety of Dickinson's formal patternings is one indication, though, that her handling of sound-and-sense relationships entails not so much a neoclassical decorum of matching word-sounds to discursive content as it does a creative interweaving of sound in a dynamic texture of poetic meaning. Notwithstanding the distinct patterns of rhyme and shifts of rhyme important in her verse, there is an experimental flexibility in her use of rhyme that leans at times in the direction of pure phonic play.

Whereas in the poems analyzed in the previous chapter her poetic procedures involve relations of contrast between conventional form and deviant form, some of her more radically deviant poems nearly transcend that dualism (of normal and deviant) as well. The majority of Dickinson's poems are structured in traditional stanza forms, but she wrote a number of poems in which rhyme functions apart from the expectations that are aroused by familiar stanza patterns. Sometimes she seems to pile on sound effects almost for pure delight, relishing the music of language. This little verse the poet sent with a cocoon to her young nephew:

> Drab Habitation of Whom?
> Tabernacle or Tomb –
> Or Dome of Worm –
> Or Porch of Gnome –
> Or some Elf's Catacomb?
> (P 893)

The poem begins with two rhyming syllables, "Drab" and "Hab-," that also rhyme with the first syllable of the second line, "Tab-." Every line is involved in an end rhyme, the first two and the last two forming full rhymes, and "Worm" at the center making a consonantal rhyme with both of those pairs. The word "Dome" tucked into line three is an internal rhyme for the last pair, and "some" in line five forms a consonantal rhyme with all the end words (as well as an eye-rhyme with "Dome"). Such abundance of rhyme in a nineteen-word poem is in part an exploitation of the sound of language for its own sake. It is the sort of thing that delights children, and it delights in adults a residual fascination with the alogical acoustic element of language, those teasing hints of meaning that elude the grasp of consciousness.[1] Here, where full rhymes and partial rhymes intermingle without any pre-set pattern, the intricate phonic play offers a mysterious pleasure of its own that is particularly apt in a poem about the miracle of life-in-death that the cocoon enacts and the riddle that the cocoon spells as a possible emblem for those other catacombs, far more drab, that humankind contemplates. There is something haunting and something merry about this slight but forceful poem, both in its theme and in its modulations of rhyme-sounds.

A longer poem with a similar phonic profusion in a pattern not orderly enough to call a rhyme "scheme" also achieves a blend of playfulness and mysteriousness:

> I know some lonely Houses off the Road
> A Robber'd like the look of –
> Wooden barred,
> And Windows hanging low,
> Inviting to –
> A Portico,
> Where two could creep –
> One – hand the Tools –
> The other peep –
> To make sure All's Asleep –
> Old fashioned eyes –
> Not easy to surprise!
>
> How orderly the Kitchen'd look, by night,
> With just a Clock –
> But they could gag the Tick –
> And Mice wont bark –
> And so the Walls – dont tell –
> None – will –

A pair of Spectacles ajar just stir –
An Almanac's aware –
Was it the Mat – winked,
Or a Nervous Star?
The Moon – slides down the stair,
To see who's there!

There's plunder – where –
Tankard, or Spoon –
Earring – or Stone –
A Watch – Some Ancient Brooch
To match the Grandmama –
Staid sleeping – there –

Day – rattles – too
Stealth's – slow –
The Sun has got as far
As the third Sycamore –
Screams Chanticleer
"Who's there"?

And Echoes – Trains away,
Sneer – "Where"!
While the old Couple, just astir,
Fancy the Sunrise – left the door ajar!

(P 289)

Full rhymes and consonantal rhymes are scattered about liberally, as if at random. Most, but not all, of the end words participate in a rhyme group. In the first strophe, full rhyme predominates, but in the second there is no full rhyme at all —just the consonance of *look/Clock/Tick/bark* and the (inexact) consonance of *Walls/tell/will*. These partial rhymes may serve onomatopoeically to suggest the muffled sounds of stealthy robbers who would "gag the Tick." The sounds of the next strophe are more obtrusive ("noisier") but without regular pattern. *Pair, ajar,* and *stir* are linked by consonance, while *pair* is also an internal rhyme matching the end rhymes *aware/stair/*

there; stir/star/stair form a group linked by rich consonance (a term designating a combination of alliteration and consonance), of which *star* makes a full rhyme for *ajar*. *Watch, Brooch,* and *match* make up still another consonantally rhyming group. There is a nervous quality to all this, with sounds recurring unexpectedly; in context, it cooperates with the sense by approximating, however remotely, the startling effect of noises in an old house at midnight. The poem is half-funny, half-somber. The line "Day – rattles – too," for example, is strange. Why "too"? Following as it does the ancient sleeping grandmama, the line implies that *she* is rattling; the idea of her staid snores is comic, but there is just an intimation of the death-rattle as well. Clocks may be silenced, but "stealth's slow," and time keeps moving inexorably toward mortality, the source of all our midnight jitters. Partial rhymes continue throughout the remainder of the poem, but full rhymes repeat and echo the key words *there!/where/there/there?/Where!* Full rhyme gives the words prominence, and the absence of predictable pattern makes them surprising when they do appear. The only other full rhyme is internal, where the screaming *Chanticleer* receives an echoing *Sneer* as the robbers turn out to be nowhere in sight. The robbers were hypothetical anyway, were they not? That is part of the playful mischief of this poem, not a great one but effective in its way. It ends happily with sunrise and the couple awake, but the final note is struck by a door mysteriously ajar and a partial rhyme (*astir/ajar*) that reverberates strangely with the same words—even the adverb "just" is repeated—in the earlier, darker part of the poem.

An uncommon abundance of rhyme in a very free pattern is also found in a playful poem about the wind:

> The Wind did'nt come from the Orchard – today –
> Further than that –
> Nor stop to play with the Hay –
> Nor threaten a Hat –
> He's a transitive fellow – very –
> Rely on that –

If He leave a Bur at the door
We know He has climbed a Fir –
But the Fir is Where – Declare –
Were you ever there?

If He bring Odors of Clovers –
And that is His business – not Our's –
Then He has been with the Mowers –
Whetting away the Hours
To sweet pauses of Hay –
His Way – of a June Day –

If He fling Sand, and Pebble –
Little Boys Hats – and Stubble –
With an occasional Steeple –
And a hoarse "Get out of the way, I say,"
Who'd be the fool to stay?
Would you – Say –
Would you be the fool to stay?

(P 316)

Lindberg-Seyersted has pointed out that the frequent rhymes here offer the "pleasure of sound repetition" and hence contribute to the gay tone of the poem (158). It should be remarked, too, that there is a strong element of threat in a wind that blows steeples down according to its whim, and the capriciousness of the wind is nicely correlated with the apparent randomness of rhymes that recur insistently but unpredictably —as end rhyme and internal rhyme, as full rhyme and partial rhyme—as if in fitful gusts. Stylistically, this poem hollers at us like the wind, "Get out of the way, I say."

In the three poems just discussed, where rhyme operates in the absence of any clear-cut stanzaic patterns, the looseness of structure means that expectations for rhyme at any particular point are minimal. Instead, a sort of free-flowing sound play is brought to the foreground. The extreme instability of pattern reduces the effect of any one rhyme and increases the attention to the generalized texture of sound; such sequences as *there/where/there/there/where* or *pebble/stubble/steeple* are made conspicuous by differentiation from that texture.

It should be noticed that the phonic play in such poems, though prominent, is never divorced from meaning but always participates in it. The foregrounding of sound draws attention to an alogical element in language, but the sounds are managed so that they bear interesting relations to the more logical, literal aspect of the poems. In poems such as these, we can observe Dickinson playing with word-sounds, allowing herself some looseness of rein, exploring the possibilities of freer forms and odder tunes, and generally destabilizing conventional fixities. Perhaps as much as any of her philosophical attitudes, her experimental approach to form links her with the Romantic movement and with its modernist heirs.

Karl Keller has written an illuminating discussion of Frost's attraction to the element of play in Dickinson's language (294, 309–26). Though Frost did not follow her in venturing outside traditional kinds of rhyme, his kinship with Dickinson is recognizable in such lines as these, from "Departmental," where rhyme proliferates:

> Yet if he encountered one
> Of the hive's enquiry squad
> Whose work is to find out God
> And the nature of time and space,
> He would put him onto the case.
> Ants are a curious race;
> One crossing with hurried tread
> The body of one of their dead
> Isn't given a moment's arrest –
> Seems not even impressed.
>
> (372)

The sounds of the rhymes in the short, three-stress lines very nearly dominate the poem, giving it a tone of levity, and Frost playfully departs from his couplet scheme when a third rhyme presents itself. The lines which begin his sonnet "Design" distantly recall Dickinson's "A Spider sewed at Night" (P 1138):

> I found a dimpled spider, fat and white,
> On a white heal-all, holding up a moth
> Like a white piece of rigid satin cloth –
> Assorted characters of death and blight
> Mixed ready to begin the morning right. . . .
>
> (396)

Frost learned, as Dickinson had, that rhyme could be haunting and that it could be comic and that those two emotional categories are not quite mutually exclusive.

Dickinson enjoyed using rhyme for humorous effect. Unlike Frost, however, she more often depends on odd *kinds* of rhyme to strike a funny note, sometimes on merely one acoustic surprise.[2] Whicher was the first to point out how the final word of a sweetly lyrical description of evening turns the poem into a "musical joke":

> Lightly stepped a yellow star
> To it's lofty place
> Loosed the Moon her silver hat
> From her lustral Face
> All of Evening softly lit
> As an Astral Hall
> Father I observed to Heaven
> You are punctual –
>
> (P 1672)

The poem "revels in a luxuriance of rippling *l*'s accompanied by the moonlight suggestiveness of such words as *silver* and *lustral*" and then "lets us down with a bump" when "punctual" wryly introduces an incongruous idea with an incongruous rhyme-sound (184).

Another wittily deviant rhyme appears in the middle of a poem that comments on the philosophical debate about the nature of reality (external, or "in the Brain"?). The unexpected sound alone, in its context, strikes a funny note:

> Within my Garden, rides a Bird
> Upon a single Wheel –
> Whose spokes a dizzy Music make
> As 'twere a travelling Mill –
>
> He never stops, but slackens
> Above the Ripest Rose –
> Partakes without alighting
> And praises as he goes,
>
> Till every spice is tasted –
> And then his Fairy Gig
> Reels in remoter atmospheres –
> And I rejoin my Dog,
>
> And He and I, perplex us
> If positive, 'twere we –
> Or bore the Garden in the Brain
> This Curiosity –
>
> But he, the best Logician,
> Refers my clumsy eye –
> To just vibrating Blossoms!
> An Exquisite Reply!
>
> (P 500)

As the hummingbird vanishes in stanza three, the rhyme *Gig/ Dog* signals what Ronald Wallace calls "one of the great comic tonal shifts in poetry." He explains:

> The first three stanzas dealing with the hummingbird purport to be light and airy, using sensory images, images of speed and exotic places, and short vowel sounds. But the last line of stanza three brings the whole airy vision back down to the real world of dogs. The slant rhyme of 'Gig' and 'Dog' is a kind of auditory joke, a shift from the

> bright and airy to the earthbound and commonplace. The
> last line of the stanza slows the whole poem down like a
> record player suddenly shifted from 78 to 33⅓ when the
> appropriate speed is 45. (92)

The sudden disappearance of the ethereal vision leaves
speaker and dog in a brief perplexity, which is resolved when
the sagacious dog settles the point with empirical evidence,
and the security of the ending is reinforced with a full rhyme.
That ending is reached, however, by way of the pivotal drop
from sublimity to practicality in the center.

A similarly comic intent to drop the reader with a thud is, I
suspect, the aim of the following poem, which exists only as
a rough worksheet:

> Risk is the Hair that holds the Tun
> Seductive in the Air –
> That Tun is hollow – but the Tun –
> With Hundred Weights – to spare –
> Too ponderous to suspect the snare
> Espies that fickle chair
> Ands seats itself to be let go
> By that perfidious Hair –
>
> The "foolish Tun" the Critics say
> While that delusive Hair
> Persuasive as Perdition,
> Decoys it's Traveller
>
> (P 1239)

Except for the last line, all three quatrains are rhymed on
exactly the same sound (*Air/spare/chair/Hair/Hair*), and there
are, additionally, an internal rhyme in line one (*Hair*) and an
additional end-rhyme in line five (*snare*)—also on the same
sound. All this monotony of rhyme lulls the reader into a complacency that is upset at last by the surprise of the off-rhyme
Traveller [var. *Passenger*]. Appropriately, the poem is about the
seductions of "Risk," which lure the unsuspecting to a fall. The

extraordinary recurrence of rhyme-sounds is "Persuasive," a technique to "Decoy" the reader into strong expectations, and the final drop into partial rhyme is a proof of the thematic point. The poem induces readers to look superciliously at the dull-witted, "ponderous" tun entrusting its bulk to an obviously "perfidious Hair"; thus, in effect, readers are enticed to seat themselves as "Critics" scoffing at a "foolish Tun" and, ironically, to repeat that gullible tun's mistake. When the perfidious final rhyme "lets go," the supercilious readers become the butt of the poetic joke. The poem is not one of Dickinson's better ones: the verse is rough, not brilliantly clever, lines three and four are unnecessarily murky, and a different last word would probably sound wittier. Still, the poem offers a glimpse of the artist at work with rhyme-sounds, exploring acoustic methods to "snare" and surprise readers in support of a poetic idea.

Partial rhymes are the most obvious of Dickinson's stylistic deviations. Scarcely noticed is her occasional use of a superabundance of full rhyme. Such apparent excesses of rhyme call attention to themselves, and they too bespeak the acoustic experimentalism of the poet. But she is less inclined than Frost to use abundant full rhymes for merriment. Partly because they are not formal "givens" in her verse, they also serve as effective support for tone and meaning in the poems where she uses them.

A five-fold rhyme signals an unusually intense firmness in this stanza:

> The lady with the Amulet – will fade –
> The Bee – in Mausoleum laid –
> Discard his Bride –
> But longer than the little Rill –
> That cooled the Forehead of the Hill –
> While Other – went the Sea to fill –
> And Other – went to turn the Mill –
> I'll do thy Will –
>
> (P 438, ll. 9–16)

The constancy of the speaker is, as it were, *heard* in the prolonged repetition of those rhymes (*Rill, Hill, Fill, Mill, Will*) as well as declared. Similarly, a series of four full rhymes forcefully urges the value of "Truth" in this poem:

> A Counterfeit – a Plated Person –
> I would not be –
> Whatever strata of Iniquity
> My Nature underlie –
> Truth is good Health – and Safety, and the Sky.
> How meagre, what an Exile – is a Lie,
> And Vocal – when we die –
>
> (P 1453)

The insistent rhymes *underlie/Sky/Lie/die* are set against the confusion of sound linked with "Counterfeit" persons in the prosodically irregular opening lines, and the repeated rhyme-sounds have the ring of the most urgent sincerity. But do they protest too much? The foregrounding in rhyme of *underlie* and *Lie* calls attention to punning possibilities of those words in relation to the lies that in hypocrites underlie "Truth." Has a "strat[um] of Iniquity" become "Vocal" in these riddling words? As in the well-known "Tell all the Truth but tell it slant" (P 1129), which avers that "Success in Circuit lies," the voice is faintly, teasingly, multivocal, undermining its own assertion and raising the question whether it is ever possible to achieve the desired "Safety" of ideal "Truth."

In both "A Counterfeit – a Plated Person" and "The lady with the Amulet," the additional rhymes apparently stretch the stanzas to a new length to make a point; Dickinson's desire for phonic reiteration, that is, seems to have dictated the stanzaic forms. Her willingness to reshape form to embody a feeling and an idea indicates an experimental artistic method. In those altered forms, one can hear significant innuendoes.

The Dickinson poem most heavily laden with full rhyme, though, is probably this one, composed in otherwise conventional quatrains:

Mine – by the Right of the White Election!
Mine – by the Royal Seal!
Mine – by the Sign in the Scarlet prison –
Bars – cannot conceal!

Mine – here – in Vision – and in Veto!
Mine – by the Grave's Repeal –
Titled – Confirmed –
Delirious Charter!
Mine – long as Ages steal!

(P 528)

The rhymes here exceed all expectations for what is normal in this stanza pattern. Both stanzas are built on the same end rhyme (*Seal/conceal/Repeal/steal*), and the first pair of these are identical in sound (an instance of *rime riche*). There are two internal rhymes (*Right/White*, and *Mine/Sign*), and six lines begin with the repeated *Mine*. All the rhyme words contain high-front vowels, *i* and *e*, and, with an added ripple of alliteration throughout, the total effect is of noisy excess. Expertly, the lyric uses statement and sound to express a mood of wildly confident exultation. Everything about it contributes to a tone of self-assertion that is *Delirious* and slightly shrill. Rhyme is crucial in producing that tone.

One of the "Wife" poems begins with exultant exclamations similarly loud with full and internal rhyme, then progresses to deviations of rhyme that are brilliantly consistent with the mordant twists of emotion in the content of the poem.

Title divine – is mine!
The Wife – without the Sign!
Acute Degree – conferred on me –
Empress of Calvary!
Royal – all but the Crown!
Betrothed – without the swoon
God sends us Women –
When you – hold – Garnet to Garnet –

> Gold – to Gold –
> Born – Bridalled – Shrouded –
> In a Day –
> "My Husband" – women say –
> Stroking the Melody –
> Is *this* – the way?
>
> (P 1072)

To support the initial tone of jubilation, the opening couplets use frequent rhyme, internal and external (*divine, mine/Sign; Degree, me/Calvary*). What seems like a clear-cut structure at first, though, begins to dissolve in lines five and six (linked with a consonantal rhyme, *Crown/Swoon*) and becomes extremely ambiguous in lines seven through nine (unrhymed? or rearranged in the mind's ear as a tetrameter couplet rhyming *hold/Gold?*). At the same time the disturbing implications of the missing *Sign,* the missing *Crown,* and the missing *swoon* become dominant. In this context (as the speaker's glorious "Title" is mysteriously deprived of fulfillment) the internal rhyme of *hold* and *Gold* may seem like a harmony heard at a distance but withheld from complete realization. The last five lines have three fully rhyming words, *Day, say,* and *way,* but they exist in a fractured structure consistent with the faltering rhythm and the tone of hesitant, faltering love implied by the words. At the heart of it all is the paradoxical experience the poem describes, epitomized in the splendidly musical sequence "Born – Bridalled – Shrouded," where the middle term is linked by alliteration to the first and by consonance to the last. The complexity of emotion here—celebration and uncertainty, pain and victorious assurance—is congruent with the subtle organization of the rhymes. Full rhymes are frequent, but since they are not in any familiar pattern, they chime in a way that seems both glad and strange. [3]

Subtle play with nuances of rhyme is a hallmark of Dickinson's style. Sometime she extends such nuances in a peculiar way throughout a whole poem, as for example in this one, which contemplates the stream of historical time from a novel vantage point:

> Funny – to be a Century –
> And see the People – going by –
> I – should die of the Oddity –
> But then – I'm not so staid – as He –
>
> He keeps His Secrets safely – very –
> Were He to tell – extremely sorry
> This Bashful Globe of Our's would be –
> So dainty of Publicity –

(P 345)

In long meter, one ordinarily finds either couplets rhyming *aabb* or an alternate scheme *abab*, but here it is impossible to tell which, if either, scheme is operative. Unaccented final -*ỳ* with a promotion stress has traditionally been rhymed with both *ī* and *ē*, but it had not (so far as I know) before been put in a context of propinquity to both at once so that the tensional pull exerted on the -*ỳ* by the stressed syllable is felt as coming simultaneously from conflicting directions. *Century* could be rhymed with *by* without raising any eyebrows, but, when *Oddity* follows, expectations are aroused for a rhyme on the long-*ī* sound to match *by* (in an *abab* pattern), something along the lines of:

> But then – He is more staid – than I.

Instead, one hears the peculiar, unbalancing "He." The next stanza does not clarify the structure, only complicates it, first with *very* and *sorry*, which end in hypercatalectic syllables receiving not even a stress promotion, and second with the final pair *be* and *Publicity*, which reverse the pattern of sound and stress of *Oddity/He* in stanza one. As it is, then, the sequence ỳ-ī-ỳ-ē-ў-ў-ē-ỳ is particularly unstable, a wavering sequence of closely related but unmatching end sounds, *all* of which are echoed by sounds within the lines. The effect is an "Oddity," playful and weird, appropriate in a poem about a passing stream of people and events considered from the abstracted viewpoint of a personified, taciturn Century. As Paul Anderson has observed, the poem "evokes the horrors of history" and "the terrible implacability of time" yet maintains a tone of "comic, bemused detachment" (77). An internal rhyme—"I should *die* of the Oddity"—lends emphasis to a casually colloquial hyperbole hiding a *memento mori* like a joke. Unorthodox as they are, the rhymes in this poem are skillfully handled, for they contribute a formal element of unease—audible, be it ever so "dainty."

A similar sequence of sounds functions somewhat differently in a different poetic setting:

> 'Twould ease – a Butterfly –
> Elate – a Bee –
> Thou'rt neither –
> Neither – thy capacity –
>
> But, Blossom, were I,
> I would rather be
> Thy moment
> Than a Bee's Eternity –
>
> Content of fading
> Is enough for me –
> Fade I unto Divinity –
> And Dying – Lifetime –
> Ample as the Eye –
> Her least attention raise on me –
>   (P 682)

Most of the end words shift back and forth between *i* and *e* as follows (with end words not part of this pattern indicated by x): ī-ē-x-ȳ, ī-ē-x-ȳ, x-ē-ȳ-x-ī-ē. Internal assonance on the same vowel sounds reinforces the emphatic alternation between the sounds. The rhyme pattern is slightly more stable in this poem than in "Funny – to be a Century" because there are no unaccented and unpromoted syllables involved in the rhymes and because the ear can perceive in the poem a latent and more conventional pattern of two long meter quatrains (rhymed ē-ỳ-ē-ỳ, ē-ỳ-ī-ē). (That the poet was herself aware of this pattern is indicated by the fact that she left a pencilled draft of the last six lines rearranged in that way, possibly sent with a flower.) Still, the effect of the unconventional, continuous shifting of closely related rhyme-sounds is curious, and not inconsistent with the thematic shifts of a gentle poem about denial and yearning and dying into life; the "Content of fading" the speaker mentions finds its acoustic parallel in the soft fading of rhyme-sounds into one another.

Such nuances or gradations of sound in partial rhymes, it seems to me, serve remarkably well in a variety of contexts to provide a delicate suggestiveness. For example, this strange dream-poem begins with six lines tied by a consonantal rhyme on *m:*

> In Winter in my Room
> I came upon a Worm
> Pink lank and warm
> But as he was a worm
> And worms presume
> Not quite with him at home
> Secured him by a string
> To something neighboring
> And went along. . . .
>
> (P 1670)

The loose stanzaic structure of the poem and the loose groups of rhyme-words contribute to the sense of informal narration. The lines contain, however, an exceptional amount of internal consonance and alliteration. Throughout the poem, the rhymes leave the reader uncertain of the formal pattern at hand and, like the speaker, "not quite at home" with what is presenting itself. The *Worm/warm/worm* sequence is especially unusual; the sounds are not harsh, but the shifting back and forth of the vowel within a consonant frame, in conjunction with the ambivalent response of the speaker to this unthreatening but vaguely repulsive pink worm, might be said to be faintly queasy. The unanticipated full rhyme on *presume* (making a pair with *Room*) gives the word a prominence it merits as a foreshadowing of things to come, for, later, the worm is transmogrified into a snake, both Miltonic and Freudian, terrifying and "ringed with power." The net effect of the rich consonantal rhyme sequence is mildly unsettling and rather fascinating, as it should be. [4]

A similar gradation works with different effect in the first strophe of a poem about a fringed gentian:

> The Gentian has a parched Corolla –
> Like azure dried
> 'Tis Nature's buoyant juices
> Beatified –
> Without a vaunt or sheen
> As casual as Rain
> And as benign – . . . .
>
> (P 1424)

Because this poem exists only as a rough draft, one cannot be sure how (or whether) the poet would have altered it before considering it finished. The stanzaic structure is very free. The opening lines present the splendid synesthetic image of "azure dried" (possibly suggested to her by Thoreau's description of the Walden ice as "solidified azure"). Those lines also yoke in a full rhyme the opposites *dried* and *Beatified*—indicating the gentian as poised on the moment of death and transfiguration of Nature each fall. This breathtaking opening is followed by a relaxation of structure and rhyme that is utterly graceful, "As casual as Rain." Instead of trying to match the powerful start with another grand effect, Dickinson has used a sequence of consonantal rhymes, *sheen/Rain/benign,* in which the vowels slide down the scale, easily, as if casually, with a pleasant musical effect. No full rhyme could accomplish as much. [5]

Dickinson, then, sometimes allowed sound gradations for onomatopoeic effect to burst the bounds of conventional stanza patterns. The form of the following poem, too, seems to have been determined not by any metrical paradigm but by the downward vowel gradation in the rhyme-words of the first five lines:

> My Reward for Being, was This.
> My premium – My Bliss –
> An Admiralty, less –
> A Sceptre – penniless –
> And Realms – just Dross –
>
> (P 343)

The initial full rhyme *This/Bliss* is in tune with the confident happiness the lines express; heard against it, the *less/penniless/Dross* sequence of consonantal rhymes—gradually coming down the scale—seems designed to sound like a voice expressively shifting from triumphant joy to disdain for mere royal power.[6] Even in somewhat more structured stanzas, Dickinson uses fluctuating consonantal rhyme sounds both to unify groups of lines aurally and to suggest subtle shifts in mood and tone of voice. (See "The One who could repeat the Summer day – " [P 307], for example, or "'Twas the old – road – through pain – " [P 344], or "Must be a Wo – " [P 571], or "The Test of Love – is Death – " [P 573].) It is an oblique method, a way of indirection, so that one cannot always be precisely sure in reading whether the nuances of meaning one perceives are *there* in the poem or in the mind "Disseminating" Dickinson's "Circumference" (P 883). We can be sure, though, that Dickinson intended just that kind of uncertainty to be part of the experience of reading her poems. A poem about the "South Wind" vividly describes her idea of an "individual Voice," with implications concerning the poetic voice she so carefully cultivated:

> A Hint of Ports and Peoples –
> And much not understood –

> The fairer – for the farness –
> And for the foreignhood.
>
> (P 719, ll. 5–8)

Elusive hints of meanings, which leave "much not under-stood," have more appeal than explicit messages publicly blared; a trace of the foreign heightens the comeliness of what is "fair" and lovely. Even here, she plays with the kindred sounds (both alliterative and consonantal) of *fair*er, *far*ness, and *for*eignhood and their tantalizing distance. It sounds strange. And right.

The variety of her rhyme experiments, as I keep saying, is impressive. She wrote one poem where she prolonged one rhyme sound (*done/begun/run/Son/done/one*) through a whole poem (P 1293), which is about the theme of stasis, and in one bizarre worksheet draft, she repeated the very same rhyme-*word* over and over:

> Through what transports of Patience
> I reached the stolid Bliss
> To breathe my Blank without thee
> Attest me this and this –
> By that bleak exultation
> I won as near as this
> Thy privilege of dying
> Abbreviate me this
>
> (P 1153)

In the continued repetition of the vague, dull pronoun *this*, she evidently is trying to achieve a "Blank" effect that will render an experience analogous to the speaker's "stolid Bliss." It is not great poetry, certainly, but it is at least an interesting experiment.

More effective are some of the poems where the whole rhyme scheme is built on one consonantal rhyme sequence, "Which is the best – the Moon or the Crescent?" (P 1315), for example, or this solemn, stately, poetic contemplation of the soul's passage through death:

> Departed – to the Judgment –
> A Mighty Afternoon –
> Great Clouds – like Ushers – leaning –
> Creation – looking on –
>
> The Flesh – Surrendered – Cancelled –
> The Bodiless – begun –
> Two Worlds – like Audiences – disperse –
> And leave the Soul – alone –
>
> (P 524)

The sublime mood here is supported by the ambiguous rhymes, low vowels modulated around one soft consonant. The rhymes (and the pattern of assonance within the lines) provide a kind of acoustic continuity between the stanzas, which are otherwise linked by parallel syntax, and they support the tone of awe.

The effect in "Departed – to the Judgment" stands in interesting contrast to the effect of similar sounds arranged differently in another eight-line poem, this one detailing the changes that take place in autumn:

> The morns are meeker than they were –
> The nuts are getting brown –
> The berry's cheek is plumper –
> The Rose is out of town.
>
> The Maple wears a gayer scarf –
> The field a scarlet gown –
> Lest I sh'd be old fashioned
> I'll put a trinket on.
>
> (P 12)

The pace of the poem is brisk and easy, and the personifications of natural objects give the season a social familiarity. The tone is light. It is not the rhyme-sounds in themselves that are of most importance here, but their arrangement in this context. The first three rhyme-words make full rhymes; only the fourth is deviant. Therefore, instead of a lingering ambiguity, the effect is of a slight but sudden shock to the reader's expectations, which have been lulled into complacency by the absolutely regular progression of everything up to that point (full rhyme, regular meter, parallel clauses in end-stopped lines, and ultra-conventional subject matter). It is noteworthy that in the copy she sent to Sue, apparently with a flower, Dickinson put an exclamation point at the end. The effect is coherent, as Paul Anderson has seen, with the tragi-comic theme—the beauty of the dying year and humankind's futile attempts to merge with nature (74). The sad note is an undertone, however, and the concluding partial rhyme works as a jest more sprightly than wry, a fillip of lighthearted frivolity in the face of time.

The variety of Dickinson's uses of rhyme and the freedom of her experimentation are centrifugal tendencies, balanced by the control she exerts as she integrates them into flexible forms of suggestive meaning. Spontaneous lyricism and conscious craftsmanship are both crucial to her art. Her radical innovations have been deprecated, on the one hand, by those inclined to prefer conventional forms and/or male authorship and valorized, on the other, by those who esteem breaking out of limits and/or female writing. Post-structuralist critical movements have fostered appreciation of linguistic play, and feminist criticism in particular has responded to the aspect of Dickinson's art that is subversive of literal, unitary (phallogocentric) meaning enclosed in definite (patriarchal) forms prescribed by the authority of convention. This emphasis is an important one, for it is sensitive to a volcanic wildness in language and in experience that Dickinson deliberately allowed herself to tap. It recognizes her rebelliousness and her readiness to give words a new freedom. As Heather McHugh has said, "To read Dickinson is to be reminded that the largest flash does not necessarily represent the greatest power, that form can be as rich in flux as in fixity, that craft is precisely NOT inert structure or coy contrivance, but an energy outbounding its visible materials, and referring through every struction (in-, con-, de-, and decon-) to the uncontainable, that intuited spirit or gist or Geist we sense as the essence, in our lives" (51). We cannot suppose that every formal feature of her style is politically motivated or that her poetry is advancing (or retreating) into a kind of indecipherable babble. Adventures in polysemic openness, in phonic play, and in the irrational are broadly characteristic of poetic uses of language, and they are prominent in some periods more than in others, in the work of some writers (and speakers) more than in others, in some poems by Dickinson more than in others. And Dickinson on the whole is a poet of tremendous control. She worked in small, relatively austere verse forms, carefully managing the effects of her technical deviations. But her phonic play tells us something about the sources of her creativity and indicates the importance to her of linguistic sound, which transcends the literal center of language. Her triumph is that she takes language from its rational, logical center toward the circumference where freer meanings play— without relinquishing the control that makes that freedom a richness of meaning rather than meaninglessness. In the felt tension between the "Carved and cool" side of her art and the other, "caper part– / An Aptitude for Bird–" (P 1046), in the interplay between the literal and the musical, Dickinson's words come alive.

FOUR

Riches of Rhyme

In a letter of 1878, Emily Dickinson wrote to Mrs. J. G. Holland thanking her for a gift of bonbons and remarking with pleasure a note from Dr. Holland: "The Doctor's Pun was happy—How lovely are the wiles of Words!" (L 555). Though poets, almost by definition, love words, the material of which poems are made, Dickinson was one of those poets who are particularly fascinated by the *wiliness* of words, their tricky elusiveness, their mysterious multiplicity. The hours she spent with her lexicon were not hours devoted to training herself to use words with mathematical precision but hours spent in companionship with words, getting to know their texture, becoming intimate with their manifold depths and facets. Her poems, as well as the manuscript variants, show that her selection of words was guided by other concerns than accuracy of denotation. Aiming to distill "amazing sense / From ordinary Meanings" (P 448), she devised ways to make familiar words spring to new vitality and reveal surprising new dimensions. She loved big, hefty words; little, simple words; and strange, evocative words; and she loved puns and riddles. Homans has discussed Dickinson's "concept of language's doubleness" and "her growing knowledge that there is no absolute truth or literal meaning," with the result that "the poet exploits the antithetical meanings of words" and shows "how richly duplicitous any word can be" (*Women* 165, 168, 210, 211). It seems not to have been noticed, however, that one of the wily, du-

plicitous maneuvers Dickinson employs in her poetry is rhyming words with other words different in meaning but identical
in sound, a practice called *rime riche* or identical rhyme, which
had been for nearly three centuries unconventional and even
unacceptable in English poetry.

Rime riche is common in French poetry, and as a result of
the French influence it is not infrequent in Chaucer's poetry.[1]
Wyatt and Spenser and other Renaissance poets used *rime
riche,* and the practice was once "looked upon as a beauty
rather than as a blemish" (Fogle 681).[2] Nevertheless, such
rhymes subsequently came into disrepute. In 1584 King James
pronounced against it in his "Ane schort Treatise conteining
some reulis and cautelis to be observit and eschewit in Scottis
Poesie." His rule, says Charles Richardson, " 'that ye rhyme
not twice in one syllable; as for example, that ye make not
prove and *reprove* rhyme together,' may be regarded as the
chronological end of a once permissible custom" (130). It can
hardly be supposed that the king's edict had sufficient power
to ensure compliance, and there must have been other reasons
for the disappearance of identical rhyme. Since the difference
of meaning between similar-sounding words is partly responsible for the allure of all rhyme (and of all phonic recurrence),
it is not entirely clear why *rime riche,* which offers a divergence
of meaning between same-sounding words, should have been
objectionable. Perhaps rhymes between words differentiated
only by a prefix seemed too facile, lacking enough difference,
acoustic or cognitive, to be interesting. That would not seem
to be the case, however, with homonyms, which offer startling
cognitive differences, and the reasons for the unacceptability
of such rhymes are subject to debate.

John Hollander has ventured the idea that *rime riche* does
not work in English for acoustic reasons alone, because of the
nature of word stress:

> The rhetorical powers of end rhyme in English—the
> ability to command and manipulate the attention of the

reading eye and the following ear—depend in good measure on the necessity of the rhyming syllable's being an
accented one. An immediate and obvious consequence of
this, for example, is that in French or even in Chaucer,
the *rime tres riche* or total homonymic rhyme is indeed an
occasion of plenitude, whereas in modern English . . .
it must always fall ridiculously flat, underlined as the
like syllables are by their stressed position" (*Vision and
Resonance* 118).

Hollander's suggestion that Chaucer's Middle English was not
heavily stressed is questionable. Though the enormous influx
of French vocabulary in that period altered the Germanic system of root stress, it seems likely that Middle English was
still characterized by heavy stress.[3] Even if he is correct in his
contention that the acoustic similarity is difficult for modern
English to handle, he must have felt considerable delight in a
clever homonymic rhyme of his own:

If it's the only rhyme that you can write,
A homonym will never sound quite right.
        (*Rhyme's Reason* 14)

The delightful thing about the rhyme in this instructive verse,
of course, is that it is *not* the only rhyme that he can write and
consequently it *is,* just exactly, "right." Paradoxically, instead
of falling flat it only sounds somewhat odd until it registers
cognitively as a rhyme that perfectly illustrates his point. (The
oddness, one may notice, is intensified skillfully by the use of
the extra internal rhyme "quite," placed just beside "right.")

It may be that the odd sound of an identical rhyme has
as much to do with the forces of convention that condition
readers' ears as it does with the system of word stress in English. Expecting acoustic difference, readers are nonplused by
acoustic sameness. Moreover, it is likely that if the effect of
a rhyme between identical syllables differing only in what is
prefixed to them seems too easy, the effect of a homonymic

rhyme seems, on the other hand, too strange, too weird, too challenging to readers' linguistic assumptions. Especially it challenges rationalistic assumptions about language. Language is not, as we sometimes think of it, a perfectly coherent system of sounds that by organized differentiation symbolize a range of discrete meanings; instead, it is, as Dickinson knew, a crotchety network of overlapping sounds and overlapping meanings that sometimes interact in unexpected, even bizarre, fashion.

English has some word groups that behave predictably according to comprehensible rules. Regular verb paradigms do, for example, and even irregular verbs have detectable patterns that make increasing sense as we grasp their origins. Clusters of similar-sounding words have similar meanings explicable either on the basis of etymological origins (*wring, wry, wrestle, wrist,* and *wrong,* for instance) or on the basis of principles that phonestheticians are still striving to explain. (The sound represented by the letter *d,* for example, according to Percy G. Adams, tends to be associated with dread, dullness, darkness, or death [31].)[4] Whatever we learn about meanings of linguistic sound patterns, however, there are—always—exceptions. "All phonic overlap encourages synonymy," says Wescott, contending that speech-sounds have intrinsic "iconic" meaning (12), but perhaps it is more accurate to say that phonic overlap encourages users of a language to seek out some degree of synonomy, to make associations of sense that correlate, however obliquely, with the sound similarity. *Dog, hog,* and *frog* seem to belong to a nicely logical group because in addition to sounding alike they are all four-legged animals; of course, a frog is more like a toad than a hog, but we ignore that and find little trouble adding *bog* to the group (it is where frogs live) and *log* as well (where frogs sit) and maybe even *slog* (what one has to do in a bog) and *flog* (which can happen to a dog) and so on according to a quirky logic that is scarcely logical but very much a part of the way we think. Coincidence of sound suggests a real or imaginary or occult coincidence of meaning, and users of a language persist in attaching semantic connections even where they are unwarranted by clear onomatopoeic, grammatical, or etymological principles. Significance thus bursts out of the rational constraints that seem to govern the sign.

To the extent that one strives to be a precise user of the language, one avoids wordplay, instead structuring statements according to the principle that for every thing there is one exact word that denotes it clearly. Utmost attention then is directed to meaning and minimal attention to the words themselves. Underlying this approach is the tacit willingness to use language as if it *were* a coherent system of signs. The more wordplay is introduced, on the other hand, the more attention is drawn to words themselves and to the disorganization that exists between words as signifiers and the multifariousness of what and how they signify. The most extreme form of linguistic confusion is the homonym.

Thus, homonyms, and homonymic rhymes especially because they foreground homonyms, produce cognitive tension.[5] All rhyme reveals phonetic equivalences between words with different meanings; though rhyme is fundamentally alogical, poetic convention has accepted that degree of irrationality as "normal." Homonymy, the total phonetic equivalence between words with different meaning, takes that principle further, to a point defined by convention as "excess." Yet the homonym merely pushes the latent, irrational fascination of all rhyme to its limit. A homonym exposes the strange chaos at the core of language. Like any riddle or paradox, a homonymic rhyme sets up a semantic gap that can induce frustration, but to those who overleap the gap with a comprehension of the philosophical appropriateness of the conflicting senses of two like-sounding words, it can also yield the pleasure of mastery. *Rime riche* is, then, a species of wit. While it lacks the acoustic tang of difference that the ear anticipates, it need not fall flat provided that the intellectual twist it proffers is sufficiently appealing.

A late poem Dickinson sent on several occasions for wedding salutations begins with these lines: "The Clock strikes one that just struck two / *Some* schism in the *Sum*" (P 1569) [emphasis added]. The wordplay, on an internal homonym, is not to be called *rime riche*, but it does illustrate Dickinson's alertness to and delight in the riddling possibilities of words with identical sounds. Her punning phrase enjoys the strange fascination of a homonym while also, indirectly, explaining it as a linguistic "schism" between two words that, like lovers united in wedlock, somehow are two and yet are joined (sumhow) as one. The wit of the lines is clever and appropriate. It is also indicative of the kind of play with acoustic coincidence that enters Dickinson's experiments with rime riche.

A homonymic rhyme is found in the introductory poem in Blake's *Songs of Innocence:*

> Piper sit thee down and write
> In a book that all may read –
> So he vanish'd from my sight.
> And I pluck'd a hollow reed.
>
> And I made a rural pen,
> And I stain'd the water clear,
> And I wrote my happy songs
> Every child may joy to hear
>
> (7)

The rhyme of *read/reed* is nicely functional in this setting: it calls attention to the transposition of the poet's songs from a musical to a written medium, and the continuity between the reed pipe and the reed pen emphasizes the music latent in the written words the reader is reading. There are few other significant uses of homonymic rhyme in this period by major poets writing in English other than Dickinson.[6]

Dickinson's poems contain fifteen homonymic end-rhymes and a great many more end-rhymes that pair identical syllables. It must be admitted that some of the rhymes are not

very successful, if one measures success by a cognitive richness that compensates for acoustic sameness. Nevertheless,
her identical rhymes provide interesting experiments in wordplay, and in a few poems the rhymes demonstrate a poetic
mastery of the very highest order.

Her earliest use of a homonymic rhyme is in "Went up a
year this evening!"[7] The poem describes someone's death in
terms of a balloon launch:

> Went up a year this evening!
> I recollect it well!
> Amid no bells nor bravoes
> The bystanders will tell!
> Cheerful – as to the village –
> Tranquil – as to repose –
> Chastened – as to the Chapel
> This humble Tourist rose!
> Did not talk of returning!
> Alluded to no time
> When, were the gales propitious –
> We might look for him!
> Was grateful for the Roses
> In life's diverse boquet –
> Talked softly of new species
> To pick another day;
> Beguiling thus the wonder
> The *wondrous* nearer drew –
> Hands bustled at the moorings –
> The crowd respectful grew –
> Ascended from our vision
> To Countenances new!
> A Difference – A Daisy –
> Is all the rest I knew!
>
> (P 93)

The last four rhyme-words in this poem (*drew/grew/new/knew*)
constitute an extended rhyme sequence and encompass a final

rhyme pair identical in sound. The final rhyme puns on the "Difference" between the *new* etherial realm to which the traveller ascends and the limitation of knowledge represented by what the speaker, left aground with an emblematic daisy to contemplate, *knew* of those far-away places. The pun is not pointless, but its interest is scarcely sufficient to redeem the ending from a somewhat limp impact.

Another early homonymic rhyme occurs in "The Wind didnt come from the Orchard – today – " (P 316), discussed in an earlier chapter. The poem so abounds in phonic play of all kinds that the *Our's/Hours* rhyme draws little attention to itself. In the main it is merely a part of the acoustic barrage that poem provides. An occult wit is attached to it, however, for the personification of the wind "with the Mowers / Whetting away the Hours" evokes the image of Father Time and his scythe. "If He [the wind] bring Odors of Clovers – " it may seem to be "His business – not Our's," but the whetting away of the "the *Hours*" subtly threatens not just the "Clovers" and "Hay" but our own human selves, who—though scarcely more able than meadow grasses to control the relentless process—may sense *that* business to be very much "*Our's*." The undertone is faint but ominous.

The success of the rhyme *too/to* at the conclusion of "For largest Woman's Heart I knew" is doubtful. The poem suggests a kinship of suffering between the speaker and the addressee:

> For largest Woman's Heart I knew –
> 'Tis little I can do –
> And yet the largest Woman's Heart
> Could hold an Arrow – too –
> And so, instructed by my own,
> I tenderer, turn Me to.

> (P 309)

The syntax in the last clause is ambiguous (I turn myself to her? or, I turn to myself?); thus, "turn Me to" at the end can be construed as like a turning to a mirror image, or to a *doppel-gänger*. The two women are linked by bonds of admiration and sympathy, and their emotional likeness is vaguely supported by the acoustic equivalence of the homonymic rhyme.[8] Whether that bit of linguistic ingenuity turns the poem into a success or not, though, is debatable.

The rhyme of *Sea/see* in "They put Us far apart," while not brilliant, is better:

> They put Us far apart –
> As separate as Sea
> And Her unsown Peninsula –
> We signified "These see" –
> > (P 474, ll. 1–4)

The poem is about the impossibility of blocking spiritual sight by mere physical means, and the words "see" and "saw" recur repeatedly throughout the poem. Thus, the play of homonyms on separation by "Sea" and the love that "sees" across all barriers initiates the theme of the poem. Because the rhyme comes at the beginning of a poem instead of at the end, it has not so much weight to bear, and the effect is not excessively flat. Instead, it introduces a linguistic intricacy parallel to the thematic subversion of ordinary logic, which holds that what is disjunct cannot be also and at the same time joined. These lovers, and this language, defy such logic.

Similarly, the rhyme of *Inn/in* in this poem is an acceptable sort of punning:

> How lonesome the Wind must feel Nights –
> When People have put out the Lights
> And everything that has an Inn
> Closes the shutter and goes in –
> > (P 1418, ll. 1–4)

One may say the same of the time-honored pun in this poem about the power of intuition:

> You'll know it – as you know 'tis Noon –
> By Glory –
> As you do the Sun –
> By Glory –
> As you will in Heaven –
> Know God the Father – and the Son.
>
> (P 420, ll. 1–4)

Here, the poem is otherwise arranged in broken tetrameter couplets, with partial rhymes (in this stanza paired as *Noon/ Sun* and *Heaven/Son*). That structure contributes an acoustic instability, across which the surprise of rich rhyme is an aesthetic treat; one might even call it an artistic "glory." The homonym, of course, underlines a parallel between this world and the next.

In another poem about the sun, described in metaphorical terms as an exemplary industrious housewife, the final stanza contains a homonymic rhyme:

> She hideth Her the last –
> And is the first, to rise –
> Her Night doth hardly recompense
> The Closing of Her eyes –
>
> She doth Her Purple Work –
> And putteth Her away
> In low Apartments in the Sod –
> As Worthily as We.
>
> To imitate Her life
> As impotent would be
> As make of Our imperfect Mints
> The Julep – of the Bee –
>
> (P 557)

If the rhyme *be/Bee* is not by itself intellectually intriguing (and perhaps it is), still the effect is pleasantly in keeping with the light tone of the poem and related in an interesting way to the theme. As a rhyme word in its own right, *be* is "impotent," but when *Bee* comes along to echo it, it is as if "be" were transformed from an ordinary, inconsequential being verb into a potent and magical "Bee," just as that industrious insect turns garden-variety mints into honeyed "Julep." The word "Julep," derived from a Persian word meaning "rosewater," may serve as a reminder that the bee's honey is distilled from the essence of the rose (as well as mint and other flowers); so too the poetry here distills the attar from language to produce something pleasantly rich and comparatively permanent (cf. P 675).

A common homonymic pair, *eye/I*, serves as the climax of "When I hoped, I recollect" (P 768) and adds considerable cognitive richness to the ideas being worked out there. The poem is structured around a logical progression from hope in the first two stanzas, to fear ("When I feared – I recollect") in the next two, to despair. The first four stanzas develop the idea that personal experience is not determined by outward conditions such as rough winds and "Sleet" or sunny days but by consciousness, which makes its own emotional climate. This is the final section:

> And the Day that I despaired –
> This – if I forget
> Nature will – that it be Night
> After Sun has set –
> Darkness intersect her face –
> And put out her eye –
> Nature hesitate – before
> Memory and I –

The contrast of "Day" and "Night" repeats the earlier idea of opposition between external circumstance and inner reality; it was day when her despair began, but despair is experienced as "Night," as "Darkness." The persistence of memory, though, a secondary theme in the earlier stanzas, becomes predominant here. "Nature" may "forget" the setting of her "Sun" before the speaker forgets the cause of her despair—by inference, the departure of the person who once had shone light and warmth into her life. The sun is nature's "eye"; analogously, the loss of the beloved is felt by the speaker as a sort of blinding. But the rhyme *eye/I* points both to the relationship of equivalence between nature and the speaker—both are benighted, deprived—and to their difference—the putting out of the physical eye does not destroy the visionary eye of "Memory" which constitutes the "I," the self.

In two poems, Dickinson incorporates a rhyme between *Hymn* and *Him*. In the earlier one, the interest of the rhyme is commensurate with the complexity of the poem:

> I rose – because He sank –
> I thought it would be opposite –
> But when his power dropped –
> My Soul grew straight.
>
> I cheered my fainting Prince –
> I sang firm – even – Chants –
> I helped his Film – with Hymn –
>
> And when the Dews drew off
> That held his Forehead stiff –
> I met him –
> Balm to Balm –
>
> I told him Best – must pass
> Through this low Arch of Flesh –
> No Casque so brave
> It spurn the Grave –
>
> I told him Worlds I knew
> Where Emperors grew –
> Who recollected us
> If we were true –

And so with Thews of Hymn –
And Sinew from within –
And ways I knew not that I knew – till then –
I lifted Him –

(P 616)

Albert Gelpi has remarked the importance of the feminine-masculine interplay in the speaker's narration of the events that transpired as she sat by the deathbed of her "fainting Prince": her strength waxes as his wanes. Gelpi's interpretation has a Jungian slant: "The lack of any felt sorrow and the growing sense of vigor and assurance indicate that this poem does not memorialize anyone's death but enacts her absorption of the animus into her psyche. Read as dream, the poem tells how he died into her ('I rose – because He sank – '), investing her with a strength both 'phallic' and spiritual. 'Thews of Hymn' joins physical and religious strength, with a pun on 'Him,' the rhyming word for 'Hymn.' His thews are then matched by 'Sinew from within – ' to become the psychic muscle and fiber through which she can lift him in 'ways I knew not that I knew – till then – " (*Muse* 254). Gelpi's analysis is acute in its stress on the physical-erotic dimension of the emotional drama, but it unnecessarily discounts the actual experience (of non-metaphorical dying) the poem relates and it does not emphasize sufficiently the *mutuality* of support between this woman and this man as she rises to the desperate occasion. As she rises in moral power, she also raises him—it is a reciprocal "Balm to Balm." There is no distinction necessary between "Thews of Hymn" and "thews of him," her strength and his. The cheering hymns she sings (it is in fact idiomatic to say "lift a hymn") are her way of encouraging the dying man and lifting "Him" through the "low Arch of Flesh" that is the passage into this life and out of it to "other Worlds." The homonymic rhyme is a linguistic union that reflects the mystical union they thus achieve.

The movement of the rhymes toward this climactic final

rhyme is noteworthy. There are no full rhymes in the first
thirteen lines, merely consonantal rhymes. After that, there
are *Brave/Grave, knew/grew/true* (with *Thews, Sinew,* and *knew,
knew* in the final stanza echoing that rhyme), and finally,
Hymn/Him. The gathering acoustic strength is like a musical
crescendo, and the poem itself is something of a hymn rising
in strength and power.

In a poem of about a year later, the same identical rhyme
appears, again at the end:

> Never for Society
> He shall seek in vain –
> Who His own acquaintance
> Cultivate – Of Men
> Wiser Men may weary –
> But the Man within
>
> Never knew Satiety –
> Better entertain
> Than could Border Ballad –
> Or Biscayan Hymn –
> Neither introduction
> Need You – unto Him –
>
> (P 746)

The structure of this poem is much tighter than that of the
other, with the two stanzas being parallel in several ways.
"Never knew Satiety" echoes "Never for Society," and "enter-
tain" in the second line of stanza two makes a full rhyme
for "vain" in the same position in stanza one. Likewise, the
contrast between the social world of "Men" and the private
world of "the Man within" in stanza one is carried out in the
second stanza by the parallel contrast between voguish social
entertainments such as the singing of popular ballads and the
more profoundly satisfying entertainment of knowing oneself
—that is, between *Hymn* and *Him.* Nevertheless, this poem
is flawed in line five: the word "Men" there interferes with

the important contrast of "Men" and "Man" in the lines before and after, and neither of the manuscript variants for that word ("One" and "Ear") conveys the meaning properly. Apart from that, the final identical rhyme does fall somewhat flat, the cognitive illumination being inadequate to compensate for the acoustic sameness. "I rose – because he sank" is clearly the superior poem.

In another pair of poems, Dickinson uses the identical rhyme of *earn* and *urn*. In both, the rhyme succeeds admirably. In the earlier of the two, the words are separated by five intervening lines, so that the effect is muted:

> Of all the Sounds despatched abroad,
> There's not a Charge to me
> Like that old measure in the Boughs –
> That phraseless Melody –
> The Wind does – working like a Hand,
> Whose fingers Comb the Sky –
> Then quiver down – with tufts of Tune –
> Permitted Gods, and me –
>
> Inheritance, it is, to us –
> Beyond the Art to Earn –
> Beyond the trait to take away
> By Robber, since the Gain
> Is gotten not of fingers –
> And inner than the Bone –
> Hid golden, for the whole of Days,
> And even in the Urn,
> I cannot vouch the merry Dust
> Do not arise and play
> In some odd fashion of it's own,
> Some quainter Holiday,
> When Winds go round and round in Bands –
> And thrum upon the door,
> And Birds take places, overhead,
> To bear them Orchestra.

I crave Him grace of Summer Boughs,
If such an Outcast be –
Who never heard that fleshless Chant –
Rise – solemn – on the Tree,
As if some Caravan of Sound
Off Deserts, in the Sky,
Had parted Rank,
Then knit, and swept –
In Seamless Company –

(P 321)

Though *Earn* and *Urn* are separated, it is worth noting that in this poem the rhymes are grouped in fours, the first and last four being vowel rhymes centered upon front vowels (long $\bar{\imath}$, long $\bar{e}$, and promoted $\ddot{y}$), the first four in the middle stanza centered upon *n*, and the subsequent four centered upon middle vowels (clearer when it is recalled that the poet would have shared the New England habit of a very light pronunciation of *r*). Lengthening the span of the rhyme in this way has the effect of unifying a larger portion of verse than usual —an octave rather than a quatrain; possibly the longer span is also intended to imitate the "phraseless Melody" of the wind, which is compared to sound that parts and knits again, "Seamless."[9] The idea of "grace" made explicit in the final stanza is introduced in the assertion that the music of the wind is part of humanity's spiritual inheritance, beyond any power either to "Earn" it or to be deprived of it. In this instance, the word *Earn* probably played a heuristic role in suggesting to the poet the dazzling idea of the "merry Dust" dancing within a funereal *Urn*.[10] For the reader, the latter rhyme word has a resonance that refers back to the earlier word and expands the conceptual range of both; the "fleshless" tune of the wind cannot be earned, nor can it be confined to any sepulcher, as the punning sense of "Beyond the Art to Urn" implies. Even the flesh, the corporeal element that *is* turned to dust and confined to urns, perhaps cannot be deprived of the "unearned" grace of the ethereal music. Because the homonymic rhyme-words are not contiguous, the rhyme lacks the piquancy of a quicker turn of wit; still, the rhyme is a long way from falling flat.

The same pair of homonyms appears in a poem dated about nine years later. Here it functions with very different purpose in the quick wit of an epigram, and its piquant force verges on bitterness:

> All men for Honor hardest work
> But are not known to earn –
> Paid after they have ceased to work
> In Infamy or Urn –
>
> (P 1193)

Incisively, this poem exploits the paradoxical, riddling quality that is fundamental both to the epigram and to *rime riche*. Men strive in desperation for "Honor," but all their labors end in death; only then they are paid for their labors, either in infamy or fame. If they are fortunate enough to receive fame, it comes in the ironic form of funereal honors, of doubtful value to the deceased. The vanity of human wishes, then, is pointed in the punning rhyme: the best one can *earn* is an *Urn*.[11] The poem might serve as a mordant epitaph.

An extraordinary poem that exists only as a pencilled draft composed about 1870, embracing several puzzling questions, also includes a homonymic rhyme, *Air/Heir:*

> Alone and in a Circumstance
> Reluctant to be told
> A spider on my reticence
> Assiduously crawled
>
> And so much more at Home than I
> Immediately grew
> I felt myself a visitor
> And hurriedly withdrew

Revisiting my late abode
With articles of claim
I found it quietly assumed
As a Gymnasium
Where Tax asleep and Title off
The inmates of the Air
Perpetual presumption took
As each were special Heir –
If any strike me on the street
I can return the Blow –
If any take my property
According to the Law
The Statute is my Learned friend
But what redress can be
For an offense nor here nor there
So not in Equity –
That Larceny of time and mind
The marrow of the Day
By spider, or forbid it Lord
That I should specify.

(P 1167)

The poem is a narration of and meditation on the encounter of the speaker and a spider in a privy, "mock-solemn" in tone, as Porter has remarked (*Idiom* 34). Porter further comments that the spider crawls on "an unmentionable part of the [privy] occupant's anatomy" and that "the victim flees without her clothes" (17). This interpretation is surely correct, and his comments imply his awareness of the pun on the difficulty of "redress" in such an awkward circumstance and also of the possible pun contained in "Assiduously" (the poet does list as alternate choices, however, "deliberately," "determinately," and "impertinently"). But there is a good deal more wordplay than this going on here. "Reticence" is a clever pun. The poet's lexicon defines "reticence" thus: "Concealment by silence. In *rhetoric*, aposiopesis or suppression; a figure by which a person really speaks of a thing, while he makes a show as if he would say nothing of the subject." [12] As she employs the word "reticence," it works with double meaning, *enacting* the rhetorical figure it also denotes. Notably, too, there is a pun in the word "Gymnasium." As her lexicon also informed her, "gymnasium" derives from the Greek *gumnos,* which means "naked." The spiders, who have taken over the speaker's abode and turned it into a gymnasium, are "inmates [var. Peasants] of the Air" and find it easy and natural to practice gymnastics naked; they thus put at a disadvantage the speaker, who shares with humankind a more sophisticated reticence about cavorting around without clothes. Much of the humor in the poem springs from the elaborate legal language brought to bear on the adventure of the speaker when she sets out bravely to re-establish her rightful claim to the privy. She comes with "articles of claim" that the spiders have no respect for at all. She wants to assert her property rights "According to the Law" and to established "Statute" and to rules of "Equity." The spiders, though, are sublimely unconcerned with the "Larceny" they have committed and with all such legalities as "Tax" and "Title." The speaker's idea of what it is to be a lawful *Heir,* then, is utterly at variance with the notion of inheritance of these ethereal beings, who live free, in the *Air.*

This peculiar homonym may have some connection with a mistaken etymology in Dickinson's lexicon. Her dictionary gives as the origin of *heir* the Norman word "hier, here," of which it explains, "The primary sense is to seize, or to rush on and take, or to expel and dispossess others, and take their property, according to the practice of rude nations." This false etymology, though opposed to the definition that follows, which properly gives the modern sense of "heir" as involving the lawful succession of property, describes exactly what the spiders (those rude peasants and airy inmates) have done. Their offense is not "in Equity," even though it has been a theft of "time and mind"—an "airy" sort of theft. The paradoxical contrast of meaning between the modern word and its supposed root may have stimulated some of the wordplay in the poem.[13]

To miss the auditory wit of the homonymic rhyme in the following poem is virtually to miss the point altogether:

> The Spirit is the Conscious Ear.
> We actually Hear
> When We inspect – that's audible –
> That is admitted – Here –
>
> For other Services – as Sound –
> There hangs a smaller Ear
> Outside the Castle – that Contain –
> The other – only – Hear –
>
> (P 733)

Obviously the poem contrasts the physical ear that registers mere "Sound" with the "Conscious Ear" that registers real meaning. Nevertheless, until the reader grasps—in addition to the paraphrasable content—the real acoustic point of the poem, it seems to be a fairly prosaic philosophical statement. Moreover, the declaration that actual hearing depends on seeing ("When we inspect – that's audible – ") appears to be nonsensical. In this poem about hearing, homonymic rhyme is functional in a way that no other rhyme could be. The rhyme makes the point. What the physical ear hears in *Hear/ Here* is an identity of sound, and since the physical ear hears only sound, it is oblivious to any difference between the two words. The crucial difference, however, is audible to the ear of consciousness—when one inspects the written words, perceives the graphic difference between them, and understands their disparate meanings. (Visual inspection is not required; a purely mental operation will do as well.) Only then is the truth "admitted" (another pun, meaning both "conceded" and "allowed to enter"). If the skeptical reader has wondered just where the ear of intuition might be, the poet locates it precisely; it is "Here," where the meaning enters in. That is the royal power contained in the "Castle."

One more homonymic rhyme is truly "rich," and it appears in a poem that has been largely ignored. The reason for the neglect is not far to seek: every one of Dickinson's editors has "corrected" her spelling. Ordinarily the first stanza appears in print like this:

> Don't put up my Thread and Needle –
> I'll begin to Sew
> When the Birds begin to whistle –
> Better Stitches – so –

Likewise, line seventeen is "corrected" this way:

> Till then – dreaming I am sewing

This, however, is what Dickinson wrote:

> Dont put up my Thread & Needle –
> I'll begin to Sow
> When the Birds begin to whistle –
> Better Stitches – so –
>
> These were bent – my sight got crooked –
> When my mind – is plain
> I'll do seams – a Queen's endeavor
> Would not blush to own –
>
> Hems – too fine for Lady's tracing
> To the sightless Knot –
> Tucks – of dainty interspersion –
> Like a dotted Dot –
>
> Leave my Needle in the furrow –
> Where I put it down –
> I can make the zigzag stitches
> Straight – when I am strong –
>
> Till then – dreaming I am sowing
> Fetch the seam I missed –
> Closer – so I – at my sleeping –
> Still surmise I stitch –

(P 617)

Johnson's variorum text does print the poem accurately, but with this note: "The spelling of 'Sow' and 'sowing' is undoubtedly a mistake for 'sewing.'" Undoubtedly, it is not. With 'Sow' emended to 'Sew,' the poem seems inchoate and full of details that do not make sense; it is no wonder that critics have taken the poem as a sincere statement by an uncertain poet about her technical inadequacies. For example, Gilbert and Gubar, in an otherwise perceptive discussion of the poems based on the sewing metaphor, mistakenly say that Dickinson "was troubled by the imperfect stitches she feared she made when her sight got 'crooked' and her mind was no longer 'plain'" (641). When the 'Sow' is properly retained, however, the poem is an intricate virtuoso display.

The weary seamstress whose voice is heard in the poem —she of the crooked stitches—is not to be equated with the masterful artist who stitches this seamless poem. In order to appreciate the finesse of the workmanship, one must keep in mind the delicate but definite distance between the two. It is quite true that Dickinson had learned fine sewing as all women did in her day (a sampler she stitched in her youth is preserved), and we should not forget that she literally fastened together her poems into fascicles with a needle and thread and that she sometimes sewed pictures or flowers onto poems she sent to friends. Still, the seamstress is not Dickinson but a "supposed person." The "zigzag stitches" the seamstress makes in the obviously misspelled *Sow* and in the awkward rhyme with *so* are, in the poet's hands, brilliantly functional. The rhyme *Sow/so* does fall absurdly flat, but only until the richness of the triple pun springs to life. The real deliberateness behind the apparent misspelling is proved by the reference to "furrow" in line sixteen: "Leave my needle in the furrow," the speaker requests, again joining together the two kinds of *sewing/sowing*. The rhyme word *so* is less important in itself than as it serves to draw attention to the pun that merges stitchery and the planting of seed as twin metaphors for the craft of the poet; even *so*, however, may accentuate the methodical nature of poetry. As "sewing" points to the meticulous putting of word and word in a fabric of elaborate design, "sowing" points to what could be called the germinative function of poetry, the sowing of seed for growth in future generations (which Dickinson refers to in P 883 as "Disseminating" poetic light).[14] Traditionally feminine and masculine arts, then, combine in the androgynous art of poetry.

Even the word "furrow" may serve as a reminder that the English word *verse* "comes to us from the Latin *versus,* a turning round as of the plow at the end of a furrow, and thus it meant also a furrow, a row, a line of writing. In verse the language turns from time to time and forms new line" (Thompson 168). The "errors" in the dreamy surmises of the apologetic seamstress contain a wisdom beyond her conscious knowledge, a superior artistry she does not need to improve upon. Though she does not know it, the "bent" stitches she regrets are worthy of a "Queen." The "sightless Knot" for which clumsy-fingered little girls are taught to strive is achieved, audibly, not with a needle but with a pen, in the splendidly mistaken rich rhyme. It is elegant embroidery—"Like a dotted Dot."[15]

Gertrude Stein could hardly have known this poem, first published in 1929, when she wrote her "Sacred Emily" (1922). Yet her poem contains a fascinating parallel to Dickinson's in these lines of praise:

> So great so great Emily.
> Sew grate sew grate Emily.
> Not a spell nicely.
> Ring.

Honoring her poetic forebear, Stein, too, rings the changes on word-sounds. Her pun discovers a mysterious link between woman's domestic work and a different greatness that verges on the sacred. Stein, who also loved the wiles of words, knew she was following in the footsteps of her "so great" exemplar.

A discussion of the identical rhymes that involve only parts of words is bound to be somewhat anticlimactic after consideration of grander feats accomplished with homonymic rhymes. Dickinson uses such rhymes so frequently, however, that one cannot ignore them. In at least one magnificent poem their success is surpassing.

Rhyme pairs that share only one syllable are less startling than homonyms; consequently, their effect is less marked. Generally, in Dickinson's hands, they are a subtle sort of wordplay. For example, when she rhymes *side* with *beside*, the rhyme is thematically significant:

> The Brain – is wider than the Sky –
> For – put them side by side –
> The one the other will contain
> With ease – and You – beside –
>
> (P 632, ll. 1–4)

The word "beside," a catachresis for "besides," literally contains the word "side" as the "Brain" figuratively contains the "Sky." The phrase "and You" points to the complexity—involving a shift from the plane of physicality to the realm of consciousness—by which the brain, a part, can contain the whole (of the self, of "You"). The idea and the idiom are reminiscent of a statement by Thoreau in the chapter "Solitude" in *Walden*, which Dickinson, of course, knew: "With thinking we may be beside ourselves in a sane sense."

Elsewhere, when Dickinson rhymes *found* with *profound*, she stirs up ambiguous cross-currents of meaning surrounding "profound" reasonings that dig deep and things too deeply buried to know, hence "not found":

> "Departed" – both – they say!
> i.e. gathered away,
> Not found,
>
> Argues the Aster still –
> Reasons the Daffodil
> Profound!
>
> (P 60, ll. 7–12)

Serious questions about loss are hardly to be answered by customary euphemism and rational attempts at definition, which Dickinson scoffs at in the abbreviation "i.e." and the subsequent terms that fail to explain anything. Deeper, truer wisdom is offered symbolically in the perennial resurrection of the aster and the daffodil, which "Argues" a *Profound*, optimistic response to the negative dead end of "*Not found*." The rhyme presents a paradox but also hints at its solution.

A poem that depicts the frost as an elusive stranger who destroys the garden "some retrieveless Night" ends with a rhyme that forces attention to the Latinate root *-fer*, "bear," and to the prefixes that distinguish two ways of dealing with the "Unproved" and the "Unknown":

> To analyze perhaps
> A Philip would prefer
> But Labor vaster than myself
> I find it to infer.
>
> (P 1202, ll. 17–20)

Philip, who asked Jesus to show him the Father (John 14:8–9), wanted evidence to be brought "before" him for analysis, but the lyric voice demands no such impossible certainties, feeling it surpassingly difficult even to bear the meaning "in." Interestingly enough, the poet's dictionary offers this definition of *infer:* "To deduce; to draw or derive, as a fact or consequence. From the character of God, as creator and governor of the world, we *infer* the indispensable obligation of all his creatures to obey his commands." Since the poem centers on the destructive power of frost, a deadly natural force that evades human vigilance, the questions raised about evidence and inference contain multiple ironies, not only about the analytic method but also about the significance of frost in regard to "the worst we fear" concerning the character of God as creator and governor of the world; the inferences that *might* be drawn are dreadful. The epistemological "Labor" is too vast, however, for there are many strange "Secrets" beyond the access of either "pre-fer-ential" analysis or "in-fer-ence."

Analysis of and inference from such linguistic intricacies is laborious, too, and at times Dickinson's cryptic, elliptical procedures can seem wearisome. Sometimes the trouble really does not seem worthwhile. (In the poem just discussed, for instance.) Her fascination with the "wiles of words" and with the labyrinthine secrets of the lexicon, though, lies close to the core of her poetic magic. Nearly every devoted reader of Dickinson has found that passages that seem exasperating at one time can later flash with meanings hitherto hidden. As she mulled over the enigmas of life and the subtleties of language, she writes primarily for those readers who enjoy doing that, too. ("The Fox fits the Hound – " [P 842].)

Sometimes her labor is more productive. She considered including some wordplay involving roots and prefixes in the famous "My life closed twice before its close."

> My life closed twice before its close;
> It yet remains to see
> If Immortality unveil
> A third event to me,
>
> So huge, so hopeless to conceive
> As these that twice befel.
> Parting is all we know of heaven,
> And all we need of hell.
>
> (P 1732)

Listed as a variant for "unveil," in line three, is "disclose." [16] With that variant, the first stanza would read like this:

> My life closed twice before its close;
> It yet remains to see
> If Immortality disclose
> A third event to me

"Disclose" is a synonym for "unveil," and both words mean "to uncover" or "to reveal." "Unveil" has the advantage of drawing in connotations suggesting the world "beyond the veil" of mortality, connotations obviously relevant here. In juxtaposition to "close," however, "disclose" has a different advantage: it attracts attention to itself as an antonym for "close" and to its own literal sense as "open," which in this context is an arresting paradox. That is, it compounds the paradox in the opening line, which pushes the reader's imagination to discriminate between two kinds of "close"—the literal ending of life, or death, and some metaphorical ending comparable to death yet prior to death and capable of recurrence an indefinite number of times. "Disclose" demands a further stretch of the mind toward conceptualization of an immensity that is simultaneously an opening and a close, a revelation or uncovering that is also a covering, a conclusion that does not conclude, thus doubly "hopeless to conceive."

The rhyme of *Seed* and *intercede* in another poem plays on different etymological elements with an uncanny phonic overlap, thus combining the idea of "*inter*ring," or burying a seed in the ground, with the idea that the seed will "intercede" (literally, "pass between"), or mediate, between one living flower and the flowers of the next generation:

> Longing is like the Seed
> That wrestles in the Ground,
> Believing if it intercede
> It shall at length be found.
> (P 1255, ll. 1–4)

The rhyme, then, like the image, reinforces the idea that burial need not preclude faith in resurrection. The *seed* may *intercede*, and what is in the *Ground* may rise to light at last and be *found*. The connection of the words by an identity of sound even implies an obscure link, in the nature of things, between longing and its fulfillment. In the second and final stanza, however, the tone is less assured:

> The Hour, and the Clime –
> Each Circumstance unknown,
> What Constancy must be achieved
> Before it see the Sun!

The *abab* rhyme scheme of stanza one yields to an *abcb* scheme here, and full rhyme is replaced by consonantal rhyme; the sound and the statement at the end strike the note of unfulfilled longing.

A poem about autumn ends with an identical rhyme that climaxes a description of the fullness of the feast (*repast*) offered by a season that is departing (almost *past*). It is significant that the prefix *re-* is used five times in a dozen lines, for the poem looks back to "review" the "residue" of a passing year that "returns" again to nature. Though it is a thing of the "past," the speaker finds the "repast" adequate, and sweet:

> With sweetness unabated
> Informed the hour had come
> With no remiss of triumph
> The autumn started home –
> Her home to be with Nature
> As competition done
> By influential kinsmen
> Invited to return
> In supplements of Purple
> An adequate repast
> In heavenly reviewing
> Her residue be past –
>
> (P 1709)

In a poem that is an exhortation to humility, the identical rhyme in the fourth stanza (*fine/superfine*) combines with an internal rhyme (*twine*) to suggest the excessive aspiration of a little wren:

> For every Bird a Nest –
> Wherefore in timid quest
> Some little Wren goes seeking round –

Wherefore when boughs are free –
Households in every tree –
Pilgrim be found?

Perhaps a home too high –
Ah Aristocracy!
The little Wren desires –

Perhaps of twig so fine –
Of twine e'en superfine,
Her pride aspires –

The Lark is not ashamed
To build upon the ground
Her modest house –

Yet who of all the throng
Dancing around the sun
Does so rejoice?

(P 143)

The partial rhymes of the last two stanzas seem to correspond with the "modesty" of the happy lark, with which the ambitious wren and its showy stunts of rhyme are implicitly contrasted.

A number of poems use the prefix *a-* in one of the words paired in an identical rhyme. The prefix *a-* is rich in its meanings, having descended from multifarious origins, and indicating among other things "not," "on," "in," "up," "away from," and "toward." In the word "ago" the prefix is merely an intensive, and in "away" the prefix literally means "on." Yet when Dickinson uses these words in rhymes with their root words, there seems to be an emphasis on privation, on absence, related to a different sense of the prefix and to her interest in what she calls in one poem our "ablative estate" (P 1741; cf. the "ablative" fruit in P 1744). The ablative is one of the oblique cases in Latin, and it indicates separation or movement away from. These rhymes on *way/away* and *go/ago* reinforce thematic emphasis on what is transitory:

Within my reach!
I could have touched!
I might have chanced that way!
Soft sauntered thro' the village –
Sauntered as soft away!
So unsuspected Violets
Within the meadows go –
Too late for striving fingers
That passed, an hour ago!

(P 90)

I said I gained it –
This – was all –
Look, how I clutch it
Lest it fall –
And I a Pauper go –
Unfitted by an instant's Grace
For the Contented – Beggar's face
I wore – an hour ago –

(P 359, ll. 8–15)

The Summer deepened, while we strove –
She put some flowers away –
And Redder cheeked Ones – in their stead –
A fond – illusive way –

(P 574, ll. 9–12)

Nor was I hungry – so I found
That Hunger – was a way
Of Persons outside Windows –
The Entering – takes away –

(P 579, ll. 17–20)

Similar is this rhyme on *drawn* and *withdrawn*, which fore-grounds the sense of the prefix *with-* (from Middle English) as "away from":

A Cap of Lead across the sky
Was tight and surly drawn
We could not find the mighty Face
The Figure was withdrawn –

(P 1649, ll. 1–4)

The aesthetic question of whether these rhymes are good rhymes, sufficiently interesting rhymes, is one I will not presume to pronounce on. It is clear, though, that they result not from the poet's recklessness but from her attentiveness to her craft. [17]

A very strange use of identical rhymes is the series of six rhymes at the end of this delicate poem in long meter couplets, couplets that recede from full rhymes (in lines 1–4) to consonantal rhymes (in lines 5–10) and conclude with "promotion identical" rhymes (the term used in the Holman-Harmon *Handbook* for identical rhymes involving a syllable ordinarily unaccented but receiving a stress promotion):

Summer begins to have the look
Peruser of enchanting book
Reluctantly but sure perceives
A gain upon the backward leaves

Autumn begins to be inferred
By millinery of the cloud
Or deeper color in the shawl
That wraps the everlasting hill

The eye begins it's avarice
A meditation chastens speech
Some Dyer of a distant tree
Resumes his gaudy industry

Conclusion is the course of All
At *most* to be perennial
And then elude stability
Recalls to immortality –

(P 1682)

The "decline" of the rhyme parallels the seasonal decline from
"Summer" to "Autumn" toward an inevitable "Conclusion."
The rhymes do not disappear altogether, though, and the
conclusion does not announce finality. Instead, it carries a reminder of what is "perennial." Not permanent, but perennial.
Paradoxically, only what "eludes stability" is called back to
"immortality." [18] Amid the instability of this oddly fascinating
rhyme sequence, words by changing stay the same—*tree/-try,
All/-al, -tỳ/-tỳ;* the effect is wonderfully congruent with the
meaning. Just as the trees put on their autumn finery, the poet
here wears her *riche* with a difference.

In all her subsequent experiments with identical rhymes,
however, Dickinson never excelled the technical achievement
of her early "These are the days when Birds come back,"
written about 1859, in common particular meter. The almost
incredible intricacies of *rime riche* in this justly famous poem
are so perfectly absorbed into the texture of the whole as to be
utterly unobtrusive, a richness to be savored by whoever will.

> These are the days when Birds come back –
> A very few – a Bird or two –
> To take a backward look.
>
> These are the days when skies resume
> The old – old sophistries of June –
> A blue and gold mistake.
>
> Oh fraud that cannot cheat the Bee –
> Almost thy plausibility
> Induces my belief.
>
> Till ranks of seeds their witness bear –
> And softly thro' the altered air
> Hurries a timid leaf.
>
> Oh Sacrament of summer days,
> Oh Last Communion in the Haze –
> Permit a child to join.

> Thy sacred emblems to partake –
> Thy consecrated bread to take
> And thine immortal wine!
>
> (P 130)

Positioned at the center of the poem is a rich rhyme, *belief/leaf*, which epitomizes the crucial conflict between the speaker's longing to believe in an immortal summer on the one hand and the all-too-visible evidence of autumnal decay (a dead leaf) on the other. The days of Indian summer are so lovely and so nearly plausible that the speaker almost can believe it *is* summer, but the seeds and the falling leaf have the force of negating belief, of proving the fraudulence of a sophistical season. The speaker, nevertheless, does not allow her skepticism to destroy utterly her will to believe but goes on to implore that she may recover the child-like state of mind (un-skeptical, ironically "in the Haze") that participates in timeless vision. Significantly, the rhyme words *belief* and *leaf* stand in perfect counterbalance.

Another rich rhyme is in the last stanza. *Partake/take* seemed objectionable to the first editors of the poem, so they emended the latter to the more logical "break." Because "consecrated bread" is irreversibly associated with the Christian ritual of breaking bread, this rhyme must have occurred to and been rejected by Dickinson. For the same reason, "break" is probably what most readers anticipate as they are hearing the poem. The unexpected repetition of "take" sends reverberations back to the earlier "take," the backward look the birds take, and also back to "mistake," those deceptive "blue and gold" beauties of Indian summer that lure the birds back. What the birds "take," then, is a "mis-take," and the echo suggests that the sacramental bread the speaker "takes" and the emblems she "partakes" are likely also to be a "mistake."

The final rhyme in the poem carries out the poised ambiguities in a remarkable way. "Join" and "wine," as Charles Anderson has pointed out, "only rhyme if the old-fashioned pronunciation, still common in hymnals, is used. Absolute faith is only possible for the old-fashioned?" (147). His surmise is enticing, but I think it is a little misleading. Absolute faith is possible only for the child, the poem indicates; later on, experience eradicates all but the tentative sort of belief expressed here. The anachronistic rhyme is best seen as it functions in the structure of the poem: if *wine* preceded *join*, one might simply give *join* the old pronunciation or some shade of it, but since *join* is first, the subsequent *wine* (reinforced by the internal rhyme *thine*) rings dissonant, as if it were a "mistake." (We might say *jine* but we cannot say *woin*.) The discord subtly tempts readers to "take a backward look" to *join* as if to re-pronounce it in their minds and thus retrieve some lost harmony, though they know it is a "cheat." The repetitions and backward echoes of the rhymes, then, like every other detail in the poem, enter into a majestic synthesis of wistful longing for lost beauty and innocence and a tremulous savoring of the precarious sacramental promise implicit in a lovely, fleeting, declining season.

Not all of Dickinson's identical rhymes are so masterful. Some are merely innovative and exploratory. All, though, show her fascination with the lively disorganization that is language and the cunning wit with which she organized the play of meaning in her poetry. All show her to have been a "philologist," a wily wordsmith who revitalized the poetic principle of the pun and its multiplicity of signification to tease the ear and mind to richer perception.

FIVE

Closure and Non-Closure

Emily Dickinson's revision of poetic structure extends to new ways of handling an ending. This feature of her poetry has been a particular object of critical indictment. Charles Anderson acknowledged her "provocative first lines" and then complained that "not one [poem] in ten fulfills the brilliant promise of the opening words" (70). Since then such critical remarks have become commonplace. Philip Larkin makes a similar accusation: "too often the poem expires in a teased-out and breathless obscurity" (367). Richard Chase argues that she simply had no concept of a poem as a "finished and formal object of art" (192).[1] As these comments suggest, the negative valuation of Dickinson's endings originates in the assumption that a poem should be a static art object that contains a clear meaning and arrives at a stable resolution of whatever uncertainties it arouses. Indeed Dickinson's practice subverts that poetic model in the interest of a more fluid, dynamic art. The irresolution of her endings is consistent not only with a general trend in poetry and the other arts away from firm closure but also with her own aesthetic principles of instability and elusiveness. The irresolution critics have called a structural weakness can be redefined as a strength when one comes to recognize its role in a poetics based on the principle that "Suspense – does not conclude" (P 705). Epistemological uncertainty and unsatisfied longings pervade Dickinson's work.[2]

Where the insecurities of persistent skepticism and persistent desire endlessly defer thematic resolutions, unclosed endings are stylistically appropriate.

There is no doubt that some of the poems are literally unfinished, some mere scraps and fragments. As far as possible, however, we should take care to discriminate unfinished poems from inconclusive poems. To infer that those that do not end with a resounding final chord are unfinished or fragmentary is to disregard abundant evidence that on the whole she deliberately avoided the authoritative voice that resolves tensions in a grand finale. A recurrent tendency in her poetry is to surprise closural expectations with abrupt stops, anticlimactic deflation, or lingering unanswered questions. Indeed, closural disruptions and closural suspensions contribute significantly to effects of wit and mystery that are central to the appeal of her poetry.[3] Rhyme is one poetic feature that she manipulates (along with other features) to achieve various degrees of closure or non-closure.

Full rhyme in itself is "neither the *sine qua non* of poetic closure nor a sufficient condition for its occurrence" (Smith 49). If it were, every rhyme would bring a full halt. Still, rhyme has closural force, and full rhyme has greater closural force than partial rhyme. Partial rhyme "avoids the violent, abrupt jerk resultant from announcing a period with the sharp pistol-crack of rime" (Herbert 438). More ambiguous and less stable in effect than full rhyme, partial rhyme may be felt in various contexts as gentler, weirder, more discordant, or more elusive. I shall examine in some detail the role of partial rhymes in the endings of Dickinson's poems, to show how they cooperate with thematic and other factors in achieving deliberately weak closure.

First, though, it is appropriate to acknowledge that a great many of her poems are firmly closed and that frequently full rhyme assists in securing that effect. Dickinson could turn an epigram when she liked, and an epigram is that maximally closed poetic form, as Barbara Herrnstein Smith says (197).

Of Heaven above the firmest proof
We fundamental know
Except for it's marauding Hand
It had been Heaven below.

(P 1205, ll. 5–8)

This stanza, in regular meter and rhyme (significantly more regular than the preceding stanza), speaks in authoritative voice of firm proof of heaven. The initial lines of the stanza set up expectations for familiar proofs of heaven such as the death on the cross, the word of the prophets, the enduring witness of faith, and the like, but the concluding lines disappoint and surprise those expectations with a delightfully bitter twist of wit: the "proof" turns out to be far more tangible—the "Hand" of heaven's rascally raids to plunder earth of its most cherished treasures. This poem not only closes: it slams shut, with a jolt.

The poet's most famous poem on the subject of closings is also brought to an end on an epigram, an epigram that imparts a subtler *frisson:*

My life closed twice before its close;
It yet remains to see
If Immortality unveil
A third event to me,

So huge, so hopeless to conceive
As these that twice befel.
Parting is all we know of heaven,
And all we need of hell.

(P 1732)

The lyric comprises two sentences—the first a long, narrative sentence and the second a brief, epigramatic summation. The long sentence reports in a short clause (line one) the fact of what has happened and speculates in a much longer, intricately complex clause (lines 2 to 6) on what may yet happen; the disproportion suggests the relative strength of the lingering "aftermath" as measured against the actual experience itself.[4] Enjambment of lines two, three, and five, along with a syntactic continuity between lines four and five that reduces the normal pause after the first stanza, helps to sustain the momentum up until the final aphorism. The conclusiveness of the last sentence derives from its force as a statement of generalized truth encapsulating the wisdom yielded by the experiences mentioned, and also from its concise assertiveness, its reference to last things (the ultimate of heaven and hell), its parallel structure, and the full rhyme with which it ends.[5] The tone of conviction is unmistakable.

The authoritative tone is to be found also in satirical poems such as "Praise it – 'tis dead" (P 1384), "We shall find the Cube of the Rainbow" (P 1484), and "Split the Lark" (P 861), mentioned previously. Full rhymes throughout these poems contribute to the stability of tone. In "Split the Lark," closure is enhanced by the word "Now," indicative of a drawing of conclusions, and also by the fact that the question it introduces is patently rhetorical; the last question is equivalent to a final "Now, are you satisfied?" Similarly, "What Soft – Cherubic Creatures" ends with contemptuous irony:

> It's such a common – Glory –
> A Fisherman's – Degree –
> Redemption – Brittle Lady –
> Be so – ashamed of Thee –
>
> (P 401)

In this instance, full rhymes appear in the first and last stanzas, with a consonantal rhyme (*refined/ashamed*) in the middle stanza. Since a return to prosodic normality after a deviation such as exists here is in fact an effective device tending toward closure (Smith 70), the final rhyme helps confirm the reader's sense that the poem has reached a definitive judgment and an appropriate stopping point.

There are many poems, less authoritative in tone, in which a return to full rhyme after a departure supports a closural effect. The return to full rhyme in "Better – than Music" (P 503), for example, discussed previously with reference to its ABA structure, lends an acoustic stability analogous to the meaning: echoing the word "alone," the last line "Drop[s] into tune – around the Throne." Another poem structured in this way ends with a gentle repose:

> Nature – the Gentlest Mother is,
> Impatient of no Child –
> The feeblest – or the waywardest –
> Her Admonition mild –
>
> In Forest – and the Hill
> By Traveller – be heard –
> Restraining Rampant Squirrel –
> Or too impetuous Bird –
>
> How fair Her Conversation –
> A Summer Afternoon –
> Her Household – Her Assembly –
> And when the Sun go down –
>
> Her Voice among the Aisles
> Incite the timid prayer
> Of the minutest Cricket –
> The most unworthy Flower –
>
> When all the Children sleep –
> She turns as long away
> As will suffice to light Her lamps –
> Then bending from the Sky –
>
> With infinite Affection –
> And infiniter Care –
> Her Golden finger on Her lip –
> Wills Silence – Everywhere –
>
> (P 790)

The image of Mother Nature tucking all her children in bed has closural force in itself, of course, by reference to nightfall, sleep, and universal silence; but the return, after ambiguous consonantal rhymes, to the relaxation of full rhymes is part of the effect as well. [6]

Even more frequent are poems in which the only full rhyme in the poem is the final rhyme. This pattern is so common it seems certain that Dickinson is availing herself of the device as a convenient means of supporting closure. (It might be argued that a lone final full rhyme does not represent a "return" to a norm on the grounds that no norm has been established earlier in the poem; this argument would be mistaken, however, because full rhyme is so pervasive in English tetrameter verse that the association of rhyme with the metrical form alone is extremely strong, especially when that association is reinforced within a poem by kinds of rhyme that, while less emphatic, point in the direction of full rhyme.)[7] This early poem, for example, has several fanciful but disturbing stanzas considering death as a strangely asocial and depersonalized person, and none of those first three stanzas is fully rhymed; a final stanza guaranteeing immortal "Rest" closes with an appropriately "restful" rhyme sound:

> Dust is the only Secret –
> Death, the only One
> You cannot find out all about
> In his "native town."
>
> Nobody knew "his Father" –
> Never was a Boy –
> Had'nt any playmates,
> Or "Early history" –
>
> Industrious! Laconic!
> Punctual! Sedate!
> Bold as a Brigand!
> Stiller than a Fleet!
>
> Builds, like a Bird, too!
> Christ robs the Nest –

Robin after Robin
Smuggled to Rest!
(P 153)

In the last stanza, the metaphysical conceit of Christ's rob-
bing birds out of the nest (like a cat or some other predator)
is surprising; nonetheless, since the birds represent souls and
the "Nest" represents darkness and the grave, the protec-
tive intent—to bring them to heavenly rest—is clear, and the
reassurance of ultimate security is manifest. Moreover, the
sound of the concluding rhyme lends an acoustic security that
supports the unambiguous tone of the close.

Similarly, in the following poem, which considers the problem of endings in multiple circumstances, the full rhyme in
the final stanza gives a sense of peaceful ending:

The Months have ends – the Years – a knot –
No Power can untie
To stretch a little further
A Skein of Misery –

The Earth lays back these tired lives
In her mysterious Drawers –
Too tenderly, that any doubt
An ultimate Repose –

The manner of the Children –
Who weary of the Day –
Themself – the noisy Plaything
They cannot put away –

(P 423)

An "ultimate Repose" is ensured here to mortals, who would,
like tired, peevish children, evade it. In another context this
perception might have been made to seem ironic, but it strikes
no irony here. Human life is pictured as a "Skein of Misery,"
best ended, and the simple harmony of the final rhyme—
because it sounds just "right"—supports the idea that in the

proper course of things a "*Day*" is meant to close with putting of things "*away*."

A poem written after the death of Elizabeth Barrett Browning, describing the experience of first reading her work, maintains a tone of exhilarated "Insanity" until the last quatrain, where the authoritative voice of reasoned conviction summarizes the abiding meaning of the experience. The formal structure of the poem is designed to enhance the thematic idea of enlightenment of the mind by the "Foreign," the potent "Magic" or knowledge defined as madness by the uninitiated. Significantly, the only full and regular rhyme is the last.

> I think I was enchanted
> When first a sombre Girl –
> I read that Foreign Lady –
> The Dark – felt beautiful –
>
> And whether it was noon at night –
> Or only Heaven – at Noon –
> For very Lunacy of Light
> I had not power to tell –
>
> The Bees – became as Butterflies –
> The Butterflies – as Swans –
> Approached – and spurned the narrow Grass –
> And just the meanest Tunes
>
> That Nature murmured to herself
> To keep herself in Cheer –
> I took for Giants – practising
> Titanic Opera –
>
> The Days – to Mighty Metres stept –
> The Homeliest – adorned
> As if unto a Jubilee
> 'Twere suddenly confirmed –
>
> I could not have defined the change –
> Conversion of the Mind

> Like Sanctifying in the Soul –
> Is witnessed – not explained –
>
> 'Twas a Divine Insanity –
> The Danger to be Sane
> Should I again experience –
> 'Tis Antidote to turn –
>
> To Tomes of solid Witchcraft –
> Magicians be asleep –
> But Magic – hath an Element
> Like Deity – to keep –
>
> (P 593)

There *is* a full rhyme in the second quatrain, *night/light*, but out of position; lines two and four, which should rhyme according to the scheme, do not (*Noon/tell*). It seems clear that Dickinson is using the dislocation of the rhyme to contribute a feeling that co-ordinates with the idea there of lunatic disorientation. Otherwise, the partial rhymes provide a musical instability compatible with the theme of enchantment, "Witchcraft," and "Divine Insanity." Only at the end does the poem arrive at a point of rest. That closure is secured by the metaphorical reference to the dead poet—"Magicians be asleep," by the affirmation that the "Magic" of poetry is bound to "keep," that is, to endure in spite of death of poets, and by the phonetic harmony of the words that make up the final, full rhyme.

A curious, and related, maneuver is effective in this poem, which depends heavily on a single rhyme for its poetic effect:

> Spring comes on the World –
> I sight the Aprils –
> Hueless to me until thou come
> As, till the Bee
> Blossoms stand negative,
> Touched to Conditions
> By a Hum.
>
> (P 1042)

Here, the last word, *Hum,* the word that makes the rhyme, not only secures closure but also enacts the point of the whole poem.[8] Paraphrased, the poem says something like this: Spring is here but it is nothing to me until you come, just as a blossom's life is blank until the bee comes to it. The structure of the poem carries out that idea beautifully. The lines are broken in such a way that no stanza pattern is apparent, and they are so rhythmically irregular that the metrical pattern is indeterminate. The reader trying to get the "feel" of the poetic movement is at something of a loss, until the last word. *Hum,* onomatopoeic in itself, also "hums" in a satisfying rhyme with "come," relaxing the reader's tensions and touching into poetic "Conditions" lines that up until that rhyme have stood "negative" and "Hueless." The arrival of the hum makes the poem itself (like the blossom, like the speaker) spring to life.

Another verse of the same year, with a similar strategy, maintains apparent chaos up till the last word:

> Dying at my music!
> Bubble! Bubble!
> Hold me till the Octave's run!
> Quick! Burst the Windows!
> Ritardando!
> Phials left, and the Sun!
>
> (P 1003)

This little poem makes merry with its own histrionics: the gasping, gurgling musician imperiously demands assistance and exclaims with gusto the particulars of her grandly operatic death. Whether her musical performance is fantasized or real is not quite clear, but as it comes to an end, the speaker's attention turns for a moment to the medicine bottles left behind and then at last to the sudden influx of sunlight. The rhyme on *Sun,* echoing *run,* gives shape to the poem and strikes the bright final chord of a triumphal and hammed-up death scene. The poem is integral and well closed.[9]

Another poem with a single full rhyme at the close, a longer poem, more complex than any of the examples of this type given previously, is "Going to Heaven!" Here, too, the concord of the final rhyme serves to allay tensions that have been built up by formal, stylistic and thematic agitations and disjunctions throughout the poem, but it does not resolve them completely.

> Going to Heaven!
> I dont know when –
> Pray do not ask me how!
> Indeed I'm too astonished
> To think of answering you!
> Going to Heaven!
> How dim it sounds!
> And yet it will be done
> As sure as flocks go home at night
> Unto the Shepherd's arm!
>
> Perhaps you're going too!
> Who knows?
> If you sh'd get there first
> Save just a little place for me
> Close to the two I lost –
> The smallest "Robe" will fit me
> And just a bit of "Crown" –
> For you know we do not mind our dress
> When we are going home –
>
> I'm glad I dont believe it
> For it w'd stop my breath –
> And I'd like to look a little more
> At such a curious Earth!
> I am glad they did believe it
> Whom I have never found
> Since the mighty Autumn afternoon
> I left them in the ground.

(P 79)

Porter correctly points out the disconcerting effect in this poem of rhythmic variations and colloquial language, which reflect the ambivalence of the speaker about faith in a life after death (*Early* 66–67).[10] It is important to note also the instability contributed by the rhymes except for the last (*how/you, done/arm, first/lost, Crown/home, breath/Earth*) and the ultimate stability contributed by that last, full rhyme (*found/ground*). The logical structure of the poem draws attention to the extreme confusions of the speaker: she is "sure" on the one hand that "it will be done" (the echo of the Lord's Prayer makes this line especially solemn) but first uncertain "when" and "how" and then unwilling to believe in heaven at all because it means surrendering "breath" and "Earth"; these confusions remain at the ending. Moreover, because of the paradoxical juxtaposition of apparent contraries—"I'm glad I dont believe it" and "I am glad they did believe it"—this ending is relatively less closed than that of some poems. It is difficult to comprehend that both statements are true. The last statement, however, is unequivocal. The diction becomes more formal, the pace is more stately, and the phonetic harmony of the rhyme gives it strength. If the last rhyme were changed to a consonantal rhyme (by substituting "Whom I could never find" for "Whom I have never found," for instance) it would have the poetic effect of undercutting the final assertion, making it sound less than whole-hearted. As they stand, however, the concluding lines carry a tone of firm conviction that faith *can* provide genuine serenity, for those persons who can believe. Even a skeptic can be glad of it. Thus, the poem achieves an uneasy balance of opposites that is splendidly intriguing.

Granted that Dickinson was capable of writing well-closed poems and did indeed write a great many, the fact remains that she also wrote a great many open-ended poems.[11] These poems are not generally inferior to the closed poems or, on the other hand, necessarily superior to them. The open-ended poems have a different kind of integrity than poems wherein ambiguities are resolved in some conclusive way. They do not achieve the same urn-like stasis. We may think of them as philosophically consistent with the poet's belief that "the unknown is the largest need of the intellect" (L 471).

Though withholding full rhyme at the end of a poem is a significant device, it is by no means her only technique of non-closure. A simple non-closural strategy she frequently uses is the asking of a final question. At the end of "Title divine – is mine!" (P 1072), for example, the tentative "Is this – the way?" leaves the lyric on a note of hesitant uncertainty. Similar endings, in varied tones of voice, contribute a lingering perplexity:

> Could it be Madness – this?
> > (P 410)

> Germ's Germ be where?
> > (P 998)

> Don't you know – me?
> > (P 497) [12]

> – Do we die –
> Or is this Death's Experiment –
> Reversed – in Victory?
> > (P 550)

> Which Anguish was the utterest – then –
> To perish, or to live?
> > (P 414)

> But where my moment of Brocade –
> My – drop – of India?
> > (P 430)

> I – do not fly, so wherefore
> My Perennial Things?
> > (P 956)

> Would you – instead of Me?
> > (P 1094)

How this be
Except by Abdication –
Me – of Me?

(P 642)[13]

Seed – summer – tomb –
Whose Doom to whom?

(P 1712)[14]

Dont you know?

(P 433)

A final question does not necessarily preclude closure. A purely rhetorical question may in fact strengthen closure, as in "Split the Lark." Even a non-rhetorical question, when it is a definitive summation of a speaker's doubts, may be relatively stable; the expressive effect of such a question, frequently, is "that sense of a lingering suspension so typical of modern closure" (Smith 248). Closure, after all, is a matter of degree, and it can be "more or less weak or strong" (Smith 211). It is worth noting that some of the examples just cited (the first six) are associated with less than full rhymes, the next four with full rhymes, and the last with a repetition (not, properly speaking, a rhyme at all). Still, the frequency of final questions in Dickinson's verse is indicative of an intent to leave unresolved some doubts and uncertainties in an art that seeks to be true to nature by being "haunted."

Another non-closural device Dickinson exploits is a final reference to something uncertain or unknown. The skeptical slant of such references, as Christopher Benfey points out, is related to Dickinson's "attraction to the access of the sublime": "For her, as for Burke or Schiller or Kant, the limits of our senses do not preclude a certain thrilling awareness of what eludes or transcends their grasp" (13). The lingering uncertainties at the end of this poem, for example, are precisely what the poem is about:

She rose to His Requirement – dropt
The Playthings of Her Life

> To take the honorable Work
> Of Woman, and of Wife –
>
> If ought She missed in Her new Day,
> Of Amplitude, or Awe –
> Or first Prospective – Or the Gold
> In using, wear away,
>
> It lay unmentioned – as the Sea
> Develope Pearl, and Weed,
> But only to Himself – be known
> The Fathoms they abide –
>
> (P 732)

Did this wife miss anything or feel a lack? In her hidden "Fathoms" were there pearls, or weeds, or both? Furthermore, how can anyone know what another person's life is really like in its private joys and sufferings? The shape of the poem lies in the progression from the definite fact set forth at the opening —"She rose to His Requirement"—and from the conventional assurance that her action is "honorable" and right, to this quiet incertitude about the "unmentioned" depths of a wife's experience. The antinomies of "Pearl" and "Weed" in the final stanza are subtly prefigured in the "rose" and "dropt" of the first line, which undermine the apparent security of the initial assertion even before the explicit questions of the second stanza.[15] But in general the poem moves from a standard assumption that the true purpose and fulfillment of a woman's "Life" is in becoming a "Wife," a notion pleasantly supported by the phonic fit of those words paired as end rhymes (they chime as if natural, ineluctable partners), to a recollection of the privations and burdens of wifehood (as "Awe" finds its partner in "away" and "Weed" reveals a kinship with "abide") and to wondering at the complexities hidden from human knowledge.

Analogous final references are common in Dickinson's work:

This timid life of Evidence
Keeps pleading – "I dont know."
(P 696)

What Deed is Their's unto the General Nature –
What Plan
They severally – retard – or further –
Unknown –
(P 742)

But Gravity – and Expectation – and Fear –
A tremor just, that All's not sure.
(P 408)

Yet – know not what was done to me
In that old chapel Aisle.
(P 183)

I know not which, Desire, or Grant –
Be wholly beautiful –
(P 801)

The Heavens with a smile,
Sweep by our disappointed Heads
Without a syllable –
(P 282)

Again, to the extent that these final lines are thematic summary statements, they have a certain closural value, but the inconclusiveness of the issues they report operates against closure. A reader may be satisfied that the point at which the poem arrives is the utmost clarity available, given the limitations of the human condition. Persistent obscurities, nevertheless, leave a purposefully irresolute effect. Partial rhymes, in all the examples just cited, contribute a corresponding acoustic instability.

Dickinson frequently destabilizes an ending with an anticlimax, first building up expectations and then casting doubt on them by a deflating phrase or clause.

As Watchers hang upon the East,
As Beggars revel at a feast
By savory Fancy spread –
As brooks in deserts babble sweet
On ear too far for the delight,
Heaven beguiles the tired.

As that same watcher, when the East
Opens the lid of Amethyst
And lets the morning go –
That Beggar, when an honored Guest,
Those thirsty lips to flagons pressed,
Heaven to us, if true.

(P 121)

The poem sets up expectations with a series of four types of longing in the first stanza: of watchers for dawn, of beggars for food, of the thirsty for drink, and—in the main clause—of tired mortals for heaven. The second stanza, with a series parallel to the first, describes hopes fulfilled: of the watcher, the beggar, the thirsty lips—thus arousing strong anticipation of a grand conclusion imaging the surpassing fulfillment of heaven. The last line does assert that heaven offers an analogous satisfaction, then immediately undercuts that assertion with the wistful conditional phrase, "if true." At the same time, the poem, structured in common particular meter, arouses prosodic expectations with a fully rhymed couplet (ll. 1–2), proceeds through consonantal rhymes that significantly tantalize and elude, sets up one more fully rhymed couplet (ll. 10–11) that coincides with the peak of the reader's anticipation for a grand finale, and then disappoints the reader's hopes with a wryly skillful failure to provide the expected rhyme sound. The aural anticlimax nicely supports the meaning, leaving the reader, so to speak, with thirsty lips on an illusory flagon. The reader's "disappointment" is translated to aesthetic surprise as the witty procedure of the poem is grasped.

An aural anticlimax combines with a conditional clause also in this short poem, purportedly a definition of prayer:

> Prayer is the little implement
> Through which Men reach
> Where Presence – is denied them.
> They fling their Speech
>
> By means of it – in God's Ear –
> If then He hear –
> This sums the Apparatus
> Comprised in Prayer –

(P 437)

"Behind the laconic precision of language," Whicher observes, "is a glint of ironic understatement and a mischievous delight in the unexpected juxtaposition of great things and small, as though prayer were a kind of pea-shooter" (273). The artfulness of the poem further includes the enjambment across the stanza break, appropriate to the idea of flinging speech across a different gap, and the use of full rhyme in the first stanza and (outside the scheme) in *Ear/hear* of the next, setting up expectations in order to disappoint them in a final partial rhyme. Likewise, men hopefully fling their voices upward with "the little implement" of prayer, but its effectiveness is problematic, for God does not necessarily hear.

A similar approach can be seen in the endings of several other poems:

> If "God is Love" as he admits
> We think that he must be
> Because he is a "jealous God"
> He tells us certainly
>
> If "All is possible with" him
> As he besides concedes
> He will refund us finally
> Our confiscated Gods –

(P 1260)

> So trust him, Comrade –
> You for you, and I, for you and me
> Eternity is ample,
> And quick enough, if true.
>
> (P 350)

England comments aptly on the lines last quoted, "I do think so conscious an artist could have thought of changing 'you and me' to 'me and you' if she had wanted true rhyme on that final chord. Rhyme and grammar [syntax, she must mean] lapse together into the conditional mode" (133). Doubt makes the final assertions ironic, precarious. [16]

Metrical irregularities at the termination of a poem, too, can disrupt the security of a close, leaving the reader with a disturbed sense of residual expectations. The correlation between such disruptions and thematic ideas in the poem is indicative that the closural weakness is part of the poetic design; what is in one sense frustrating thus becomes aesthetically satisfying.[17] The metrical deficiency in the final line of this poem, for example, is a calculated shock:

> One need not be a Chamber – to be Haunted –
> One need not be a House –
> The Brain has corridors – surpassing
> Material Place –
>
> Far safer, of a Midnight Meeting
> External Ghost
> Than it's interior Confronting –
> That Cooler Host.
>
> Far safer, through an Abbey gallop,
> The Stones a'chase –
> Than Unarmed, one's a'self encounter –
> In lonesome Place –
>
> Ourself behind ourself, concealed –
> Should startle most –

Assassin hid in our Apartment
Be Horror's least.

The Body – borrows a Revolver –
He bolts the Door –
O'erlooking a superior spectre –
Or More –

(P 670)

The poem dramatizes the terrors of psychological reality, and
it tries to give the reader a shiver at its abrupt end.[18] In the last
line, the reader had anticipated four syllables, so that when
only two appear, the end seems premature, startling. The va-
cancy echoes. This version of the poem was a fair copy sent
to Sue and written about 1863, Johnson states in the variorum
edition. The fascicle copy, which he dates about a year earlier,
has a slightly different version of the last stanza containing
several variants:

The Prudent* – carries a Revolver –
He bolts the Door –
O'erlooking a Superior spectre – +
More near

*v. The Body
+v.1 A Spectre – infinite – accompanying –
+He fails to fear –
+v.2 Maintaining a Superior Spectre –
+None saw –

Two of the three earlier alternative last lines share the metrical
deficiency of the final version, and all three of them have a
partial rhyme, unlike the final version. A partial rhyme contributes an additional element of instability at the end, an
instability appropriate to the meaning and reflected in the
poet's initial intent. Her rejection of that strategy suggests
that she found the untimely full rhyme more sudden, more
jarring. The rhyme-pairs *Door/near* and *Door/More* share the

consonantal ending *r* with the end-words *Revolver* and *Spectre*, and the phrase "Superior Spectre" repeats the sounds *s-p-r*, *s-p-r*; the phonic effect is slight, but not negligible. [19]

The breaking off at the end of an earlier poem is somewhat heavy-handed, but there can be little doubt that the lame effect is intentional:

> You're right – "the way *is* narrow" –
> And "difficult the Gate" –
> And "few there be" – Correct again –
> That "enter in – thereat" –
>
> '*Tis* Costly – so are *purples*!
> 'Tis just the price of *Breath* –
> With but the "Discount" of the *Grave* –
> Termed by the *Brokers* – "*Death*"!
>
> And after *that* – there's Heaven –
> The *Good* Man's – "*Dividend*" –
> And *Bad* Men – "go to Jail" –
> I guess –
>
> (P 234)

The inadequacy of that last line culminates the irony in the poem directed against the difficulty of attaining salvation, the proportional meagerness of reward, and the paltriness of the whole divine scheme of accounting. England's interpretive comment is accurate: "The rhyme word to be matched is *Dividend*, and one supposes that its mate should properly have been *end*. But it is the poem that ends. It breaks off short in mid-line. No rhyme. No meter. No comment" (136). The text under consideration in this poem is formidable: nothing less than the Sermon on the Mount. The speaker manages to be undaunted, even saucy, at the outset, but his tone grows progressively weaker as the poem proceeds. Despite the attempt to reduce it by terminology to a mere "Discount," death remains awesome. Similarly, the effort to evade the threat of hell by converting it to the milder "jail" is patently unsuc-

cessful—"hell" echoes in the mind. The ironic inequities of
the divine economic system are finally overshadowed by the
ironic fact of human impotence within that almighty system;
against it impudence is no defense. The ineffectual "I guess"
with which the speaker leaves off combines an effort to be
playfully derisive with sheer helplessness.

A poem may appear to be firmly closed when in fact its ambiguities are intensified rather than diminished by a "close"
that is patently illusory. In this interior monologue, the an-
nounced finality of the last exclamation fails to resolve the
bewilderment preceding:

> I'm "wife" – I've finished that –
> That other state –
> I'm Czar – I'm "Woman" now –
> It's safer so –
>
> How odd the Girl's life looks
> Behind this soft Eclipse –
> I think that Earth feels so
> To folks in Heaven – now –
>
> This being comfort – then
> That other kind – was pain –
> But why compare?
> I'm "Wife"! Stop there!

(P 199)

Pondering her own identity, the speaker betrays a perturbed
ambivalence. The apparent assurance of her declaration that
she is "Czar" is belied by the hesitancy of her speech, by
the fearfulness implicit in the phrase "It's safer so," by the
ironic purport of the phrase "This soft Eclipse," by her persistent retrospection, and by her difficulty in convincing herself
that her former state was "pain." For Gilbert and Gubar, "The
stops and steps of the mind that give this dramatic monologue its strength clearly indicate Dickinson's ironic view of
her speaker's anxious rationalizations. 'This being comfort –

then' one must *infer* that 'That other kind – was pain,' since there never was (or so the poem implies) any real evidence of pain. The equally anxious question 'But why compare?' reinforces our sense that a comparison might indeed be odious, with the wrong term coming out ahead. Hence the speaker . . . must almost forcibly restrain herself from letting her thoughts . . . go further" (589). Closure is declared, not achieved. "Stop there!" The only full rhyme in the poem indicates closure, but the jerk of the unexpectedly brief final lines undermines it. Above all, the ending does not resolve the issues that have been raised. As there is no conversational remark more tantalizing than "I must not say anything more," so the speaker's "Stop there" leaves us wondering what other ambivalences she is hiding and why. Telling herself to cease this train of thought does not mean that she has come to terms with her conflicting feelings about her condition. She feels "safe," but she also feels dead.

An abrupt ending can have various semantic purposes. In another poem, a too-abrupt end stops a reader short with the shrewd common sense of the impudent child-persona:

> So I pull my Stockings off
> Wading in the Water
> For the Disobedience' Sake
> Boy that lived for "Ought to"   (var. or'ter)
>
> Went to Heaven perhaps at Death
> And perhaps he did'nt
> Moses was'nt fairly used –
> Ananias was'nt –
>
> (P 1201)

I have tried to avoid choosing among Dickinson's variants, but here the boy is characterized more vividly, I think, by the slang variant. Like Huck Finn, he can spot sham in revered places such as the Bible, and he has no use for obedience to rules of grammar or of conduct. The poem is not "closed" when the laconic statement is finished. Latent questions linger thick in the air for the adult part of the reader, left stuttering mental *but*'s and *ought*'s and *why*'s and *wherefore*'s that cannot possibly answer the questions. The reader's obstreperous child-self, meanwhile, can scarcely fail to be delighted.

A poem may have an open-ended effect, too, if it begins a sequence that implies a conclusion but stops before reaching it. Each vivid detail of this poem, for example, reveals a cocoon-bound speaker straining toward the condition of the butterfly—fresh air and free flight:

> My Cocoon tightens – Colors teaze –
> I'm feeling for the Air –
> A dim capacity for Wings
> Demeans the Dress I wear –
>
> A power of Butterfly must be –
> The Aptitude to fly
> Meadows of Majesty concedes
> And easy Sweeps of Sky –
>
> So I must baffle at the Hint
> And cipher at the Sign
> And make much blunder, if at last
> I take the clue divine –
>
> (P 1099)

The speaker's yearning for release from the cocoon serves metaphorically, of course, to suggest the soul's desire for release from the dark constraint of the body into an immortal "Sky," and the poem leans toward some such finale. The reader is left with a sense of expectant reaching in the direction of a fulfillment not yet achieved, perhaps not even achievable, but the achievement of which seems to be of overriding importance. Closural and anti-closural forces at the end work in opposite directions. The poem stops, but the sequence is not yet finished. The phrase "at last" suggests finality, but the word "if" resists finality. The terminal phrase "clue divine" suggests the ultimate goal, but it also makes the goal seem vague and elusive. Moreover, although there is a full rhyme in the final stanza, its conclusive effect is minimal since the preceding stanzas also contain full rhymes. This poem, rich in assonance and alliteration, is very musical, but it does not provide a resolving chord. The absence of resolution imparts to the reader the sense of unsatisfied desire that is the essence of this lyrical moment.

Another anti-closural device I will mention is the repeated refrain. The terminal modification of a refrain is common as a closural device in song and poetry (Smith 59); an *un*modified refrain unsettles the end of this poem:

> I reason, Earth is short –
> And Anguish – absolute –
> And many hurt,
> But, what of that?
>
> I reason, we could die –
> The best Vitality
> Cannot excel Decay,
> But, what of that?
>
> I reason, that in Heaven –
> Somehow, it will be even –
> Some new Equation, given –
> But, what of that?
>
> (P 301)

The insouciant refrain dismisses the sorrows of life in stanza one and the sorrows of death in stanza two; this is all within the tradition of *contemptus mundi,* where it is combined with the affirmation that such sorrows are inconsequential in the face of heavenly salvation. A reader familiar with the tradition is led to expect a conclusive shift to some such affirmation, which the first three lines of the last stanza, with their reference to heaven's "new Equation," seem to be headed towards. Conventionally, the refrain should be modified, probably from a question into an answer. The mere repetition of the refrain, without modification, is an ironic surprise, a blend of acid skepticism and devil-may-care puckishness.

Rhyme alone can work against closure. Dickinson is adept at the acoustic anticlimax. A final word that does not rhyme as the reader has been led to suppose it will frequently succeeds in ending a poem on a note that is designedly unsettling—variously sour, ironic, witty, yearning, or mysterious. Depending on the context and the way the rhymes are handled, the effect may be strongly anti-closural or it may be mild, merely muting the effect of closure. For example, in a poem that turns religious commonplaces upside down, a final off-key rhyme co-ordinates with the deliberately outrageous claim:

> My Faith is larger than the Hills –
> So when the Hills decay –
> My Faith must take the Purple Wheel
> To show the Sun the way –
>
> 'Tis first He steps upon the Vane –
> And then – upon the Hill –
> And then abroad the World He go
> To do His Golden Will –
>
> And if His Yellow feet should miss –
> The Bird would not arise –
> The Flowers would slumber on their Stems –
> No Bells have Paradise –
>
> How dare I, therefore, stint a faith
> On which so vast depends –
> Lest Firmament should fail for me –
> The Rivet in the Bands
>
> (P 766)

It is written, "I will lift up mine eyes unto the hills." But is it not also written, "If ye have faith as a grain of mustard seed, ye shall move mountains"? Then where does stability reside? In the cosmic order or in the human mind? England describes the "shock tactics" here: "The abrupt slanting of the rhyme is part and parcel of the tactics. Look to the hills? Let the hills look to me, 'The Rivet in the Bands'" (134).[20] It is noteworthy that the final quatrain is in the form of an impish, mock-modest question: "How dare I . . . ?" The doubts raised throughout the poem about the permanence of nature (hills, sun, birds, flowers) and of the supernatural (Paradise, in danger of losing its bells) are hardly resolved by this question. In the question lurks a boundless anxiety at the existential burden borne by human consciousness amid a tottering cosmos. The thematic insecurity is aligned with the acoustic insecurity of the last rhyme. Following the full rhymes of the previous stanzas, the final consonantal rhyme (*depends/Bands*) sounds not firm but—shall we say?—faintly wobbly.

A similar tactic is apparent in this poem, which starts out with a jingling meter and rhyme and then becomes progressively more strange:

> A Dying Tiger – moaned for Drink –
> I hunted all the Sand –
> I caught the Dripping of a Rock
> And bore it in my Hand –
>
> His Mighty Balls – in death were thick –
> But searching – I could see
> A Vision on the Retina
> Of Water – and of me –
>
> 'Twas not my blame – who sped too slow –
> 'Twas not his blame – who died
> While I was reaching him –
> But 'twas – the fact that He was dead –
>
> (P 566)

The nursery-rhyme flavor of the opening gives way to the complex, haunting image on the tiger's retina and finally to the blunt terminal fact "dead," made harsher by the clash of rhyme (a rich consonance): *died/dead*. "The concluding line is flat," John Crowe Ransom has said, "like some ironic line by Hardy. Its blankness cancels out the expostulation we had expected, and pure contingency replaces the vicious agent we would have blamed, and there is nothing rational to be said" (10).

Rich consonance is a peculiarly striking type of partial rhyme. This kind of rhyme, where the vowel changes while the consonantal frame is retained, was used systematically by Wilfred Owen in about a dozen poems and in Owen criticism is commonly called "pararhyme." [21] Dickinson used this sort of rhyme occasionally, but never consistently throughout a whole poem; in her hands it serves to focus auditory attention and cooperates in a variety of effects. [22] In some poems, like the perennially anthologized "I like to see it lap the Miles" (P 585), where we find *peer/pare* and (internally) *like-lick* and *stop-step*, it is a phonic part of a general playfulness. In some, its arresting strangeness is obscurely suggestive of meaning, as in "Like Eyes that looked on Wastes" (P 458), where the rhyme *Ought/Night* is echoed by the next line "Just Infinites of *Nought*," which accomplishes a linguistic merger of the sounds of "Ought" and "Night."

At the end of a poem, a rich consonance is especially prominent and unsettling. In the last stanza of "Crisis is a Hair," for example, the "hair's difference" between *Hair* and *Here* is properly felt as disturbingly insecure:

It – may jolt the Hand
That adjusts the Hair
That secures Eternity
From presenting – Here –
(P 889)

At the end of "I saw no Way – The Heavens were stitched," a rich consonance enhances the awe accompanying a magical transformation of the universe, which enables the speaker's experience of timelessness:

> And back it slid – and I alone –
> A Speck upon a Ball –
> Went out upon Circumference –
> Beyond the Dip of Bell –
>
> (P 378)

At the end of "Remorse – is Memory – awake," the antithetical force of the rhyme-words *heal* and *Hell* combines with their oddly discordant sound to intensify the starkness of the idea:

> Remorse is cureless – the Disease
> Not even God – can heal –
> For 'tis His institution – and
> The Adequate of Hell –
>
> (P 744)

Similarly, in "It was not Death," the bleakness of the ending is made bleaker and more compelling by the mysterious acoustic nearness and distance between *Spar* and *Despair:*

> But, most, like Chaos – Stopless – cool
> Without a Chance, or Spar –
> Or even a Report of Land –
> To justify – Despair.
>
> (P 510)

Dickinson certainly was not employing rich consonance in any systematic way, but she clearly was aware of the peculiar intensity of word-pairs so linked and exploited it with powerful effect to unsettle some of her endings.

An ironically "sour" last rhyme marks a large number of her poems, including this well known one:

> Apparently with no surprise
> To any happy Flower
> The Frost beheads it at it's play –
> In accidental power –
> The blonde Assassin passes on –

The Sun proceeds unmoved
To measure off another Day
For an Approving God.

(P 1624)

Except for that last word, meter and rhyme here are as regular
as the relentless processes of nature. Tracing its course from
frost to the power behind the frost, the poem ends on a jarring
thematic and acoustic discord: *God*. We are meant to wince.[23]
(The word *Approving* intensifies the effect. As it partly echoes
unmoved, it possibly might have been worked into a full end
rhyme, but not quite rhyming and appearing not at line end,
it increases the effect of an order gone awry.)

After four perfectly rhymed stanzas, the consonantal rhyme
at the termination of this poem is a major destabilizing factor:

One Blessing had I than the rest
So larger to my Eyes
That I stopped guaging – satisfied –
For this enchanted size –

It was the limit of my Dream –
The focus of my Prayer –
A perfect – paralyzing Bliss –
Contented as Despair –

I knew no more of Want – or Cold –
Phantasms both become
For this new Value in the Soul –
Supremest Earthly Sum –

The Heaven below the Heaven above –
Obscured with ruddier Blue –
Life's Latitudes leant over – full –
The Judgment perished – too –

Why Bliss so scantily disburse –
Why Paradise defer –

Why Floods be served to Us – in Bowls –
I speculate no more –

(P 756)

All but the last stanza emphasize the delight of the persona in
the "Blessing" and the "Bliss" of a supreme experience that is
totally satisfying; after that, the phrase "no more" is certainly
a strong element tending toward closure. If the final rhyme
were exact, the ending would ring almost with conviction.
As it is, though, *defer/more* (or its variant, *demur/more*) sounds
ambiguous, enough so that those three last *Why*'s seem ominous. If the speaker is indeed thoroughly contented, why do
those troubling questions obtrude themselves? Why *is* bliss
so scantily distributed? The nagging questions (which the
speaker professes no longer to consider) reflect back on the
preceding ambiguities such as the "paralyzing" effect of this
bliss, its likeness to "Despair," and its obscuring of "Heaven
above." One is left pondering these unresolved issues, and
the poem is stronger as a result of its non-closure and the
unease of its final rhyme.

A final shift away from full rhyme, similarly, is a significant
aspect of an abrupt transition of tone in the last two lines of
this poem:

The only Ghost I ever saw
Was dressed in Mechlin – so –
He had no sandal on his foot –
And stepped like flakes of snow –

His Mien, was soundless, like the Bird –
But rapid – like the Roe –
His fashions, quaint, Mosaic –
Or haply, Mistletoe –

His conversation – seldom –
His laughter, like the Breeze
That dies away in Dimples
Among the pensive Trees –

Our interview – was transient –
Of me, himself was shy –
And God forbid I look behind –
Since that appalling Day!

(P 274)

The ghost here seems as gentle and appealing a ghost as was ever invented. Similes compare him to snowfall, a bird, a deer. He steps softly and laughs "like the Breeze"—a breeze that fades into "Dimples," no less! (A variant word has the pensive trees as "smiling Trees.") He is quaintly dressed in delicate lace. Moreover, he is shy. The easy meter is lilting, and the full rhymes are mellow, four long *o* sounds plus *Breeze/Trees*. The off-key last rhyme is as unexpected as the sudden revelation that accompanies it: the speaker's meeting with this shy ghost was somehow horrific. A reader, surprised to have misapprehended the ghost, is impelled to review (to "look behind" at) the earlier portion of the poem in order to see what details have been overlooked. Does "soundless," possibly, imply stealth? Does "snow" imply "the cold fearful silence of death" (Porter, *Early* 79)? Is the reference to "Mistletoe" intended to associate this ghost with Druid rites of sacrifice? Even if the answer to all those questions is yes, none of the clues indicates that our first reading was a misreading; *if* the ghost is to be understood as death personified (Chase 233; Johnson 220), still the point of the poem seems to reside in the contrast between the apparent harmlessness of the ghost —as experienced by the reader and by the persona—and the appalling reality that ensues, terror for the speaker, anxiety for the reader. The lack of specificity concerning what exactly happened is part of the mystery. I am inclined to think that a similar lack of specificity about what the ghost is—death or a hidden aspect of the psyche or some other kind of visitant —is also intentional. Unlike the poem "I am alive – I guess," discussed above, where everything odd and ambiguous retrospectively snaps into clear and comprehensible place with a conclusive shift, *this* poem has everything that seemed clear abruptly blur into ghostliness. The unresolvedness is designedly "appalling."

Even more powerfully discordant is the bizarre rhyme that ends this poem, a poem about music:

> The fascinating chill that music leaves
> Is Earth's corroboration
> Of Ecstasy's impediment –
> 'Tis Rapture's germination
> In timid and tumultuous soil
> A fine – estranging creature –
> To something upper wooing us
> But not to our Creator –
>
> (P 1480)

This tightly condensed verse, concise to the point of obscurity, is based on the paradox that music stimulates the growth of rapture and simultaneously sharpens the sense of distance from ecstasy; music woos and estranges. The antithetical mixture here of upward striving and the earth-bound has to do, I think, with the ineffable beauty of music as Dickinson conceived it, its testimony to what mortals can glimpse but not reach, experience but not hold. "Earth," which corroborates the "impediment" to ecstasy, is yet the same "soil" in which the purer spirit apprehended in music germinates. The rhyme pattern supports the theme. The first rhyme, *corroboration/germination*, is a mellifluous, full, and double rhyme. (Double rhymes are quite rare in Dickinson's poetry.) This rhyme, pleasantly harmonious, in no way prepares the reader for the striking discord that follows in *creature/Creator*. "Creature" refers initially to the tumultuous effect of music stirring in the souls of human beings, but it also serves as a reminder of humanity's status as created beings, subordinate to God and tied to Him by bonds of creaturely piety. The two rhyme-words are a pair that seem by rights of linguistics and logic to belong together. But when the final line, "But not to our Cre-

ator," places the word *Creator* in rhyming position with *creature,* the effect is grotesque. The differing accentuation of the
two words is made by the rhyme to seem acute, a wrenching
incongruity of relationship that no manner of pronunciation
can restore to harmony. The rhyme, then, provides an aural
figure of the estrangement between man and God, and the effect wrought on the reader is a sort of "fascinating chill." The
unresolved questions the poem arouses and the final clash of
rhyme are non-closural, and stirring.

A similar final rhyme, also made bizarre by the difference
of accents, appears in this poem:

> A Word dropped careless on a Page
> May stimulate an eye
> When folded in perpetual seam
> The Wrinkled Maker lie
>
> Infection in the sentence breeds
> We may inhale Despair
> At distances of Centuries
> From the Malaria –
>
> (P 1261)

In comparison with "A fascinating chill" this poem is de-
cidedly lucid. But as the poem is about the mysterious power
of words, the dynamics of the poem depend on the progression from the almost prosaic first two lines (as *if* these words
themselves were "dropped careless") to increasing figurality
and conceptual strangeness. Congruent with that progression, the first rhyme, *eye/lie,* is easy and conventional, while
the last one is startling. No kind of pronunciation (regardless
of how people in Western Massachusetts pronounced their
r's) can make the words rhyme comfortably. The rhyming syllable of *Despair* falls on the third metrical beat, while the third
metrical beat of the last line falls only on -*a.* The phonetic
similarity (equivalent to a full rhyme) between -*spair* and -*lar-*
(on the second metrical beat of the line, the second of four

syllables in the other rhyme word) is very strong, however, so that considerable tension is felt between the metrical paradigm and the rhyme paradigm, the latter of which is flagrantly violated. The discordant sound is appropriate to the idea of diseased emotions, tucked away for centuries, released with the opening of a book. The sound, as much as the idea, is responsible for the unsettling effect of the ending.

Though Dickinson's transitions of tone are not always so sudden, the pattern of thematic clarity yielding to ambiguity accompanied by a shift away from full rhyme recurs in a host of poems. We may recall "A Bird came down the Walk," "A Spider sewed at Night," "I got so I could hear his name" (all discussed in a previous chapter), or this splendidly musical lyric:

> Oh Sumptuous moment
> Slower go
> That I may gloat on thee –
> 'Twill never be the same to starve
> Now I abundance see –
>
> Which was to famish, then or now –
> The difference of Day
> Ask him unto the Gallows led –
> With morning in the sky
>
> (P 1125)

An assonantal sequence of long o's, alliterated s's, and full rhymes contribute to the sustained lyricism of the first stanza, where the persona savors a "Sumptuous moment." Even in the midst of this experience of joy, however, enters the recognition that it cannot last and that present abundance will make future deprivation a keener suffering. The second stanza ponders the unanswerable question: is the more intense life felt by someone about to die a more intense "famishing" as well? Implicit is the whole paradoxical admixture of ecstasy with anguish, exemplified by the ambiguous "difference" perceived by one doomed to be hanged as he glimpses last the daily phenomenon of morning, presumably a "mourning" also, in all its unaccustomed sumptuousness. The superb ambiguousness of the final departure from full rhyme in *Day/sky* is unanticipated, surely, but whether it is a "sour note" or a finer sweetness it is impossible to say. The sequence of vowels here is unusual and unstable; a decline of pitch tends to be relaxing, closural, but here a reversal of the more normal order of a high vowel followed by a low vowel augments the instability of the rhyme.[24] The high, bright *i*—emerging out of the darker sounds preceding and coinciding with the idea of a keenly felt bright morning—seems to me profoundly affecting.

Because partial rhyme resists the resolution that full rhyme represents, it co-ordinates well with a theme, central in Dickinson's work, that Eberwein calls the "theme of primal insufficiency" (61). In this poem, for example, the last rhyme, unaccented and promoted, with unmatching vowels, does not provide the acoustic plenitude the pattern of the verse leads the reader to anticipate:

> "I want" – it pleaded – All it's life –
> I want – was chief it said
> When Skill entreated it – the last –
> And when so newly dead –
>
> I could not deem it late – to hear
> That single – steadfast sigh –
> The lips had placed as with a "Please"
> Toward Eternity –

(P 731)

The theme of the poem is yearning, and the yearning sigh the speaker hears (with the ear of imagination) emanating from dead lips is echoed for the reader by the insufficient rhyme —actually an artfully sufficient one. As the deferral of fulfillment throughout a lifetime of longing is extended indefinitely into eternity, the fulfillment towards which the reader's listening ear leans is deferred indefinitely into the silence beyond the poem.

A similar effect is achieved in another poem, also allied thematically, where all the rhyme-words except the last end on the same sound (*die*/*by*/*supply*—then *Immortality*):

> We thirst at first – 'tis Nature's Act –
> And later – when we die –
> A little Water supplicate –
> Of fingers going by –
>
> It intimates the finer want –
> Whose adequate supply
> Is that Great Water in the West –
> Termed Immortality –
>
> (P 726)

An internal rhyme in the initial clause piques the ear and slows the pace of the line. The ensuing lines quicken in movement, as the caesurae become fewer and monosyllables give way to more polysyllabic diction. The first rhyme, *die*/*by*, meets conventional expectations, in effect satisfying a reader's initial thirst. But *supply*, by chiming on the same rhyme sound, builds a crescendo of expectation, which the final rhyme does not fully meet. The lingering acoustic irresolution mirrors the idea of an elusive if not illusive goal. The reader may hear at the end the sound of unsatisfied desire. [25]

The ending of these two poems on the grandly abstract words "Eternity" and "Immortality" is not untypical, and a fairly large number of poems end with such words. The reason, I believe, is that they offer at once closural and nonclosural value. As ultimates, they provide an appropriate termination to any logical sequence, and as illogical and vague in themselves, they are mysterious enough to avoid being pat. A parody of Dickinson, one supposes, ought to have "Eternity" at the end. Yet it is true that such endings are often extremely powerful. Allen Tate praises the deservedly famous

"Because I could not stop for Death" (P 712), which ends with the rhyme *Day/Eternity*, for its superb lack of closure: "she has presented a typical Christian theme in all its final irresolution, without making any final statement about it" (15). Her opening lines may be more memorizable, but these endings can be haunting.

On the whole Dickinson is less interested in asserting solid convictions than in capturing the evanescent moment, subtle shades of emotion, and the mystery of things. A master of the muted close that is not quite closed, she often aims at a suggestive indefiniteness she associates with poetry itself.

> I held a Jewel in my fingers –
> And went to sleep –
> The day was warm, and winds were prosy –
> I said " 'Twill keep" –
>
> I woke – and chid my honest fingers,
> The Gem was gone –
> And now, an Amethyst remembrance
> Is all I own –
>
> (P 245)

The initial, unthinking assumption of the speaker that treasures will last is, like the "winds" of the first stanza, a "prosy" view of life. Awakened to loss, the speaker gains in place of the gem a wistful but enhanced poetic vision, "an Amethyst remembrance." The movement of the rhyme from the secure and ordinary to ambiguity is appropriate.

Dickinson wants to reveal the infinitude of the commonest drama around us and within us—what she once calls "Finite Infinity" (P 1695). And she often finds an acoustic equivalent in the more elusive types of rhyme. A leisurely description of sunset, for example, ends with a rhyme (consonantal, with a slight difference in stress) that does not click a close:

> The Mountains stood in Haze –
> The Valleys stopped below

And went or waited as they liked
The River and the Sky.

At leisure was the Sun –
His interests of Fire
A little from remark withdrawn –
The Twilight spoke the Spire,

So soft upon the Scene
The Act of evening fell
We felt how neighborly a Thing
Was the Invisible.

(P 1278)

The suggestion of death in the last quatrain is, like evening, closural, but ever so softly. The rhyme seems gentle, too, a little strange but hardly a deprivation, maybe even a quiet enrichment.

Similarly, the muted rhymes of the following poem seem perfectly suited to treatment of the "harrowing Grace" of a passing season:

As imperceptibly as Grief
The Summer lapsed away –
Too imperceptible at last
To seem like Perfidy –
A Quietness distilled
As Twilight long begun,
Or Nature spending with herself
Sequestered Afternoon –
The Dusk drew earlier in –
The Morning foreign shone –
A courteous, yet harrowing Grace,
As Guest, that would be gone –
And thus, without a Wing
Or service of a Keel
Our Summer made her light escape
Into the Beautiful.

(P 1540)

Summer ends here, like the poem, with a whisper. Yet it does not quite end, either; it seems to make an "escape" into another condition, which one can almost apprehend in the silence that lingers after the last delicate rhyme. Who could possibly wish such a poem to be more "properly" rhymed, more emphatically closed?

The beauty of elusiveness and the paradox of painful joy inform another lyric, little noticed, that impresses me as subtle and perfect. In one sense, it is a self-reflexive poem about Dickinson herself as poet, for it is the sort of song it also describes, a "lonesome Glee":

It is a lonesome Glee –
Yet sanctifies the Mind –
With fair association –
Afar upon the Wind

A Bird to overhear
Delight without a Cause –
Arrestless as invisible –
A matter of the Skies.

(P 774)

Seemingly artless, the poem is much richer than it seems, turning on repeated alliances of opposites. It relates the simplest of events, hearing a bird singing in the distance. But it reveals the spiritual dimension of that ordinary experience as the bird's song "sanctifies" the listener. The song is a blessing without cause, like grace, and without ending ("arrestless"), like infinity. Still, it comes in a mode that mortals can apprehend, a "matter" that mysteriously transcends matter, as it is celestial—"of the Skies"—"invisible" and immaterial, yet manifest to the listening ear. The phonetic closeness and distance of *fair* and *Afar* helps link the idea of "fair association" in a paradox with the idea of distance, remoteness; the beauty of the song and its elusive distance seem inseparable. Likewise, the lonesomeness and the glee are indistinguishable, and they belong at once to songbird and listener. The whole shape of the poem appears unpremeditated, and the consonantal rhymes too seem utterly casual. The ending is marked by a period, but the absence of full rhyme—"invisible" and "Arrestless"—sounds a distance that prevents finality. The ending drifts off, lingering.

Dickinson could write firmly closed poems when she liked, and often did. Her more open-ended poems, though, generally spring from artistic aims rooted in a conviction that

> This World is not Conclusion.
> A Species stands beyond –
> Invisible, as Music –
> But positive, as Sound –
>
> (P 501, ll. 1–4)

Her conception of poetry as musical and of music as something that reaches "beyond" prosaic language and beyond "This World" led her to create lyrics that by their very inconclusiveness, achieve "Invisible . . . / But positive" evocations. Her art is a transitive art, designed to affect: to "stun" a reader "With Bolts of Melody" (P 505) or to leave a lingering attar. Thus, she restructures the lyric toward a different, and often open, end. Revising common notions of poetic form, her unclosed endings reach across the confines that sometimes are suggested to be the limits of the poetic object, and they beckon readers "Beyond the Dip of Bell" (P 378), toward a boundless, ambiguous realm of mystery. As she wrote to Susan Dickinson, "In a Life that stopped guessing, you and I should not feel at home – " (L 586).

Conclusion

Ears are fashioned differently, and it is never possible to be quite sure that the precise mood one apprehends in a poem, a musical composition, or a tone of voice is exactly what someone else might hear there. Dickinson herself recognized that what one ear hears as a "Rune" latent with poetic hints of profound significance may be to another ear no rune at all and possibly even an unwelcome "din." Reading has a subjective dimension, and it requires a creative play of ear and mind answering to the creative play of ear and mind the poet brings to language. Dickinson's poetry more than most demands such activity on the reader's part. Hers is a "haunted" art of shifting surfaces and riddling depths, of questions and mysteries, gaps and sudden surprises. Her way of telling the truth indirectly, or "slant," requires a "rare Ear" equal to her foxy methods:

> Good to hide, and hear 'em hunt!
> Better, to be found,
> If one care to, that is,
> The Fox fits the Hound –
>
> Good to know, and not tell,
> Best, to know and tell,
> Can one find the rare Ear
> Not too dull –
>
> (P 842)

If the sound of her poetry is not so odd to our ears as it was to those of her first readers, it retains a quality of strangeness. The strangeness is designed, and it has designs on us. The evocative play of linguistic sound—especially sound foregrounded in rhymes—is a verbal music intended to enchant and appall, to suggest and startle, and ultimately to delight the reader. Rhyme is a crucial part of her verbal dynamics.

Skepticism properly wonders how or what pure sound can mean. A cry, or a laugh, perhaps, or a moan or a jolly whistle—but a *rhyme?* That seems to violate common sense. Dickinson's poetry indicates, though, that there are ways that rhyme-sounds can undergird meaning and even constitute meaning. Not in the simplistic way we might have supposed: full rhymes are not necessarily happy and partial rhymes not necessarily sad. Nor can we work out a system whereby consonantal rhymes ending in voiced stops have some particular emotional shading while rhymes between two unaccented but promoted syllables ending in unlike vowels have some other specific emotional shading, and so on. That kind of systematic approach to language violates the nature of poetry—and the nature of language.

What we discover in Dickinson's poetic practice, however, is in principle still quite simple, if complex in application. Namely, "internal difference" is where the meanings are. Just as a musical note—G, say, or E-flat—has no meaning in isolation but acquires meaning in combination, so rhyme-sounds acquire meaning as they are combined. Three G's and an E-flat make the powerful theme with which Beethoven's *Fifth Symphony* opens, and in combination with other tones those notes gather in the course of the symphony tremendous and complicated meanings, meanings that elude language. Similarly, the sound of a partial rhyme in itself may have little meaning. In blank verse or prose we do not even attend to such rhymes when they by chance occur. But in verse forms associated with full rhyme, the appearance of a partial rhyme begins to seem significant. Within a poem, if a partial rhyme follows full rhymes, or is followed by full rhymes, or even by other partial rhymes, the acoustic difference gathers meaning —influenced, of course, by what all the words of the poem are signifying discursively, figuratively, rhythmically, and so forth. The sound of the word *swim*, for example, does not carry much meaning beyond the level of a dictionary definition, but when *swim* is combined with *seam* at the end of "A Bird came down the Walk" the internal difference of sound between those two words has acquired an evocative resonance of breathless desire and distance that not only suits the final mood of awe but contributes to it. An ending of that poem on a full rhyme (*trim/swim*, possibly, or *seam/gleam*) would be empty in comparison.

There is no need to suppose that Dickinson is doing something subtle and intricate with rhyme in every one of her poems. Probably it is not possible to suit sound and sense always, and overt attempts to do so are apt to seem heavy-handed. In a great many of her poems the rhymes can only be said to be fairly unobtrusive, not impeding the flow of her verse. Many poems, especially the earliest, adhere to conventional practice in employing a predominance of full rhymes with a few modestly traditional departures from full rhyme intermixed. Many more poems throughout her career use a larger proportion of partial rhymes, replacing the familiar chime of ordinary rhymes with a moderate acoustic instability and ambiguity. In a large number of her poems, though, it is plain that she is remarkably bold and experimental in her rhymes, exploring and exploiting rhyme differences either in daring individual rhymes that command attention for a striking effect or in progressions and dynamic modulations of rhyme that help shape and support the structure and movement of whole poems.

In some instances, where the acoustic distance between rhyming words is slight, it is difficult to be positive that the difference is indeed significant. In "The Soul selects her own Society" (P 303), for example, ought one to hear the final rhyme (*One/Stone*) reverberating dully in some vaguely haunted way, or does the fact that it had been for centuries a common, acceptable eye rhyme make the difference in sound inconsequential? Is the "Degree" of auditory distance between the conventionally rhymed words "given" and "Heaven" part of the point in a verse such as the following?

> Lest this be Heaven indeed
> An Obstacle is given
> That always guages a Degree
> Between Ourself and Heaven.
>
> (P 1043)

Or, in "A Light exists in Spring" (P 812), is the odd rhyme *Fields/feels* (more than assonance, more and less than consonance, not quite full rhyme, yet very nearly a homonym) intentionally such a rhyme as "Science cannot overtake / But Human Nature feels"? No doubt one can overdo this sort of thing, tune up one's ear to such fineness that one is pursuing exquisite but imaginary effects. Nonetheless, because Dickinson so often demonstrates that nuances of sound are evocative of meaning and because readers in the past have been too little attentive to her subtleties, such questions are not inconsequential but merit discussion and debate.

For on the whole the stylistic deviations in Dickinson's poetry are effective estranging devices, wielded with sensitive intelligence by an artisan who practiced "Gem-Tactics" (P 320) until her words came "alive." The interest and the affective power of the play of sound in her poetry, I suspect, has something to do with the emotional appeal and accessibility of her verse even prior to intellectual comprehension of it. The fascination of those odd rhymes contributes to its perpetual appeal. Though Higginson disapproved of her prosody, we notice, he kept coming back, and in the end, more or less, she won him over. The phonic gaps of her shifting rhymes tease us with difference, guide our inferences, and implicate us in the poetic effort toward the ineffable meanings just beyond the reach of language. They touch us with meanings not contained in words but hovering at their circumference.

Looking again at those two poems with which I began, "I felt a Funeral, in my Brain" and "I felt a Cleaving in my Mind," one can see that it is in large part the different *sound* of the poems that makes for their difference in tone. The metric and phonetic disruptions of "I felt a Funeral" make it sound more troubled, more haunted, while the more conventional form of "I felt a Cleaving," with its steady rhythm and chiming rhyme, makes it sound more straightforward in statement. The past tense of "I felt a Cleaving" seems appropriate to the narration of a past disturbance by a speaker who is now reconciled and controlled; the aberration is seen to have been temporary, possibly just the truancy of ordered thought familiar to everyone. One senses in these lines the normality of abnormality. The past tense of "I felt a Funeral," on the other hand, is problematic: the voice that declares it has "Finished knowing" is a voice that knows and speaks, with dark, wondering intensity, and the past disturbance lingers palpably in the texture of the present narration. The conclusive period and the full rhyme in "I felt a Cleaving" contrast with the inconclusive dash and partial rhyme at the end of "I felt a Funeral." The linguistic play in "I felt a Cleaving" is playful, intellectually teasing. But the linguistic play in "I felt a Funeral" arouses profound uncertainties—existential and epistemological—and is emotionally unsettling. The acoustic structure of the two poems, apparently so much alike in theme, then, really works towards very different expressive ends. The composed voice telling in seamless sequence the impossibility of matching seams or managing sequence gives a touch of reflective humor to a poem that is bound to seem a little thin unless a reader attends to the multiple meanings of its words. But "I felt a Funeral" conveys a powerful disturbance from the very first reading, and on repeated readings it touches ever deeper levels of human uncertainties.

Dickinson evades our attempts to reduce her to philosophical coherence. Possibly "Each Life converges to some Centre," as she wrote (P 680), and each artist's work doubtless has its centering characteristics and themes. Too often, though, urgent attempts to define this poet, to place her in a narrow niche, result in the overlooking of what is most poetic in her work, her richness, her lyrical diversity. Her artistic goal was not to resolve mysteries but to vivify them in compelling language. The subtle shadings or dramatic shifts of her tone, the witty intellectual twists and turns, the leadings out to the edge of awe—all these are clearer when a reader attends to the music of her verse. The more attentively one reads, the more impressive her artfulness. The more closely one listens, the finer the resonances.

Notes

Introduction

1 The Johnson-Ward numbering of Emily Dickinson's letters is adopted from *The Letters of Emily Dickinson*, ed. Thomas H. Johnson and Theodora Ward. Letters are identified by the letter L followed by the letter number.

2 William Dean Howells's was a dissenting voice: "Occasionally, the outside of the poem, so to speak, is left so rough, so rude, that the art seems to have faltered. But there is apparent to reflection the fact that the artist meant just this harsh exterior to remain, and that no grace of smoothness could have imparted her intention as it does" (320).

3 Earlier critics had made the same point about adding variety to the hymn stanza, notably Albert Gelpi (*Mind* 148) and David Porter (*Early* 107).

4 *The Poems of Emily Dickinson*, ed. Thomas H. Johnson. Poems are identified in the text by the letter P followed by Johnson's number.

5 Curiously, Miles calls this rhyme (*before/Floor*) a "three-quarters rhyme" (which she defines as "an echo of the final consonant . . . and the substitution of a long for a corresponding short vowel, or of a short for a corresponding long") and argues that this is "exactly right" as a phonic equivalent of "the silly evasiveness alike of the fallen knitting-ball and of the slipped thought" (147). But *before* and *floor* constitute a full rhyme, not a partial rhyme.

6 One further complication connected with this poem is the stanza, apparently a variant of stanza 2, that appears as poem 992 in the variorum edition. The words "Dust" [with "behind"] and "Disk" [with "before"] darken the meaning, but the jingling rhythm and rhyme remain.

7 Rhymes of the former type are frequent in Dickinson's verse, the latter infrequent but generally more pronounced in effect. Also appearing occasionally in her verse are rhymes belonging to a third sub-group of "unaccented rhyme"; these involve similar syllables both of which are un-

stressed (*chestnut/present, didn't/wasn't*). The *Handbook* suggests the label "puny" for such rhymes (431).

8 Detailed explanation of the procedures Johnson followed in dating the poems can be found in the introduction to the variorum edition, lx–lxii.

Franklin explains his procedures in revising that dating in *The Manuscript Books of Emily Dickinson*, xv–xvi and Appendix 3.

9 Morris properly excludes from his count both "a small number of poems in a 'free-rhyming' verse that rhymes erratically, with no regular meter or rhyme-scheme" and poems that are "fragmentary or in very rough drafts" (30). Precise determination of what is finished and what is not, however, is an unattainable goal.

10 A concise, informative discussion of the subject appears in Percy G. Adams's *Graces of Harmony*, 199–211.

11 Poems without a consistent metrical scheme present more complex problems, as for example does this poem:

> Precious to Me – She still shall be –
> Though She forget the name I bear –
> The fashion of the Gown I wear –
> The very Color of My Hair –
>
> So like the Meadows – now –
> I dared to show a Tress of Their's
> If haply – She might not despise
> A Buttercup's Array –
>
> I know the Whole – obscures the Part –
> The fraction – that appeased the Heart
> Till Number's Empery –
> Remembered – as the Milliner's flower
> When Summer's Everlasting Dower –
> Confronts the dazzled Bee.
>
> (P 727)

Stanza one is a long meter stanza in which lines two, three, and four are exactly rhymed. Stanza three is a common particular meter stanza with exactly rhymed couplets (one with a single, one with a duple rhyme) and the unaccented rhyme of *Empery* and *Bee*. Stanza two is not a familiar stanza at all (6-8-8-6 syllables), and an analyst would have to judge whether to consider it unrhymed (by analogy to the *abcb* pattern predominant in Dickinson's four-line stanzas) or to take note of the consonantal rhyme *Their's* and *despise* and/or the partial vowel rhyme *now* and *Array*. It is possible, too, to note the internal rhyme *Me/She/be* in line one and the coincidence of *Bee* in the last line in a homophonic rhyme with *be* of line one. Any one instance of this sort may be relatively simple to resolve, but as such cruxes and the number of decisions proliferate, the value of any statistical "count" becomes increasingly dubious. Other poems presenting difficult choices about which lines to count include 156, 183, 204, 237, 273, 288, 380, 411, 576, 598, 629, 661, 759, 831, 1035, 1288, 1355, 1400, 1572, and 1724.

In "Precious to Me – She still shall be – " the pattern of rhyme progresses from rhyme within the line (in line 1), to rhyme between adjacent lines (in lines 2, 3, and 4), to the complex pattern of the final stanza, which is adumbrated by lines 3 to 8. The stanzaic division "obscures" the common particular meter that is faintly perceptible to the reader's ear in lines 3 to 8; the repetition of the common particular meter pattern in the last stanza in effect absorbs the "Part" that stands as a formally ambiguous second stanza into a larger "Whole." Conceivably, the reader's progression from the satisfactions of small formal patterns to a more comprehensive pattern is purposefully connected to the thematic idea of "the fraction" that appeases until a grander "Whole" appears. If so, the reader's mind can perhaps grasp the final *Bee* as a sound that brings the otherwise externally unrhymed first line, ending in *be*, into a larger unity; thus, the fractional is echoed and "Remembered" at last in a rather dazzling poetic performance. Such intricate pyrotechnics might seem to be little more than a prosodic stunt if they were not all so unobtrusive.

12 In P 1604, for example, the last line appears in the variorum text as an aberrant seven-stress line in a poem otherwise composed of regularly alternating four- and three-stress lines. The manuscript (at Amherst College), however, shows a line division after the fourth stress, where it belongs according to the prosodic scheme; Johnson's editing here is evidently in error. The issue is not quite so simple as that, though, since there are numerous other line breaks (two within what appears in Johnson's text as line 1, two within line 5, and one within every other line); under such circumstances editorial decisions are extremely difficult. Because the metrical pattern is regular and consonantal rhymes (*divine/return/vain/gone*) recur so as to indicate an arrangement of eight lines of common meter, it seems likely that narrow paper and large handwriting brought about many of the divisions, but it might also be argued plausibly that this "poem" was really a casual and rhythmic piece of prose, not properly a poem at all.

"Would you like summer?" (P 691) never appears as a poem in Dickinson's manuscripts; instead, it occurs in a letter to Samuel Bowles (L 229), and in the printed text of the *Letters* is separated by the editors as a verse definitely distinct from the prose of that letter. I am grateful to Karen Dandurand for pointing out to me that that is not at all how it is in the actual letter, where it is barely distinguishable from the prose: the lines are not indented (unlike the printed text), and except for spaces left after "Down," "looked on," and "Medicine" the line divisions are not indicative of verse and do not correspond closely with those of the printed version. Something that verges upon poetry emerges from the prose of that letter, but the printed text is misleading.

For the most part Johnson's editorial rearrangements are necessary and admirable, and such problems need not be exaggerated. But one ought to be aware of them generally. Other poems requiring judgments about line arrangement and rhyme include 417, 489, 584, 586, 592, 622, 640, 918, 1050, 1072, 1109, 1320, 1604, and 1606.

13 Lindberg-Seyersted, 134–35: "in her suggested variants for words or phrases, Dickinson maintained—with infrequent exceptions (e.g. in No. 500)—the rhythm she had first set down, both in the direction (rising vs. falling rhythm) and the span (number of syllables) of the metrical units."

14 This version of the poem differs so widely from the original that George Monteiro argues they ought to be considered as separate poems altogether (224). His analytical comments on the poem and on "circumference" are also of considerable value.

15 Lindberg-Seyersted writes: "Identical rhymes, that is, rhymes which are made up of different, but identically sounding words (or parts of words), occur infrequently in her verse and do not characterize it in any important way" (160).

One. A Musical Aesthetic

1 For this idea I am indebted to Mary G. De Jong and her paper "Frances Osgood, Sara Helen Whitman, and 'The Poetess.'"

2 Ann D. Wood, considering the "scribbling women" of the nineteenth century, discusses the popular descriptions of women writing "heedless of any sense of literary form," from "instinctive womanly nature," "because they cannot help it." At the origin of such descriptions, she explains, was a taboo against competition by women, especially economic competition in the marketplace: "women's motives in writing are being stripped [by these descriptions] of all aggressive content" (18–19).

3 M. H. Abrams discusses the importance of music in the expressive theory of aesthetics in *The Mirror and the Lamp*, 91–94.

4 This poem, about the pine at her window which the wind rushes through, ends "Apprehensions – are God's introductions – / To be hallowed – accordingly." The poem may owe something to Emerson's "Woodnotes," which also associates the wind with the breath of the primal mind.

5 In a letter to H. S. Boyd, postmarked August 13, 1884, Browning wrote:

"And now I must explain to you that most of the 'incorrectnesses' you speak of may be 'incorrectnesses,' but are not *negligences*." She goes on to ask "why you rhyme (as everybody does, without blame from anybody) 'given' to 'heaven' when you object to my rhyming 'remember' and 'chamber'? The analogy is all on my side, and I *believe* that the spirit of the English language is also" (*Letters* 1: 183–84).

6 The Earth-Song in "Hamatreya" is an instance where Emerson's deviation is functional; as Hyatt Waggoner puts it, "The free use, and breaking, of traditional verse forms is as effective in 'Hamatreya' as in any poem Emerson ever wrote" (153). But complaints about Emerson's "ear," his carelessness of prosody, are valid, I think. Similar complaints about Dickinson are not.

7 England is not mistaken in noticing an allusion. Watts's hymn speaks of seeing "the Canaan that we love, / With unbeclouded eyes!" while in P 168 Dickinson also refers to Moses, to Canaan, and "beclouded Eyes." But her poem shows no intent to parody or criticize Watts's. Further, his poem is in common meter, whereas hers is in trochaic eights and fives. It is nearly as plausible to emphasize the parallel with Burns's "Comin' through the Rye," which is in the same meter and works with the same "If"-this-happens-"Need"-this-happen structure.

8 Wolosky asserts that P 1491 is a parody of Watts' Hymn 158, "Broad Is the Road that Leads to Death" (76). Again, the irregular short lines of Dickinson's poem are sharply divergent from the long meter of Watts's poem, and there is no common phraseology in the two poems; consequently, the connection seems too remote to be called parody. I would agree with Timothy Morris that "Far from being constrained by her form or immured within the tradition of the hymn, she escaped that tradition completely, to the point where most of her poems no longer bear even a parodic or contrasting relationship to hymns" (27).

Davidson claims that the "distant strains of triumph" coming to the "defeated – dying" in Dickinson's "Success is counted sweetest" (P 67) owes something to Watts's Psalm 49:

> Laid in the grave, like silly sheep,
>   Death feeds upon them there;
> Till the last trumpet breaks their sleep,
>   In terror and despair.

The argument strikes me as shaky.

9 The song lyrics, by Andrew Cherry, with accompanying tune by John Davy, first appeared in the ballad-opera *Spanish Dollars* in 1805. The refrain is included as an epigraph to a chapter in James Fenimore Cooper's *The Pioneers*. Interestingly, in that novel, Marmaduke Temple speaks with

amusement of his domestic servant, who loves to brag of his adventures on the high seas and who loves to sing that song, as having sung "part of it" at an evening church service, whereupon another character launches pompously into a "dissertation . . . on the subject of psalmody, which he closed by a violent eulogium on the air of the 'Bay of Biscay, O.' . . ." The episode underlines the interrelationship of hymn-meters and the meters of popular songs and dances. The Puritans appropriated secular tunes to sacred words for psalms and hymns, with the result that, in the early days, some people cried out against hearing profane ballad and dance tunes in church. The music accompanying the first half of each stanza in "The Bay of Biscay" has a hymn-like cadence, but the latter half is pure music-hall material. Sigmund Spaeth reports that Davy "is said to have taken" the melody "from some Negro sailors in London" (51).

10   Margaret Freeman, who has conducted an extended study of Dickinson's metrics, writes: "The poems have usually been categorised in terms of the forms found in hymnody, also according to the number of syllables per line. The limitation of grouping the poems by syllable number alone, however, is that it becomes only a rough approximation for many of the poems that bear little, if any, resemblance to the strict forms of hymn metre. . . . In metrical terms, it is perhaps ironic that Watts is still most generally accepted as the major influence on Emily Dickinson's form, since Watts himself, a true product of eighteenth century syllabic theory, used only a few of the hymn forms ascribed to him. Most of his metrical psalms and hymns adhere to 'common' metre, many to 'long' metre, and a few to 'short' metre. Of the remaining, the most common is the extension of 'long' metre to six-line stanzas (scarcely a major metrical change) and 'sixes and fours' in the pattern 6-6-6-6-4-4-4-4. The other variations —pentametre lines and what is known as 'short particular' metre (6-6-8-6) [Freeman's error for 6-6-8-6-6-8]—occur rarely and only in the psalms. Watts never uses trochaic metres in the hymns. It is, in fact, in the 474 'Hymns selected from Various Authors' included in Worcester's edition of Watts that the trochaic and anapestic metres as well as hymns with much more flexibility in syllable count can be found" (81–82).

11   Scholars have remarked the influence on Blake of Protestant hymns, particularly those of Charles Wesley and Isaac Watts (See England 43–112 and Saintsbury 3:14). It is worth remembering, though, that Blake was familiar with literary ballads and enjoyed ballads as song, too, as B. H. Fairchild explains (3).

12   For examples of each, see "If you were coming in the Fall" (P 511), "A Light exists in Spring" (P 812), "A Prison gets to be a friend" (P 652), or "It was not Death, for I stood up" (P 510), and "Pink – small – and punctual – " (P 1332). In these, and indeed in most of her poems, Dickinson is operating out of a lyric tradition broader than that of the hymn.

13 Consonantal rhymes are frequent in Watts's psalms and hymns, not only eye rhymes such as *good/food, gone/atone, have/grave,* and *Lord/word,* but also (and more frequently) such consonantal rhymes as *blood/God, sin/clean, Lamb/name, adore/power, Son/down, known/Son, tombs/comes, cup/hope, maladies/arise, lost/dust,* and *tread/exceed.* Dickinson has a great many rhymes of the same type. Extremely rare in hymns are any combinations involving a final consonant blend rhymed with a non-identical consonant blend or a single consonant (*thoughts/faults* is a rare instance in Watts); she, on the other hand, frequently pairs such words as *rides* and *is, around* and *Head,* or *endured* and *Beloved,* and even sometimes such remote pairs as *Death* and *enough* (in this case, both end in fricatives) or *Equinox/intercourse.* Rhymes including an accented syllable with metric promotion such as *thee/immortality* or *eyes/vanities* are infrequent in Watts's practice and abundant in Dickinson's—pushed to such further lengths as *beyond/satisfied, extinct/thanked/Retrospect, woe/Italy, Flail/burial, gash/Countenance,* or (doubled) *Melody/Eternally, privacy/infinity, Brigadier/Troubadour,* or (tripled) *Immortality/Strategy/Physiognomy.* Other more experimental rhymes she used, such as rich consonance (*Birds/Bards*) and identical rhymes (*Sow/so*), are practically non-existent in hymnody.

14 George Sullivan Woodman was a student at Amherst College who later received an M.D. from Harvard. He had studied with Lowell Mason, the president of the Handel and Haydn Society in Boston and the major organizer in the U.S. of music instruction for schoolchildren and their teachers. Mason published dozens of songbooks for children (beginning with *The Juvenile Lyre* in 1831) as well as for adult choirs. Singing schools, "common in New England before the end of the eighteenth century," taught a variety of music, such songs as "Old Hundred," "Indian Converts," "Romish Lady," or "Captain Kidd," and "[t]he line between religious and secular music was tenuous," according to Irving Sablosky (*American* 67). Though Sablosky gives no specific information about how Lowell Mason's influence altered the material sung in the schools, he implies that it gradually became more sophisticated and diverse (70–74). Material about George Woodman was made available to me by the staff of the Archives at Amherst College (*Amherst Biographical* 128).

15 From a volume of recollections, entitled "Memorabilia of Mary Lyon," found in the archives of Mount Holyoke College, this excerpt is by Amelia D. Jones, class of 1849. Her comments indicate something about the breadth of musical kinds sung in the singing schools.

16 Harriet Hawes is listed in the *Annual Catalogue of the Mount Holyoke Female Seminary* for 1847–48 (Amherst: J. S. and C. Adams, 1848).

17 Susan Dickinson's sketch "Two Generations of Amherst Society," written before her death in 1913, recalls the Senior Levee given annually by the president of Amherst College: "There was music, with the piano," and

she mentions women singing there such songs as "O Summer Night!" and "Wert thou in the cauld blast." She tells, too, of a typical party at the Sweetsers, where "voices somewhat decadent sang sweetly though with a timid tremulo, 'Are we almost there? Said the dying girl,' 'Coming Through the Rye,' etc., or a resident basso of solemn mien, with a tone really below any pitch known to musical necessity, was prevailed upon after the habitual prolonged urging to give us, 'Rocked in the Cradle of the Deep,' the refrain being held with such sustained power I am sure the glasses in the corner cupboards tinkled from the jar. By this time music was in the air, and aroused to an almost vivacious gaiety, all stood about the piano and sang together, 'Lest auld acquaintance be forgot,' 'America,' and 'Scotland's burning!' " (171, 176). (Martha Dickinson Bianchi's version of this sketch identifies the voice singing "Are we almost there?" as Lavinia Dickinson's, but without reference to either sweetness or decadence [35–38].)

18 Referring to the performance of Jenny Lind in a letter, Dickinson's rhetoric stands in sharp contrast to the inflated praise of Dwight (and most of the American public), but she does admit to being impressed by "some notes from her 'Echo [Song]' – the Bird sounds from the 'Bird Song' and some of her curious trills" (L 46). Of the Germania Orchestra, she said, "I never heard [such] *sounds* before" (L 118); that sentence has a more Dickinsonian ring and probably conveys her meaning better without Johnson's bracketed editorial insertion.

19 Leyda 272–73. Leyda dates this event in June 1877. He takes his account from Green's article in *The Bookman* 60 (Nov. 1924). Dickinson mentions hearing the song in a letter to Higginson in January 1878 (L 533).

20 Green was right in expressing doubt about whether it was Anton Rubinstein the poet had heard. Dickinson *was* deeply impressed with the celebrated composer and performer; in a letter of 1873 she wrote to Frances Norcross, "Glad you heard Rubinstein. . . . He makes me think of polar nights Captain Hall could tell! Going from ice to ice! What an exchange of awe!" (L 390). (Hall was an explorer who died in the Arctic in 1871.) But she could not have heard Rubinstein perform. He did not come to the United States until 1872, after she had ceased to leave Amherst. It is not clear what pianist she might have mentioned to Green. She may have attended concerts during other trips to Boston; few letters survive from the months she spent in Boston in 1864 and 1865. In any case, her extravagant praise of Rubinstein indicates that she maintained a vivid interest in the musical life beyond her seclusion. (See also L 907, where she asks to know what tunes please her cousin.)

21 A comparable idea in British romantic poetry may be found in the second book of Wordsworth's *Prelude:*

One song they sang, and it was audible,
Most audible, then, when the fleshly ear,
O'ercome by humblest prelude of that strain,
Forgot her functions, and slept undisturbed.
(59)

22 The same idea is found in Shelley, as for example in his "To Jane: 'The Keen Stars Were Twinkling'":

Though the sound overpowers,
Sing again, with your dear voice revealing
    A tone
    Of some world far from ours,
Where music and moonlight and feeling
    Are one.
(204)

23 He cites Wordsworth's Mount Snowdon passage, "where the visionary prospect becomes penetrated by 'the roar of waters,'" Keats's nightingale and twittering swallows, Shelley's skylark, and Blake's "fantastic synesthesias."

24 In both these poems, alliteration on the sound of *r* hints of meaning. In "A Route of Evanescence" it suggests a whirr of wings. The much longer sequence of alliteration, consonance, and rhyme involving *r* in "I Years had been from Home" lends almost a low roar to the first five stanzas. James E. Miller gives a sensitive analysis of two versions of the latter poem, with attention to the rhymes, in *Quests Surd and Absurd* 154–58.

25 Elizabeth Phillips points out that "Country people say, when they first hear them [the cricket songs], that it will be six weeks until frost" (153).

26   To pile like Thunder to it's close
    Then crumble grand away
    While Everything created hid
    This – would be Poetry –

27 Actually, Emerson's attitude toward language is more complex than Hagenbüchle's article acknowledges. A recent article by Leonard Neufeldt and Christopher Barr, discussing the essay "Circles," treats those complexities more fully.

28 Other poems where Dickinson uses the word *key* in a musical sense include P 1775 and P 470, both discussed in subsequent chapters.

29 Kenneth Burke sagely advises that "There is an indeterminate realm between the conscious and the unconscious where one is 'aware' in the sense that he recognizes a special kind of event to be going on, and yet is not 'aware' in the sense that he could offer you an analytic description

and classification of this event. The first kind of awareness we might call consciousness of method, the second a consciousness of methodology. And I presume that we should not attribute the second kind to an artist unless explicit statements by the artist provide us with an authorization." Even then, he warns, the act precedes the analytic formulation, so the absence of an artistic manifesto does not argue the absence of artistic control (38). That Dickinson was 'aware' in at least the first sense is evident in her poems.

30 Claude Levi-Strauss articulates a similar idea that in myth and music meaning "becomes actual . . . through and by the listener" (30). He notes the "reversal of the relation between transmitter and receiver . . . since in the last resort the latter discovers its own meaning through the message from the former: music has its being in me, and I listen to myself through it. Thus the myth and the musical work are like conductors of an orchestra, whose audience becomes the silent performers" (17). His attempt to dissociate poetry from this pattern is unconvincing; words do make poetry less indeterminate than music, but his claim that "any adequately educated man could write poems, good or bad; whereas musical invention depends on special gifts, which can be developed only where they are innate" (18) makes an untenable distinction.

31 In P 1750, for example:

> The words the happy say
> Are paltry melody
> But those the silent feel
> Are beautiful –

Two. Structural Strategies

1 For information about this version, see Charles Anderson 324–25.
2 Yvor Winters rightly praises the poem: "the false rhymes are employed with unusually fine modulation; the first rhyme is perfect, the second and third represent successive stages of departure, and the last a return to what is roughly the stage of the second. These effects are complicated by the rhyming, both perfect and imperfect, from stanza to stanza. The intense strangeness of this poem could not have been achieved with standard rhyming" (160).

Cameron makes the musical connection explicit in her discussion of the poem, referring to "the minor key song of the crickets" and calling attention to the allusions to the music attending the celebration of mass, "directly and indirectly invoked as a 'Canticle' (the song sung at vespers), [and as] a '[G]radual' (the chant that dominates the Proper of the Mass) . . ." (182).

Another poem where Dickinson is apparently punning on the musical sense of "minor" is P 565: "One Anguish – in a Crowd – / A Minor thing – it sounds."

3 A similar shift is to be found in P 1530 where the initial harmony of "things that *sing*" in the "*Spring*" is followed by a series of partial rhymes that seem to sound the disharmony of pang-stricken "Minds." In the same way, after the full rhymes in the first stanza of P 732, the partial rhymes suggest the something missing in the wife's new life, a loss "unmentioned" but audible.

4 Heiskänen-Mäkelä comments on the ambiguity of the third stanza, "the last stanza makes the poem turn on an axis of irony: the optimistic absurdity of insect toil . . . is illustrated by utmost human heroism, the hope of immortality, which is, again, referred to absurdity by it" (176).

Salska explains the way in which this poem "undercuts its own major device": though the poem is "structured by analogy," "the sudden leap" between the part devoted to the spider and the part given to the analogue stresses "the arbitrary character of the association." Since "the speaker remains outside the poem" and the past tense in the last stanza "carefully disclaims the validity of the analogy as a general law," the emphasis is on the inscrutability of the creative process (78–79).

5 Admittedly, the line arrangement is somewhat distracting. It is possible that the line divisions in Johnson's edition do not accurately reflect the poet's intent. A look at the poem in R. W. Franklin's edition of the manuscript books shows that the paper has no room for more words on individual lines; even "Bride" in line 2 is moved to a separate line. Perhaps "No more ashamed" and "No more to hide," for instance, *should* go on one line, though it is not uncommon in Dickinson's practice (or that of other poets) to divide a line into half-lines to emphasize a parallelism. Still, one thing is definite amid the questions concerning her lineation: we need to *listen* harder to what is going on.

6 In the manuscript of this poem, the structure of this stanza is even vaguer than it appears here because "O'ertook by Blast" is a separate line (line 3). It is possible that she could not fit all that on one handwritten line and would have arranged it as Johnson does. But we cannot be sure.

7 The approach and effect, it seems to me, are comparable to that in Emerson's "Hamatreya," where the long, irregular, and barely rhymed medial section is followed by a concluding stanza with a full rhyme:

> When I heard the Earth-song
> I was no longer brave;
> My avarice cooled
> Like lust in the chill of the grave.
>
> (37)

In both poems, the final rhyme, like the sense, is jarring.

8 Oddly, although it describes a tune that is not "contained—like other stanza," this poem *is* "contained" in stanzas of long meter; oddly too, the sections that treat the "Keyless Rhyme" are rhymed conventionally, while the digression about lost paradisal melodies is rhymed more freely and thus from one vantage point has more claim to be considered "Keyless," liberated from the restrictions of conventional "keys." Perhaps the freedom of the medial section is connected to the better melodies of Eden, dim recollections of which are yet our link to the essential truth at the heart of legends of a lost paradise. Just as in Wordsworth's "Ode" shadowy recollections are "as master-light of all our seeing," this "Keyless rhyme" would be the master-tune of all our hearing, our link to supernal reality. In any case, full rhyme succeeds here in giving a sense of exhilarated affirmation and of a return, after departure, to a joyful "tune."

9 The final consonantal rhyme *Grace/Price* is made to seem an emphatic refusal to rhyme "properly" by the consonantal sequence that runs through the words *Grace/reduce/Disgrace/Price* and particularly by the play on the words *Grace* and *Disgrace*, which underscores the speaker's contempt for the compromise of selfhood that publication involves.

10 William Harmon, in his *Handbook*, refers to an "eccentric critical dogma" according to which "poetry is distinguished by the foregrounded presence of hieronymy [names] and its antithetical complement, onomatopoeia" (237). "Bobolink" is a word in which those antithetical complements are united. The critical dogma, his own, he elaborates in an article in *Parnassus*.

11 The manuscript, from fascicle 34, has the numerals 2 and 1 before lines 8 and 10 respectively, which Johnson identifies as marks made by Dickinson. The marks evidently mean she considered arranging the lines in a more conventional way:

> Brave Bobolink –
> Whose Music be His
> Only Anodyne –

This pattern would provide a regular rhythm but preserve the consonantal rhyme *gone/Anodyne*. While that is not bad, and more softly wistful in tone, the sharper disjunctures of the primary arrangement seem to me to make a superior poem. Maybe Dickinson wondered whether it was too extreme; we are destined here as elsewhere always to wonder what her final choices would have been.

12 Another poem in which Dickinson's prosodic feet imitate human feet is P 431, where the first and last stanzas are quatrains composed of trimeter couplets. Between them is this detached dimeter couplet:

> The Saints forget
> Our bashful feet –

The little stanza apparently is meant to be shrinking and "bashful" in effect.

13 In her manuscript, the numbers 1, 3, 2, and 4 placed before the first four lines of the second stanza show that Dickinson considered an arrangement even further deviant from either prosodic paradigm:

> The Feet, mechanical, go round –
> A Wooden way
> Of Ground, or Air, or Ought –
> Regardless grown,
> A Quartz contentment, like a stone –

This variant arrangement indicates the care with which the poet weighed the stylistic disruption of this medial stanza.

14 Very similar is the withheld rhyme in P 1237, a worksheet draft:

> My Heart ran so to thee
> It would not wait for me
> And I affronted grew
> And drew away
> For whatsoe'er my pace
> He first achieve thy Face
> How general a Grace
> Allotted two – . . .

The speaker's withdrawal is supported by the apparent retreat of the rhyme-word *drew*.

15 In one stanza of the famous "There came a Day at Summer's full" (P 322), there may be an attempt at some such effect:

> And so when all the time had leaked,
> Without external sound
> Each bound the Other's Crucifix –
> We gave no other bond –

The phrase "without external sound" seems to point to the internal rhyme *bound*, which echoes *sound* (and forms a rich consonance with *Bond*).

16 Dickinson alludes to "The Charge of the Light Brigade" in a letter of 1862 as well. For her cousins Louise and Frances Norcross, she describes the return of the body of Frazer Stearns, slain in battle, to his hometown: "Classmates to the right of him, and classmates to the left of him, to guard his narrow face" (L 255).

17 The initial couplet has something less than a full rhyme by the narrowest

definition because the rhyming syllables do not receive a full stress in ordinary speech, but, given a stress promotion, they represent no departure from common poetic practice. Since the syllables are identical, and since the rhymed words are both nouns and very closely allied in meaning, they help set up expectations for the continuation of something stylistically very ordinary.

18   A footnote to Hymn 124, "'Tis not the law of ten commands," in Emily Dickinson's father's copy of Watts's hymns points out the relationship: "Joshua *same with* Jesus, and signifies *a Savior*" (449).

Three. Experiments in Sound

1   On the predominance of phonological similarity over rational lexis in children's language play, see Roman Jakobson and Linda Waugh, *The Sound Shape of Language*, 217–20.

2   Keller's discussion of Frost's mixed admiration and criticism (and envy) of Dickinson's technique is worth reading in full. Here, though, is a crucial excerpt:

> Emily Dickinson played away, too, but a little too fast and freely for Frost's taste, a little too "easy in [her] harness." Frost wrote in a letter, "A real artist delights in roughness for what he can do to it," that is, for how he can control it. But Emily Dickinson was interested in what she could do *with* the roughness, that is, what possibilities there were for a voice of her own within the ordering. Herein lies the major difference between the two. Frost could not handle such "compromises" himself, he said, but he granted that *she* could (316–17).

3   Juhasz argues that the tone of the poem is pure affirmation: "the tone of exclamation, of celebration is one aspect of the poem that is both clear and consistent, from start to finish" (111). The rhyme structure is evidence that this interpretation is not quite accurate.

A later version of the same poem arranges the lines so that *hold* and *Gold* make an external rather than an internal rhyme. (The line divisions given in the Johnson variorum edition do not accurately represent those in the manuscript at the Houghton Library.) It also places after line 11 the additional line "Tri Victory," which regularizes the rhythmic structure somewhat. Exclamation points and the final question mark disappear as well, so that generally the tone is calmer and more assured than in the earlier version.

The line divisions of the earlier version, also, do not correspond precisely with those in the manuscript at Amherst College. The paper is narrower than the line length, as has been said before. A certain amount of editorial relineation is clearly indicated in both instances, but the divisions Johnson made in the earlier version are more defensible than those he made in the later (Houghton) version.

4   With a little feminist critical ingenuity, one can envision all this verbal fluidity, here and throughout the poem, too, as a defensive weapon against the masculine power that snake represents. Whether that fluidity can be identified as a feminine principle generally, however, is doubtful. The snake is pretty fluid himself.

5   The second strophe, more regular in structure, alludes directly to William Cullen Bryant's "To the Fringed Gentian." His stanza, the third, is marked with a pencilled X in the copy of Bryant's poems, inscribed "To Miss Gilbert," in the Dickinson collection at the Houghton:

> Thou waitest late and com'st alone,
> When woods are bare and birds are flown,
> And frosts and shortening days portend
> The aged year is near his end.
>
> (214)

Dickinson's stanza repeats Bryant's phrase "aged year" and closes, like his, on the rhyme-word *end:*

> When most is past – it comes –
> Nor isolate it seems
> It's Bond it's Friend –
> To fill it's Fringed career
> And aid an aged Year
> Abundant end –

As if in answer to Bryant's, her poem says the gentian does not seem lonely.

6   In the second strophe, the acoustic progression of consonance in the line "Dominions dower*less* beside *this Grace*" extends the rhyme-sounds from the first strophe.

> When Thrones accost my Hands –
> With "Me, Miss, Me"
> I'll unroll Thee –
> Dominions dowerless – beside this Grace –
> Election – Vote –
> The Ballots of Eternity, will show just that.

On the whole, though, this poetic experiment is not very successful; the contrast between democratic electoral government and autocratic rule is insufficiently integrated into the poem, and the final couplet, rhymed

Vote/that, is pointlessly flat. The poet herself must have thought so, too, because a later version reworks the second strophe like this:

> When Thrones – accost My Hands –
> With "Me – Miss – Me" –
> I'll unroll – Thee –
> Sufficient Dynasty –
> To Peer this Grace –
> Empire – State –
> Too little – Dust –
> To Dower – so Great –

This version preserves the virtues of the first version and adds a full rhyme in the middle and another at the end that sounds properly emphatic.

Four. Riches of Rhyme

1 The first verse paragraph of *The Canterbury Tales* ends with a famous identical rhyme:

> The hooly blisful martir for to seke,
> That hem hath holpen whan that they were seeke.

After the introductory description of the beauties of returning spring, pilgrims seeking holy shrines seem a natural part of the season and its burgeoning animal activities; the word *seeke* [sick], however, abruptly shifts the tone and the conceptual focus to human weakness and mortality and thus to the spiritual reasons for pilgrimages. Other of Chaucer's identical rhymes are mentioned by Brown (104n) and by Schipper (273). An identical rhyme in *The Complaint of Mars,* ll. 76–77, punningly enjoys the ironic distance between the *armes* (arms) with which Mars embraces Venus and the *armes* (armaments) he is god of. This rhyme is a homograph as well as a homophone.

2 See Schipper (273) for citation of instances.

3 Stress in Middle English is not well understood. Generally it violates common sense to suppose that the language moved from a heavily stressed system in Old English to a heavily stressed system in Modern English by way of a period between in which stress was not important. Norman Eliason's consideration of stress in Chaucer's verse supports a tentative conclusion that it *was* strongly stressed. Eliason ponders the "unanswerable question" of Chaucer's manner of reciting his own verse: "Did he emphasize the meter, beating it out strongly and insistently and producing a tum-ta, tum-ta effect that would appall us today? I suspect he did. But aside from his concern about the regularity of the meter—which is

not a negligible consideration—the only evidence I can think of is the likelihood that this was the traditional way of reciting verse, handed down from the Old English scops, whose meter virtually demanded such recital . . . , and also the fact that certain linguistic changes [vowel lengthening in open syllables] at the time indicate that stress was uncommonly strong in disyllabic words like *tale* and *name,* which were very numerous then" (55).

More recently Suzanne Woods has also argued the importance of accentuation in Chaucer's work: "While there is no evidence that poets of Chaucer's time thought rimed syllables must inevitably be accented, Chaucer's practice is consistent in riming accented syllables" (39).

4 Adams is properly tentative in his speculations and skeptical about the effect of phonesthemes when unaided by lexical associations. Other material on phonesthemes includes Wescott's *Sound and Sense* and David Masson's articles in *The Princeton Encyclopedia of Poetry and Poetics,* especially "Tone Color."

5 Harmon discusses identical rhyme, which he terms "redundancy," as "the most sophisticated sort of rhyme (as may be demonstrated by its importance to so advanced and difficult a poet as Mallarmé)." It is at once "a rhyme and more than a rhyme but also not exactly a rhyme." Such rhymes, he writes, are "irreducibly complex, since . . . both mind and ear have to be involved as they need not be involved in *perfect* and *deficient* rhyme" ("Rhyme" 387, 390–91).

6 Poe's "To Helen" rhymes *roam/home/Rome.* The first two terms are antithetical in import, and in context the third achieves something of a synthesis of those opposites.

William Keach points out the rhyme of *vale* and *veil* in Shelley's "Mont Blanc," which he says "signals the precarious balance and interaction between skepticism and visionary imagination." Since the words are thirteen lines apart, it is doubtful whether the listening ear can pick up the identity and hence whether there is much poetic effect attaching to this rhyme (except for a carefully scrutinizing eye). Keach acknowledges the remoteness of the rhyme, noting that it is as " 'inaccessible' as Mont Blanc itself" (198–99).

Wordsworth rhymes *one* and *won* in a couplet in "The Happy Warrior," but the rhyme has no significance that I can discern.

7 The homonymic rhymes occur in verse as early as 1859 and as late as 1877. No two appear in the same fascicle. There are more in the poems dated 1862 than in other years.

8 Homans discusss this poem as one of several concerning "two female figures" and contends that in these poems "[t]he thematic emphasis . . . is on similarity and equivalence, indeed, on sameness" ("Vision" 121). Without necessarily refuting Homans, one can note that "I tried to think

a lonelier Thing" (P 532) is based on a like idea, detailing the speaker's search for a "Duplicate," "Horror's Twin," a fellow in suffering and in pity, and that there the twin is referred to with masculine pronouns.

9 Dickinson repeats the idea of seamlessness in "A Bird came down the walk" (P 328), written in the same year. It may be significant that the line there containing the words "Too silver for a seam" are also grouped by a consonantal rhyme link into an octave. Such larger rhyme-groups are not rare in her poetry, however, and such speculations as this must remain tentative.

10 See Shapiro and Beum, 102–3, for a discussion of the heuristic value of rhyme.

11 There is a possible parallel between this poem and a pair of lines marked with a marginal pencil line in Susan Gilbert's copy of Elizabeth Barrett Browning's *Poems*, which bears her signature, dated 1853. The lines, from "A Vision of Poets" are these: "They are scorned / By men they sing for, till inurned."

12 Willis J. Buckingham has identified Dickinson's lexicon as Webster's *American Dictionary of the English Language,* published in 1844 in Amherst by J. S. and C. Adams. This dictionary is available at the Houghton Library. Few other copies survive. On this subject see also Richard Benvenuto's article in *ESQ.*

13 The most perplexing of the questions about this poem is raised in Johnson's note in the variorum edition: "Pasted onto the center of the front half of the half-sheet of notepaper on which the poem is written there is an unused three-cent postage stamp of the issue of 1869. Beneath one side of the stamp are two small strips clipped from *Harper's Magazine* for May 1870. One bears the name 'George Sand' and the other 'Mauprat'— the title of the novel by George Sand published in 1836. The poem was written after the stamp and strips were pasted onto the sheet, for the lines accommodate themselves to the occupied space."

14 A two-line passage in "A Vision of Poets" in Susan Gilbert's copy of Elizabeth Barrett Browning's *Poems,* marked with a marginal pencil line, says of Marlowe, Webster, Fletcher, and Ben Jonson:

> Whose fire-heart sowed our furrows, when
> The world was worthy of such men.

Browning's figure of poets as sowers may have influenced Dickinson's.
   Possibly relevant as well is a passage, marked in Dickinson's own copy of *Aurora Leigh,* pointed out by Jack Capps (86):

> By the way
> The works of women are symbolical.

> We sew, sew, prick our fingers, dull our sight,
> Producing what? A pair of slippers, Sir,
> To put on when you're weary – or a stool
> To stumble over, and vex you . . . "Curse that stool!"
> Or else at best, a cushion, where you lean
> And sleep, and dream of something we are not
> But would be for your sake. Alas, alas!
>
> (1: 455–63)

15　An interesting pun on "sow" and "sew" also appears in another poem of 1862, P 339, of which the first stanza reads:

> I tend my flowers for thee –
> Bright Absentee!
> My Fuschzia's Coral Seams
> Rip – while the Sower – dreams –

The speaker, literally a gardener and figuratively a seamstress, is a sower-sewer who tends the fuchsia but dreamily neglects to mend its ripped seams or to plant its seeds. In lush, sensuous images, the poem draws an extended, implied parallel between the gardener and the "Absentee," who similarly neglects his "Daisy," as the speaker of the poem calls herself.

　　Both of these poems (P 339 and P 617) are insightfully interpreted by Gertrude Reif Hughes as subversions of the cult of domesticity prevalent in Dickinson's day; she is correct in arguing that they suggest "a female poetics in which processes and products of womanly work serve as metaphors for her poetry itself and for her attitudes to the conventions that prescribe and evaluate her daily life" (19–20).

16　Since no autograph copy of this poem exists, it is not clear whether this variant (crossed out in the transcript) was rejected by the poet herself or merely by Mrs. Todd.

17　Sometimes she appears to be using identical rhyme in an attempt to suggest onomatopoeically an effect of numbness or stasis. Poem 358 has two identical rhymes in an *abab* pattern: *standing/Understanding* and *rose/arose*. Poem 364 rhymes *on/upon;* poem 612 rhymes *remove/move;* poem 786 rhymes *firm/confirm*. In these instances, the various prefixes contribute less to the meaning than the repeated syllable; in context, the effect of the repetition supports a thematic sense of uncomprehending immobility.

18　No manuscript of this poem survives, and the date of its composition is unknown. There is an interesting parallel, though, between its final stanza and the letter that seems to have been Dickinson's last: "Little Cousins, Called Back." The last phrase is inscribed on her tombstone.

Five. Closure and Non-Closure

1 Likewise, Porter laments the failure of her endings to resolve the suspense and perplexity inaugurated in the first lines (*Idiom* 93–94); "Like impressionist music," he says subsequently, "Dickinson's poems search for a resolving chord, but the poet seems not to have undertaken the complicated work of achieving it" (*Idiom* 110). There is no reason to conclude that what was a powerful stylistic innovation for impressionist composers was for her a clumsy inadvertence, but Porter indirectly offers a glimpse of what the poet is up to.

2 Salska appropriately emphasizes "the discontinuous character of Dickinson's vision": "the polarities of Dickinson's oppositions do not gradually blend into each other. Instead, they are locked in an unresolvable confrontation" (130).

3 Eleanor Wilner has said that the "equivocal moment of closure—impetus and hesitation" is the focus of Dickinson's poetic genius (126). This statement is made in a discussion of the expressive function of the dash, to which I do not wholly subscribe; nevertheless, the observation has merit.

    Wolosky argues convincingly the expressive value of Dickinson's syntactic discontinuities, and she remarks "ironic incompletion" in some poems (14).

4 See Porter, *Idiom* 9–24, for a discussion of the importance of the "aftermath" of experience in Dickinson's poetry.

5 Smith cites "a high incidence of formal parallelism," when it occurs at the end of a poem, as a device lending strong closural force (171).

6 For similar examples, see P 126, P 737, and P 943. In the last of these, the rhyme gives the poem a closural effect counterbalancing the anti-closural statement that anyone who gives a friend to the grave will have "Circumference without Relief – / Or Estimate – or End – ."

7 James Bailey, who also provides a statistical tabulation of rhyme patterns in ten major writers of English iambic tetrameter verse, writes, "the English iambic tetrameter is almost exclusively a rhymed meter" (66).

8 Cf. Smith 175: "It must often happen, in fact, that the *donnee* of a poem is its conclusion, that the poet began with the end, and that what the reader perceives as an ending determined by the poem's thematic structure may, from the poet's point of view, have been what determined that structure in the first place."

    Poe, in "The Philosophy of Composition," makes a comparable statement, quoting Charles Dickens in support of it.

9 Weisbuch thinks the poem "may be the worst of all kinds of poems, unintentional self-parody" (154). On the contrary, I think, the theatrics

are surely intentional, a comic parody not only of some of her poems (see especially P 238, which also has dying bubbles) but also of a type of poetry in general. (I think, for example, of Shelley's "I fall upon the thorns of life! I bleed!") It is possible, after all, to be desperately serious about something at one moment and to find it pretty ridiculous at another.

10 Porter's remarks about the "hymn form" of this poem (*Early* 64, 68), however, are rather strained. As he admits, the lines are not arranged in the conventional hymnal manner, and the meter is only a rough approximation of hymn meter. His broader contention, though—that the poem holds in tension religious subject matter and conversational idiom, faith, and skepticism—is quite valid.

11 The pattern of partial rhymes followed by a single full rhyme in final position, according with thematic and other closural effects, is found in several poems discussed in the previous chapter, in the famous "I heard a Fly buzz" (P 465), and a very large number of others. See especially also P 291, P 392, P 405, P 701, P 925, P 1033, and P 1194. In P 1277, the consonantal rhymes of stanza one, *fear/fair*, interlock inversely with those of stanza two, *Despair/here*, before the tension of those stanzas is relaxed in the more normal rhyme, *new/through*, of the third and last.

12 This is one of the partial rhymes "corrected" by Mabel Loomis Todd.

13 Salska cites this poem as representative of Dickinson's unresolved confrontations within the self (135).

14 Franklin argues that these lines do not end this poem, that five lines now printed as part of P 443, having been separated in the vicissitudes of manuscript shuffling over the years, properly conclude this poem. The five lines in question begin "'Twould start them" (See *Editing* 40–46). The irresolution of the lines I quote is not, however, untypical of Dickinson's endings.

15 Cristanne Miller has observed that "it is virtually impossible to read the first line metrically, that is, giving "Requirement" three syllable positions. Partly because of the dash following it and partly because so many of Dickinson's lines end in polysyllables, 'Requirement' seems to fill the line (to take four syllables), and 'dropt' is as much a metrical surprise as it is a thematic one. By the end of the first line, the poet has already undercut her initial claim that the wife's new 'honorable' position involves any real elevation" (43).

16 Similar examples of anticlimax include P 652 and P 700.

17 Smith states: "If, for one reason or another, we are confident that the closural weakness is part of that design (again, in the two meanings of structure and intention), it will be successfully incorporated into our total experience of the poem" (233).

18 Weisbuch's comment is accurate: "This parody of a cheap gothic ballad attempts to rescue Burkean sublimity from the genteel shudder. It internalizes 'Haunting' and devalues external horrors in comparison to self-inflicted ones" (139).

19 "The Soul has Bandaged Moments" (P 512) offers another powerful instance of an ending with a deliberate formal disruption:

> The Soul's retaken moments –
> When, Felon led along,
> With shackles on the plumed feet,
> And staples, in the Song,
>
> The Horror welcomes her, again,
> These, are not brayed of Tongue –

The quatrain form breaks off into a fragment of itself—a couplet concluding with a consonantal rhyme. The spondaic rhythm of "plumed feet" conveys a plodding sense of shackled poetic feet, and the stapled "Song" is echoed in a broken ending with a dissonant rhyme. Curiously, *song* and *tongue* have often been rhymed in English poetry although the words themselves have never rhymed. Similar metrical disruptions are effective in P 293, P 355, P 403, and P 1024.

20 Arguing a thesis that Dickinson's work is strongly influenced by Watts's hymns, England compares the musical effect to that of the hymn tune *Tierce de Picardie*, "which revolves [resolves?] a minor tune on a final major chord . . . [that] suddenly thrusts the hymn into an exotic musical convention." It seems to me unlikely that the effect is traceable to any particular source.

21 Gertrude White observes, "In only fourteen poems did he use half-rhymes, and of these thirteen were written in the last twenty months of his life" (97). The fact that most of these are bitter war poems has encouraged the false notion that such rhymes invariably connote frustration and despair.

The fascination of these rhymes may be connected with linguistic patterns of vowel alternation in a root word to indicate grammatical relationships, as in the *died*/*dead* rhyme, mentioned above; our fundamental linguistic habits trigger a mental response that reaches for a semantic link built into such rhyme-pairs even when the words come from different roots. Wescott's discussion of the "catchy" effect of vowel gradation—in humorous verse, in tradenames, and in slang—is interesting (306–16).

22 Other instances in Dickinson's verse of rich consonance used as rhyme include *dawn*/*down* (P 51), *fast*/*fist* (P 218), *smile*/*small* (P 223), *Dawn*/*down* (P 236), *Book*/*back* (P 344), *man*/*men* (P 350), *Home*/*Him* (P 425), *did*/*Dead* (P 426), *Wheel*/*while* (P 451), *Love*/*live* (P 468), *Noon*/*none* (P 469), *hid*/*Head*

(P 494), *Bells/Balls* (P 639), *Moon/Mine* (P 643), *Steel/still* (P 666), *soul/seal* (P 777), *Deed/Dead* (P 878), *time/tomb* (P 906), *live/Love* (P 961), *steep/step* (P 1010), *broad/Bread* (P 1077), *fight/feet* (P 1113), *Seed/sod* (P 1288), *Feet/Fate* (P 1318), *Life/Loaf* (P 1374), *Leaf/Life* (P 1437) *Birds/Bards* (P 1466), and *Dyes/days* (P 1673). Some of these are final rhyme pairs. Other examples of rich consonance in her verse incorporate words of more than one syllable (e.g., *chagrin/Green* in P 1379). In addition, there are other such word-pairs appearing within a line of verse (e.g., *Last* and *Least* in P 573).

23 In "I know that He exists" (P 338) a similar strategy is apparent. The poem begins with full rhyme and ends with a consonantal rhyme, *stare/far*, which accompanies the final question, an accusation against God. Lindberg-Seyersted's analysis of the rhymes in the poem differs in detail from my own, but she agrees that the diminution of the rhyme is important in creating an artfully disturbing ending (167–68).

24 "Tick" precedes "tock" for immutable reasons not clearly understood. A "sense of closure is in part a product of the general configuration of relaxation and quiescence, melodically speaking, relaxation is associated with the decline in tension which is effected when pitches are lower—when a progression descends at its close" (Meyer 139). Perhaps for the same reasons the majority of consonantal rhymes in Owen's poetry and in Dickinson's follow that progression. Another instance where Dickinson violates that order with superb and ambiguous effect is the final rhyme of P 598, *lulled/lived*.

25 Cristanne Miller comments on Dickinson's fondness for using polysyllabic words at the end of a poem: "Because in English few polysyllabic or latinate words of more than two syllables have a final stressed syllable, Dickinson's poems often end on a secondary or tertiary stress." When this weakly stressed syllable is also part of a slant rhyme, Miller says, "her poems end on a mediate, holding note, with a chord quietly or only partially resolved . . ." (44).

Works Cited

Primary Sources

Dickinson, Emily. *The Letters of Emily Dickinson*. Ed. Thomas H. Johnson and Theodora Ward. 3 vols. Cambridge: Belknap-Harvard UP, 1958.

———. *The Poems of Emily Dickinson: Including Variant Readings Critically Compared with All Known Manuscripts*. Ed. Thomas H. Johnson. 3 vols. Cambridge: Belknap-Harvard UP, 1955.

Franklin, R. W., ed. *The Manuscript Books of Emily Dickinson*. 2 vols. Cambridge: Belknap-Harvard UP, 1981.

"Title divine, is mine." Dickinson ms. 361. Houghton Library, Harvard U.

"Title divine – is mine!" Leyda ms. 678. Frost Library, Amherst College.

"You remember the little 'Meeting.' " Leyda ms. 677. Frost Library, Amherst College.

Secondary Sources

Abrams, M. H. *The Mirror and the Lamp: Romantic Theory and the Critical Tradition*. New York: Norton, 1958.

Adams, Percy G. *Graces of Harmony: Alliteration, Assonance, and Consonance in Eighteenth-Century British Poetry*. Athens: U of Georgia P, 1977.

Allen, Gay Wilson. *American Prosody*. New York: American Book, 1935.

Amherst College Biographical Record of the Graduates and Non-Graduates, Class of 1846. Amherst, Mass., 1927.

Anderson, Charles R. *Emily Dickinson's Poetry: Stairway of Surprise*. New York: Holt, 1960.

Anderson, Paul W. "The Metaphysical Mirth of Emily Dickinson." *Georgia Review* 20 (1966): 72–83.

Anderson, Peggy. "Dickinson's *Son of None*." *Explicator* 41 (1982): 32–33.

Annual Catalogue of the Mount Holyoke Female Seminary. Amherst: J. S. and C. Adams, 1848.

Babbitt, Irving. *The New Laokoon*. Boston: Houghton, 1910.

Bailey, James. *Toward A Statistical Analysis of English Verse: The Iambic Tetrameter of Ten Poets*. Lisse, Netherlands: de Ridder Press, 1975.

Benfey, Christopher E. G. *Emily Dickinson and the Problem of Others*. Amherst: U of Massachusetts P, 1984.

Benvenuto, Richard. "Words within Words: Dickinson's Use of the Dictionary." *Emerson Society Quarterly* 29 (1983): 46–55.

Bianchi, Martha Dickinson. *The Life and Letters of Emily Dickinson*. Boston: Houghton, 1924.

Blake, William. *The Poetry and Prose of William Blake*. Ed. David V. Erdman and Harold Bloom. Garden City, NY: Doubleday, 1965.

Brown, Calvin S. *Music and Literature: A Comparison of the Arts*. Athens: U of Georgia P, 1948.

Browning, Elizabeth Barrett. *Aurora Leigh*. New York: C. S. Francis, 1859.

——— . *The Letters of Elizabeth Barrett Browning*. Ed. Frederic G. Kenyon. Vol. 1. London: John Murray, 1898.

——— . *The Poems of Elizabeth Barrett Browning*. 2 vols. New York: C. S. Francis, 1852.

Bryant, William Cullen. *Poems by William Cullen Bryant*. Philadelphia: Carey and Hart, 1849.

Buckingham, Willis J. "Emily Dickinson's Dictionary." *Harvard Library Bulletin* 25 (1977): 489–92.

Burke, Kenneth. "On Musicality in Verse." *Poetry* 57 (1940): 31–40.

Cameron, Sharon. *Lyric Time: Dickinson and the Limits of Genre*. Baltimore: Johns Hopkins UP, 1979.

Capps, Jack L. *Emily Dickinson's Reading, 1836–1886*. Cambridge: Harvard UP, 1966.

Carlyle, Thomas. *On Heroes, Hero-Worship and the Heroic in History*. Oxford: Geoffrey Cumberlege, 1904.

Carpenter, Frederic I. "Emily Dickinson and the Rhymes of Dream." *U of Kansas City Review* 20 (1953): 113–20.

Chase, Richard [Volney]. *Emily Dickinson*. American Men of Letters Series. New York: Sloane, 1951.

Coppee, Henry. *A Gallery of Distinguished English and American Female Poets*. Philadelphia: E. H. Butler, 1860.

Davidson, James. "Emily Dickinson and Isaac Watts." *Boston Public Library Quarterly* 6 (July 1954): 141–49.

De Jong, Mary G. "Frances Osgood, Sara Helen Whitman, and the 'Poetess.'" Meeting of the Philological Association of the Carolinas, Greensboro, NC. March 13, 1987.

Derrida, Jacques. *Dissemination*. Trans. Barbara Johnson. U of Chicago P, 1981.

Dickinson, Susan. "Two Generations of Amherst Society." *Essays on Amherst's History*. Ed. Theodore P. Greene. Amherst: Vista Trust, 1978. 168–88.

Diehl, Joanne Feit. *Dickinson and the Romantic Imagination*. Princeton: Princeton UP, 1981.

———. "Ransom in a Voice: Language as Defense in Dickinson's Poetry." *Feminist Critics Read Emily Dickinson*. Ed. Suzanne Juhasz. Bloomington: Indiana UP, 1983. 156–75.

Donoghue, Denis. *Emily Dickinson*. Pamphlets on American Writers 81. Minneapolis: U of Minnesota P, 1969.

Eberwein, Jane Donahue. *Strategies of Limitation*. Amherst: U of Massachusetts P, 1985.

Eliason, Norman E. *The Language of Chaucer's Poetry*. Copenhagen: Rosenkilde and Bagger, 1972.

Emerson, Ralph Waldo. "Merlin." *Poems*. Vol. 9 of *The Complete Works of Ralph Waldo Emerson*. Ed. Edward Waldo Emerson. Boston: Houghton, 1903–4. 12 vols. 120–24.

———. "The Poet." *Essays: Second Series*. Vol. 3 of *The Collected Works of Ralph Waldo Emerson*. Text established by Alfred R. Ferguson and Jean Ferguson Carr. Cambridge: Belknap-Harvard UP, 1983. 1–24.

England, Martha Winburn and John Sparrow. *Hymns Unbidden: Donne, Herbert, Blake, Emily Dickinson and the Hymnographers*. New York: New York Public Library, 1966.

Fairchild, B. H. *Such Holy Song*. Kent: Kent State UP, 1980.

Fogle, Stephen F. "Pun." *Princeton Encyclopedia of Poetry and Poetics*. Ed. Alex Preminger, 681–82. Princeton: Princeton UP, 1965.

Franklin, R. W. *The Editing of Emily Dickinson: A Reconsideration*. Madison: U of Wisconsin P, 1967.

Freeman, Margaret Helen. "Emily Dickinson's Prosody: A Study in Metrics." Diss. U of Massachusetts, 1972.

Frost, Robert. *Complete Poems of Robert Frost*. New York: Holt, 1949.

Frye, Northrop. *Sound and Poetry*. New York: Columbia UP, 1957.

Gelpi, Albert J. *Emily Dickinson: The Mind of the Poet*. Cambridge: Harvard UP, 1965.

———. "Emily Dickinson." *The Tenth Muse: The Psyche of the American Poet*. Cambridge: Harvard UP, 1975. 217–99.

Gilbert, Sandra M., and Susan Gubar. *The Madwoman in the Attic: The Woman Writer and the Nineteenth-Century Literary Imagination*. New Haven: Yale UP, 1979.

Hagenbüchle, Roland. "Precision and Indeterminacy in the Poetry of Emily Dickinson." *Emerson Society Quarterly* 20 (1974): 33–56.

———. "Sign and Process: The Concept of Language in Emerson and Dickinson." *Emerson Society Quarterly* 25 (1979): 137–55.

Harmon, William. "Bashō and Proust: A Note on the Nature of Poetry." *Parnassus* 11 (1983–84): 186–91.

————. "Rhyme in English Verse: History, Structures, Functions." *Studies in Philology* 84 (1987): 365–93.

Hecht, Anthony. "The Riddles of Emily Dickinson." *New England Review* 1 (1978): 1–24.

Heiskänen-Mäkelä, Sirkka. *In Quest of Truth: Observations on the Development of Emily Dickinson's Poetic Dialectic.* Jyväskylä, Finland: K. J. Gummerus Osakeyhtiön Kirjapainossa, 1970.

Herbert, T. Walter. "Near-Rimes and Paraphones." *Sewanee Review* 45 (1937): 433–52.

Higginson, Thomas Wentworth. "Preface from *Poems,* 1890." *Collected Poems of Emily Dickinson, Original Editions Edited by Mabel Loomis Todd and Thomas Wentworth Higginson.* New York: Avenel, 1982. xix–xxii.

————. "An Open Portfolio." *The Christian Union* 42 (25 September 1890): 392–93.

Hollander, John. *Rhyme's Reason.* New Haven: Yale UP, 1981.

————. *Vision and Resonance.* New York: Oxford UP, 1975.

Holman, C. Hugh, and William Harmon. *A Handbook to Literature.* New York: Macmillan, 1986.

Homans, Margaret. "'Oh, Vision of Language!': Dickinson's Poems of Love and Death." *Feminist Critics Read Emily Dickinson.* Ed. Suzanne Juhasz. Bloomington: Indiana UP, 1983. 114–33.

————. *Women Writers and Poetic Identity: Dorothy Wordsworth, Emily Bronte, and Emily Dickinson.* Princeton: Princeton UP, 1980.

Howells, William Dean. "The Strange *Poems* of Emily Dickinson." *Harper's Magazine* 82 (January 1891): 318–21.

Hughes, Gertrude Reif. "Subverting the Cult of Domesticity: Emily Dickinson's Critique of Women's Work." *Legacy* 3 (1986): 17–28.

Jakobson, Roman, and Linda Waugh. *The Sound Shape of Language.* Bloomington: Indiana UP, 1979.

Johnson, Thomas H. *Emily Dickinson: An Interpretive Biography.* Cambridge: Belknap-Harvard UP, 1955.

Jones, Amelia D. "Memorabilia of Mary Lyon." Archives of Mount Holyoke College.

Juhasz, Suzanne. *The Undiscovered Continent: Emily Dickinson and the Space of the Mind.* Bloomington: Indiana UP, 1983.

Keach, William. *Shelley's Style.* New York: Methuen, 1984.

Keller, Karl. *The Only Kangaroo Among the Beauty: Emily Dickinson and America.* Baltimore and London: Johns Hopkins UP, 1979.

Kerman, Joseph. *Contemplating Music.* Cambridge: Harvard UP, 1985.

Lanier, Sidney. *The Science of English Verse.* New York: Scribner, 1880.

Larkin, Philip. "Big Victims: Emily Dickinson and Walter de la Mare." *New Statesman* 79 (1970): 367–68.

Levi-Strauss, Claude. *The Raw and the Cooked: Introduction to a Science of My-*

thology: I. Trans. John and Doreen Weightman. New York: Harper and Row, 1969.

Leyda, Jay. *The Years and Hours of Emily Dickinson*. 2 vols. New Haven: Yale UP, 1960.

Lindberg-Seyersted, Brita. *The Voice of the Poet: Aspects of Style in the Poetry of Emily Dickinson*. Cambridge: Harvard UP, 1968.

Malof, Joseph. *A Manual of English Meters*. Bloomington: Indiana UP, 1970.

Martin, Wendy. "Emily Dickinson." *Columbia Literary History of the United States*. Ed. Emory Elliot. New York: Columbia UP, 1988. 609–26.

Masson, David. "Tone-Color." *Princeton Encyclopedia of Poetry and Poetics*. Ed. Alex Preminger, 856–58. Princeton: Princeton UP, 1965.

May, Caroline. *The American Female Poets: with Biographical and Critical Notices*. New York: Leavitt and Allen, 1869.

McHugh, Heather. "Interpretive Insecurity and Poetic Truth: Dickinson's Equivocation." *American Poetry Review* 17.2 (March/April 1988): 49–54.

Meyer, Leonard B. *Emotion and Meaning in Music*. Chicago: U of Chicago P, 1956.

Miles, Susan. "The Irregularities of Emily Dickinson." *London Mercury* 13 (1925): 145+.

Miller, Cristanne. *Emily Dickinson: A Poet's Grammar*. Cambridge and London: Harvard UP, 1987.

Miller, James E., Jr. *Quests Surd and Absurd*. Chicago: U of Chicago P, 1967.

Mills, Elizabeth M. "Wording the Unspeakable: Emily Dickinson and A. R. Ammons." Diss. U of North Carolina at Chapel Hill, 1985.

Monteiro, George. "In Question: The Status of Emily Dickinson's 1878 'Worksheet' for 'Two Butterflies went out at noon.'" *Essays in Literature* 6 (1979): 219–25.

Moore, Thomas. "What the Bee is to the Floweret." *Irish Melodies*. Philadelphia: E. H. Butler, 1865. 57–58.

Morris, Timothy. "The Development of Dickinson's Style." *American Literature* 60 (1988): 26–41.

Neufeldt, Leonard N., and Christopher Barr. "'I Shall Write Like a Latin Father': Emerson's 'Circles.'" *New England Quarterly* 59 (1986): 92–108.

O'Donnell, Brennan P. "Wordsworth's Verse Forms: A Descriptive Catalogue." M.A. Thesis. U of North Carolina at Chapel Hill, 1983.

Pater, Walter. *The Renaissance: Studies in Art and Poetry. The 1893 Text*. Ed. Donald L. Hill. Berkeley: U of California P, 1980.

Phillips, Elizabeth. *Emily Dickinson: Personae and Performance*. University Park and London: Pennsylvania State UP, 1988.

Poe, Edgar Allan. "Letter to Mr. ———." *Edgar Allan Poe: Poetry and Tales*. Library of America Series 19. 1984. 10–17.

Porter, David T. *The Art of Emily Dickinson's Early Poetry*. Cambridge: Harvard UP, 1966.

————. *Dickinson: The Modern Idiom*. Cambridge: Harvard UP, 1981.

Ransom, John Crowe. "Emily Dickinson: A Poet Restored." *Perspectives USA* 15 (Spring 1956): 5–20.

Reeves, James. Introduction. *Selected Poems of Emily Dickinson*. New York: Barnes, 1966.

Richardson, Charles F. *A Study of English Rhyme*. Hanover, NH: n.p., 1909.

Sablosky, Irving. *American Music*. Chicago: U of Chicago P, 1969.

————. *What They Heard: Music in America, 1852–1881; From the Pages of "Dwight's Journal of Music."* Baton Rouge: Louisiana State UP, 1985.

Saintsbury, George. *A History of English Prosody*. 3 vols. London: Macmillan, 1908.

Salska, Agnieszka. *Walt Whitman and Emily Dickinson: Poetry of the Central Consciousness*. Philadelphia: U of Pennsylvania P, 1985.

Schipper, Jakob. *A History of English Versification*. Oxford: Clarendon, 1910.

Sewall, Richard B. *The Life of Emily Dickinson*. New York: Farrar, 1974.

Shapiro, Karl, and Robert Beum. *A Prosody Handbook*. New York: Harper, 1965.

Shapiro, Michael. *Asymmetry: An Inquiry into the Linguistic Structure of Poetry*. Amsterdam: North Holland Publishing Co., 1976.

Shelley, Percy Bysshe. *The Complete Works of Percy Bysshe Shelley*. Ed. Roger Ingpen and Walter E. Peck. Vol. 4. New York: Gordian P, 1965.

Smith, Barbara Herrnstein. *Poetic Closure*. Chicago: U of Chicago P, 1968.

Spaeth, Sigmund. *A History of Popular Music in America*. New York: Random House, 1948.

St. Armand, Barton Levi. *Emily Dickinson and Her Culture: The Soul's Society*. Cambridge: Cambridge UP, 1984.

Stein, Gertrude. "Sacred Emily." *Geography and Plays*. 1922. New York: Something Else P, 1968. 178–88.

Stevenson, Robert Louis. *The Complete Poems*. New York: Scribner, 1923.

Tate, Allen. *Reactionary Essays on Poetry and Ideas*. New York: Scribner, 1936.

Thompson, John. "Linguistic Structure and the Poetic Line." In *Poetics, Poetyka, ΠΟΞ TNKA*. The Hague: Mouton, 1961. 167–75.

Thoreau, Henry D. *A Week on the Concord and Merrimack Rivers*. Ed. Carl F. Hovde et al. Princeton: Princeton UP, 1980.

Verlaine, [Paul Marie]. "Art poétique." *Oeuvres Poétiques Complètes*. Ed. Jacques Borel, 326. Paris: Gallimard, 1962.

Waggoner, Hyatt H. *Emerson as Poet*. Princeton: Princeton UP, 1974.

Walker, Cheryl. *The Nightingale's Burden: Women Poets and American Culture before 1900*. Bloomington: Indiana UP, 1982.

Wallace, Ronald. *God Be With the Clown: Humor in American Poetry*. Columbia: U of Missouri P, 1984.

Walsh, John Evangelist. *The Hidden Life of Emily Dickinson*. New York: Simon, 1971.

Watts, Isaac. *The Psalms, Hymns, and Spiritual Songs, of the Rev. Isaac Watts, D. D.: To Which are Added Select Hymns from Other Authors; and Directions for Musical Expression*. Ed. Samuel Worcester. Boston: Crocker and Brewster, 1834. (Owned by Dickinson's father.)

Webb, G[eorge] J[ames], and Lowell Mason. *The Odeon: A Collection of Secular Melodies Arranged and Harmonized for Four Voices, Designed for Adult Singing Schools, and for Social Music Parties*. Boston: J. H. Wilkins and R. B. Carter, 1839.

Webster, Noah. *An American Dictionary of the English Language*. 2 vols. Amherst: J. S. and C. Adams, 1844.

Weisbuch, Robert. *Emily Dickinson's Poetry*. Chicago: U of Chicago P, 1975.

Wellek, René, and Austin Warren. "Euphony, Rhythm, and Meter." *Theory of Literature*. New York: Harcourt, 1956. 158–73.

Wells, Henry W. *Introduction to Emily Dickinson*. Chicago: Packard, 1947.

Wescott, Roger Williams. *Sound and Sense: Linguistic Essays on Phonosemic Subjects*. Lake Bluff, IL: Jupiter P, 1980.

Wesling, Donald. *The Chances of Rhyme: Device and Modernity*. Berkeley: U of California P, 1980.

———. *The New Poetries*. Lewisburg: Bucknell UP, 1985.

Whicher, George Frisbie. *This Was a Poet: A Critical Biography of Emily Dickinson*. New York: Scribner's, 1938.

White, Gertrude M. *Wilfred Owen*. New York: Twayne, 1969.

Wilner, Eleanor. "The Poetics of Emily Dickinson." *English Literary History* 38 (1971): 126–54.

Wimsatt, W[illiam] K[urtz]. "One Relation of Rhyme to Reason." *The Verbal Icon*. Lexington: U of Kentucky P, 1954. 153–66.

Winters, Yvor. "Emily Dickinson and the Limits of Judgment." *Maule's Curse*. Norfolk, CT: New Directions, 1938. 149–65.

Wolff, Cynthia Griffin. *Emily Dickinson*. New York: Knopf, 1986.

Wolosky, Shira. *Emily Dickinson: A Voice of War*. New Haven: Yale UP, 1984.

Wood, Ann D. "The 'Scribbling Women' and Fanny Fern: Why Women Wrote." *American Quarterly* 23 (1971): 3–24.

Woods, Suzanne. *Natural Emphasis: English Versification from Chaucer to Dryden*. San Marino: Huntington Library, 1985.

Wordsworth, William. *The Fourteen-Book Prelude*. Ed. W. J. B. Owen. Ithaca: Cornell UP, 1985.

Index of Poems Cited

General Index

Anthon, Kate Scott, 51
Arnold, Matthew, 59

Blake, William, 5; rhymes of, 71–72, 145
Browning, Elizabeth Barrett, 31, 181, 238 (n. 11), 238 (n. 14); rhymes of, 40–41
Browning, Robert, 31, 40
Burke, Edmund, 187
Burns, Robert, 45
Byron, George Gordon, Lord, 24–27

Chaucer, Geoffrey, 141, 142, 236–37 (nn. 1, 3); Wife of Bath, 46
Closure, role of rhyme in, 94, 175–85
Coleridge, Samuel Taylor, 47, 61

Dickinson, Emily Elizabeth: critical reputation of, 1–8; as woman poet, 1, 3–4, 31–34; letters of, 2, 5, 29, 30, 31, 38, 43–44, 48, 50, 51, 55, 59, 76, 105, 117, 140, 186, 214, 228 (nn. 18, 19, 20), 233 (n. 16), 239 (n. 18); process of composition of, 2, 21–24; stanza forms of, 26, 41, 44–47, 75, 118, 139; and defiance of conventional rules, 29, 117; aesthetic aims of, 29–30, 55–56, 60–61, 214, 220; songbird imagery of, 29, 30, 31, 33–36, 38, 39, 43, 68, 84–85, 104–5, 111, 112, 167–68, 213; auditory imagery of, 30, 52–55, 58–59, 62, 63–66, 68, 69, 70, 77, 78, 92–94, 119–20, 154–55, 181, 182–83, 206; and ideas about music, 37–38, 60–61, 64–66; and use of word *hymn*, 43–44; musical experience of, 45, 48–52 (*See also* Music, Dickinson's experience of); and skepticism about language, 59–61, 173; and love of language, 63, 140, 173; understanding of reader's activity, 67–70; lexicon of, 140, 157, 158, 164, 238 (n. 12); diversity of, 220
Dickinson, Lavinia (sister), 228 (n. 17)
Dickinson, Susan Gilbert (sister-in-law), 214
Dickinson, William Austin (brother), 2

Emerson, Ralph Waldo, 40, 55, 61; rhymes of, 41, 42, 225 (n. 6)
Endings, critical indictment of Dickinson's, 27, 102, 174–75, 239 (n. 1)
Epigram, 26, 175–76
Esling, Catherine H., 32
Eye rhyme, 17, 18, 218, 222 (n. 10), 227 (n. 13)

French symbolists, 36
Frost, Robert, 28, 123–24, 234 (n. 2)

Germania Musical Society, 50, 228 (n. 18)
Gilman, Caroline, 32